KU-261-105

To: sue@s-sco.demon.co.uk
From: Hamzah <bnh@hamzah.demon.co.uk>
Subject: The UK Internet Book
Date: Fri, 6 Jan 1995 19:27:42 +0000

Great Book. I had to buy it in the end because I couldn't afford
another 3 hours at Waterstones to finish reading it.

Why did I buy it for?. I wanted to set-up an account with Demon and
was looking for a book for setting up the software etc. but in a way
I was slightly disappointed. However, I managed to set up Trumpet
Winsock using the Appendix in your book. Great I thought, I should
be able to set up my mail now. Alas, I realised this is not the book
for those sort of instructions.

I also did want to find out about what the Internet does, the
technical bits and pieces, and where to go etc. Your book is great
for this. I am not what you call a 'Guru' but I did learn a lot.

So on balance I would say it was well worth the money.

BTW (see I learnt something!), I did not get to use the free month
sub from Demon because I enrolled before I got your book. Never
mind!!

Keep up the good work.

Cheers

Hamzah

===

Date: Fri, 23 Sep 1994 23:14:21 +0700
To: sue@s-sco.demon.co.uk
From: Robert Firmin <bob@bljswap.demon.co.uk>
Subject: Getting Started with MACS

I bought a copy of your book yesterday, which I am enjoying very
much. It's a nice change to read a book about the Internet from an
English angle.

I got my package from demon, including the software and the Internet
Starter Kit. I successfully loaded the software, which for me was
nearly a miracle, not being computer minded.

Regards from Bob Firmin

===

Sue
I've just got back to work after my holiday to discover "The UK
Internet Book" on my desk. Very nice indeed.

Mike
—
Michael Bernardi   mike@childsoc.demon.co.uk

===

```
Date: Mon, 02 Jan 95 18:00:13 GMT
From: Louise Morse <louise@morsepts.demon.co.uk>
Organization: The Morse Partnership
To: sue@s-sco.demon.co.uk
Subject: The UK Internet Book.

Dear Sue,
Read your book — still reading it and I think it's brilliant. Don't
understand it all, but hopefully, getting there. Only been connected
3/4 days and at the moment have more questions than answers.
Probably everyone else flies it the moment they're connected, but I'm
still getting my head round the software.

Question 1: have you written other books? Titles, ISBN's?

Question 2: is there a kind of local news pin-board for
Cambridgeshire?

Happy new year.

Louise Morse
The Morse Partnership
louise@morsepts.demon.co.uk

==================================================================

Date: Wed, 21 Sep 94 19:33 BST-1
From: Peter Reid <preid@cix.compulink.co.uk>
Subject: the uk internet book
To: sue@s-sco.demon.co.uk

Just bought your book today, it looks excellent so far, I must have
browsed my way through about half of it! It is about time we all
insisted on proper UK sourced books on the Internet instead of
filling the pockets of all these Americans.

best wishes
peter

==================================================================

Date: Wed, 2 Sep 92 12:54:07 GMT
Organization:
From: Bill Lockley <block@faqer.demon.co.uk>
To: Sue@s-sco.demon.co.uk
Subject: UK Internet Book

Enjoyed your book immensely, also your sense of humour! Given the
implementation problems I had, I don't know what I would have done
without your book. Hope you make lots of money.

Best regard and thanks,

Bill lockley.

[One of your (hopefully +ve) stock replies would do fine.]

==================================================================
```

What the Cybernauts say about it ...

```
====================================================================
```

From: Stephen Soghoian <stephens@drjazz.demon.co.uk>
Subject: Review Copy of ur Book recd-Thanks
To: sue@s-sco.demon.co.uk
Date: Mon, 12 Sep 1994 01:24:02 +0100 (GMT+0100)

Hi There Sue

I just received a review copy of your new Addison Wesley UK Internet
Book. I've read two chapters, it's very informative and user
friendly. Perhaps I can write a brief review of it for the Internet
alt.books.review newsgroup?

I think the book is very useful to NET users in the UK because it
deals effectively with the nuts and bolts of how to get connected to
UK internet providers, none of that material is covered by the
plethora of American Internet books on the market.

Best of Luck with your new book. I hope it goes to the top of the
charts for the Sunday Times Non-Fiction.

Cheers
—
Stephen Soghoian
American Journalist — London, England
reporter, "The American" Newspaper
stephens@drjazz.demon.co.uk

```
====================================================================
```

Date: Thu, 15 Sep 1994 11:11:23 +0000
To: sue@s-sco.demon.co.uk
From: Chris Davis <cdavis@smouse.demon.co.uk>
Subject: Magnum opus

Sue,
The herds of crocodiles snapping at my lower portions have prevented
me from writing to you sooner to convey my delighted thanks for the
UK Internet Book, which arrived a few days ago.

What a terrifically useful thing to have around: UK-based, plenty of
Mac-oriented information, and very comprehensive stuff about Demon!
The book has now taken up residence on my bedside table, and is
consulted every morning and evening.

You have a really excellent writing style. I've always liked
technical stuff written with an (apparent) grin — the spoonful of
sugar to help the didacticism go down.

Best wishes,

Chris

```
====================================================================
```

Date: Sat, 08 Oct 1994 10:31:07 GMT
From: peter batty <batty@dedrum.demon.co.uk>
Reply-To: batty@dedrum.demon.co.uk
To: sue@s-sco.demon.co.uk
Subject: Hello

hello sue

A note to say thanks very much for the UK Internet Book. It
encouraged me to take the plunge into this strange world and, most
important of all, explained how! Brilliant!

Still completely fazed by it all (first logon yesterday), don't
understand what I'm doing, but somehow have managed to get news
(well, not "get" exactly — it seems to happen automatically), ftp
some files, even seem to have got Cello up and running! (Did it
really connect me to CERN and to somewhere-in-the-US-I've-forgotten-
already at 02.30 this morning?)

All questions received by yours truly along the lines of "Wot's this
Internet thing, then?" (yes, most of my friends are entirely at home
in the Information Age) are now being answered with "Well, there's
this really good book ..." and exhortations to BUY IT!

Sorry to trouble you with this inconsequential rambling, but in the
book you did invite people to send you email. Regretting it yet? I
would appreciate a reply of some sort, if only to discover that
email actually works. The sad truth is — I don't know anyone else
to ask :-)

peter batty

===

Date: Tue, 27 Sep 1994 10:47:48 +0000
To: sue@s-sco.demon.co.uk
From: Nicholas Wilson <njrw@njrwgsy.demon.co.uk>
Subject: The UK Internet Book

I have recently bought your book (yesterday evening). I have noticed
that on pp. 138—139 you mention the "Summa" project. Could you tell
me the address of the Summa project please. Thanks in advance. BTW,
I like your book. Although I am only half way through (I read
voraciously) I would have prefered it to Engst's ISK when I was
trying to configure MacPPP and MacTCP.
Well done.

Regards

Nicholas Wilson
Guernsey

===

The UK Internet Book

Revised Edition

Sue Schofield

ADDISON-WESLEY PUBLISHING COMPANY

Wokingham, England • Reading, Massachusetts
Menlo Park, California • New York • Don Mills, Ontario
Amsterdam • Bonn • Sydney • Singapore • Tokyo • Madrid
San Juan • Milan • Paris • Mexico City • Seoul • Taipei

© 1995 Addison-Wesley Publishers Ltd.
© 1995 Addison-Wesley Publishing Company Inc.

All rights reserved. No part of this publication may be reproduced, stored in a retrieval system, or transmitted in any form or by any means, electronic, mechanical, photocopying, recording or otherwise, without prior written permission of the publisher.

The programs in this book have been included for their instructional value. They have been tested with care but are not guaranteed for any particular purpose. The publisher does not offer any warranties or representations, nor does it accept any liabilities with respect to the programs.

Many of the designations used by manufacturers and sellers to distinguish their products are claimed as trademarks. Addison-Wesley has made every attempt to supply trademark information about manufacturers and their products mentioned in this book. A list of the trademark designations and their owners appears below.

Cover designed by Designers & Partners of Oxford
and printed by The Oxted Colour Press Ltd, Oxted, Surrey.
Text designed by Sally Grover.
Cartoons by Martyn Jones.
Typeset by Wyvern Typesetting Ltd.
Printed in Great Britain at the University Press, Cambridge.

First edition published 1994. Reprinted 1994 and 1995.
Revised edition printed 1995.

ISBN 0-201-87731-7

British Library Cataloguing in Publication Data
A catalogue record for this book is available from the British Library.

Trademark notice
IBM PC/XT/AT/PS2 are trademarks of International Business Machines Corporation
Chameleon is a trademark of Netmanage Inc.
CompuServe is a trademark of CompuServe Inc.
MS-DOS and Microsoft Windows are trademarks of Microsoft Corporation
System 7.1 and Macintosh are trademarks of Apple Computer Inc.
Lotus 123 is a trademark of Lotus Corporation
Unix is a trademark of AT&T Bell Laboratories
Versaterm Pro and Versatilities are trademarks of Abelbeck Software

This is the single most useful tool – apart from your computer – in getting up and running on the Internet, and once you are there, in learning how to get the best out of it. Sue Schofield has brought together all the information which you need, and provides up to date contact details. What is more, this is not a US or 'international' book full of American phone numbers. Buy it, read it, and keep it with you. It will save you a lot of time and tears.

Howard Oakley
'MacAgony' columnist in
The Mac magazine

For Tatz, who made it,
and Black Woolly, who didn't.

Preface

'Don't expect this
book to turn you
into an Internet
expert overnight...'

The first edition of *The UK Internet Book* generated hundreds of messages from readers saying that we had got them started on the Internet ('we' includes the editorial, production and sales teams at Addison-Wesley who did such a fine job). Those readers told us that the start-up Appendices were vital, and the content of the rest of it about right. So I've kept the book much as it was for this 1995 revision, although phone numbers and site details have been updated, and new Chapters and Appendices and a free disk added. My heartfelt thanks go out to all of the correspondents who took the trouble to write – and especially to those new users who sent me their first email messages.

Many more Internet providers have arrived on the scene since last year and readers are advised to shop around for a good deal. Look for a local phone number for access near you and remember that it's not recommended that you pay time based charges for access to what is still the world's greatest free information resource.

We have revamped some of the offers in the book – but we have maintained the excellent relationship with Demon Internet Services. The only moans we heard of from the people who joined that service using this book were about busy lines. Demon are now using Energis to provide a higher modem-to-customer ratio to alleviate this and the lines were in place as we went to print.

Additions to this reprint include a disk of text files covering some of the lists we couldn't publish in the book for various reasons, space being the major one. The files are on the disk in their original electronic format.

I've also rewritten and illustrated Appendix 5b: 'Setting up NetManage Chameleon for Windows' to make it a more general set of get-you-started instructions, and illustrated it with screen shots. You can use the instructions for setting up Chameleon with any TCP/IP based provider. The new Appendix covers version 4.1, released in December 1994 but is relevant for earlier versions. I've also twiddled with some of the services and sites which disappeared the day the first edition appeared in print. The offers included with the book are also revised, and you should be able to recoup the cost of this book by using the coupons supplied within.

As before, don't expect this book to turn you into an Internet expert overnight but there's all the information you need to get started, and a special suck-it-and-see offer so you can try the Internet for yourself. As with all books promoting the Internet the hardest decisions were about what to leave out, not what to include, and the book remains a start-up guide for new users by public demand, rather than an encyclopedia of US-centric Internet trivia.

I've covered Windows, DOS, Mac and Amiga computers, but focused on comput*ing*, rather than comput*ers*. I've used as many screen shots as necessary to highlight significant differences between the various computers and operating systems, but don't be disappointed if you don't see a screen shot for your particular computer in every chapter. This is because much of the Internet is currently based on terminal emulation, which looks the same regardless of the computing platform in use, and I've illustrated most of the places where it doesn't.

Many of the advanced Internet services are moving rapidly towards a Graphical User Interface (GUI). Services such as Gopher, WAIS and the World Wide Web all benefit from this approach, making the possibility of transferring sound and vision over the 'Net a reality. I've gone along with this trend – there is now little development for the older character based interfaces such as DOS, and the world of personal computers is ever more a point and click world. This is mirrored in the book, which steers deliberately away from Unix interfaces wherever possible.

Users of terminal accounts with their character based interfaces will find the basic concepts in the book useful, but terminal based services such as CIX and CompuServe will one day have to give in and move over to TCP/IP working in full colour, if only to retain market share. The days of the 7-bit ASCII terminal, like DOS, are now numbered.

Using this book

This book is a basic introduction to the Internet and it's for users of the sort of personal computer you might buy in the High Street. The text is kept to a minimum but each chapter contains step-by-step screen shots showing you what to expect from the various Internet services.

Getting started – full Internet access

If you want to get started with the minimum of delay then read Part 1 for a grounding in what you need. Then go to the Appendices which tell you how to locate the software and set it up. You'll find that I've concentrated on services and software providing full TCP/IP access. This is because you'll need a full TCP/IP connection to get the most from the Internet.

Getting started - partial 'terminal' access

If you use a terminal service like CIX, Delphi or CompuServe, then you can go straight to Part 2. It tells you how to use the Internet tools available to you. If you need help to get started with those services then Appendix 2 teaches modem basics.

All users

Details of useful sites are included at the end of each chapter. These show where you can get all of the extra information you need. Unlike other Internet books I haven't included lists of information taken from the Internet because they would be out of date within weeks, but there are pointers to those lists on the enclosed disk so you can choose for yourself once you're hooked up.

Free disk

The disk included with the book contains lots of lists in PC text format. Mac users can read the disk with either Apple File Exchange, or PC exchange bundled with System 7.5. The three million or so characters of extra information on the disk include up-to-date details of Internet providers, and sample texts from the Internet so you can decide whether the Internet is for you before parting with money. To give you a full flavour would take about 10 terabytes. I left off WWW pages due to space limitations – readers can get good WWW demos from an Internet equipped friend, or at any of the trade shows and exhibitions.

Hardware and software used to produce this book

Pre-production and authoring: Macintosh LCIII 12/80/Ethernet, 'Graphic Convertor' shareware program for image manipulation, cropping and conversion. 486 DX 33 8/500/Reveal SoundFX/ NE2000 Lan card. Windows screen shots via 'Clipmate' shareware program.

Word processing: Apple PowerBook 165 8/80/Focus EtherLan SC, 'Nisus Compact' and 'Write Now' word processors.

Networking and communications: Novell 3.11 file-server/NE2000 Ethernet adapter, used for inter-computer file transfer and mail. Thanks to Charles Schofield (CNE) for providing the Novell facilities.

Modems: Hayes Optima 28800 V.FC + Fax modem – used for the comms from Macs and PCs – courtesy Hayes Microcomputer Products, UK. Pace Microlin Fx 9600 – used for portable dial-up from the PowerBook – courtesy Pace Micro Technology Ltd. Both modems are highly recommended.

Printers: Hewlett Packard DeskJet 300c, DeskWriter 510, Portable DeskWriter 310.

Backups: Bernoulli Mac Transportable drive, APC Back-UPS 250, APC Back-UPS 600, Syquest 44 removable drive.

Project Tracking: Apple Newton MessagePad 100.

Suppliers

Internet provider: Demon Internet Ltd, Finchley, London.

Macintosh supplier: Mygate Computing Ltd – tel: 0181 318 1424.

Certified Novell Engineer: Charles Schofield.

CD-ROM references

The Hackers Chronicles – P80 Systems

Forbidden Subjects – Forbidden Productions

InfoMagic UseNet CDROM – InfoMagic Inc.

InfoMac Archives – August '93

All from CONFIG.SYS – Ohio (mail joe@config.com).

Recommended commercial software

Macs

'VersaTerm with VersaTerm Link' software – Synergis.
This is an integrated suite of Internet utilities for the Mac which provides off-line Usenet news, encrypted POP3 mail, FTP and telnet access and the vital MacTCP control panel. It's now available from MacLine in the UK, tel: 0181 401 1111.

Windows

'NetManage Chameleon 4.1' software – Ethix.
Chameleon is a fine Windows program aimed squarely at dial-up Internetters. It will work with the majority of UK Internet providers. See the coupon in the book for a special offer.

All of the Shareware used in the production of this book was registered.

Acknowledgements

My thanks to:

> Grahame Davis (gbd@demon.net)
> – for Demon Internet Services.

> All the staff at Demon Internet Services
> – for being there.

> Charles Schofield CNE (chas@s-sco.demon.co.uk)
> – for hot beer, cold take-aways, warm heart.

> Editor Nicky Jaeger, Addison-Wesley
> (100020.554@compuserve.com)
> – for enthusiasm, and a small Piglet.

> Michelle Nath, Synergis USA (hnath@synergis.com)
> – for Versaterm Link software.

> Stuart Reay of Ethix (sales@calibra.demon.co.uk)
> – for NetManage Chameleon version 4.1.

Hayes Microcomputer Products (hayes@cix.compulink.co.uk)
– for handsome modems (Optima 28800 V.FC+Fax).
(Hayes bbs +44 (0) 1252 775 599)

Pace Microcomputers Limited
– for small handsome modems (Microlin 2400)
Pace bbs +44 (0) 1274 537 043

Music for this book supplied by Apple QuickTime GX.

Finally

If you get stuck with anything in the book and you have an
electronic mail account, you can email the Author for help at:

sue@s-sco.demon.co.uk

Your mail will be passed to someone who can help out with
your problem.

Sue Schofield
March 1995

About the author

Sue Schofield writes for the UK computer press, in between books.
Her work has appeared in *Focus Magazine*, *PC Plus*, *PC Magazine*,
PC Answers, *PC Direct*, *Teleworker Magazine*, the *Independent*
newspaper, *Mac User* and *Mac World* magazines, amongst many
others. Her work also appears regularly on the Internet in the
Privacy Forum Digest. She is a member of the Society of Authors
and the RSPCA, and is the author of the award winning *Modem &
Communications Guidebook*. Sue was born in the Year of the Cat,
and is currently owned by five felines. She opened her first
electronic mail account in 1981 and looks forward to the time when
UK service providers finally get the hang of Apple computers.

Sue commutes electronically from the depths of Sussex, and
can be freely contacted as *sue@s-sco.demon.co.uk*.

Contents

Part 2 Internet tools

Part 3 Finale

One of the favourite maxims of my father was the distinction between the two sorts of truths. Profound truths can be recognized by the fact that their opposites are also a profound truth, in contrast to trivialities where their opposites are equally absurd...

Neils Boer, 1967

Part I

Internet basics

1 Internet basics

'Internet providers
have started to
spring out of the
ground like worms
on a damp day...'

In the beginning there was the cold war, the Kennedy administration, and the Defense Department, spelt with an 's'. Out of that came the Internet as we know it, a sprawling network of networks, spiralling around the world like a thing spiralling around the world. There are connections to it in almost every country of the world, there are no charges for using it, and no limitations on the amount of data you can take from it, or copy from it. At the moment the Internet is the greatest free knowledge base on the planet, with the emphasis on the words 'at the moment'.

It's a bit of a mystery why the Internet has taken so long to reach the consciousness of the UK computer-owning public. And why the sudden interest now? Perhaps it's the rapid increase in the ownership of cheap computers, or is it the fact that Internet providers have started to spring out of the ground like worms on a damp day? Whatever the reason, the Internet is this year's flavour of the month, to mix an already poor metaphor, and this book hopes to get you set up along with the other 20 million people who are already plugged into the thing. It's rumoured that Internet connections are selling at the rate of two per second, so don't be surprised if you find that things are a tad busy, once you get there.

What you need

All you need to hook into the Internet is a telephone modem or an Ethernet cable which ties in with an 'Internet provider' (IP). At the basic level you might just have a simple mail connection via a bulletin board, at the top level you might have full access via a suite of software on your computer which knows about something called TCP/IP. (Don't worry about the jargon – yet.) This latter method is a bit different from the sort of computer based communications you might be used to. If you have a CompuServe or other dial-up bulletin board account you'll be familiar with terms like 'downloading', 'file transfers' and ASCII, which will provide a good grounding for using the Internet. But as you'll see, the Internet interacts with the user's computer in a different way to almost anything else you've come across, and you'll need a guiding hand in the early days while you're still fighting with impenetrable jargon

Computers can communicate with each other over bits of wire. That's the simple bit. The complicated bit is getting the hang of the Internet by picking up some of the technical jargon that surrounds it. This is because the Internet is a heap of computers which use a particular set of utilities and programs to communicate with each other, and occasionally with human beings. As things stand at the moment, the computers on the Internet have the upper hand, and you can't just plug yourself into a socket on the wall and get going, which you can do with almost every other consumer product. So you can deduce from this that the Internet isn't yet a consumer product, although it will be in a couple of years' time. And because it's not a consumer product, you, dear reader, have to fight with the impenetrable language of the computer-geek or the UNIX Dweeb, but not for long.

It should be said early on that users do not have to get involved with any of the technicalities of hooking up to the Internet, because there are any number of commercial companies who will come along and connect you up in exchange for a brown envelope full of fivers. But many of the UK people on the Internet have chosen to get involved with TCP/IP software because they like mucking about with computers. However, it's possible for non-technical users to get hooked up, as we are about to see.

Starting out

Let's start at the beginning. The first thing you need for access to the Internet is an Internet access account. It takes the form of provision of an access point to the 'Net, and generally speaking, you'll pick up that node – or permission to use it – from an Internet provider (IP in the jargon). These people supply connections to the Internet in the same way as a telecomms provider supplies a telephone service, and there are a growing number of them in the UK.

If you're a student, or an employee of a large company, you might already have an Internet connection available to you – as your educational body or employer will have registered a block of addresses with the Internet authorities. In that case you just need permission to use the node, which will generally appear to the user as a number, such as 158.152.24.106. The number is the 'address' of the computer on the Internet, and it's assigned to the TCP/IP software on the machine for the same purpose as a telephone number is assigned to a telephone. Once the address has been assigned, the computer becomes a 'network node' which can then access a TCP/IP network locally via Ethernet or LocalTalk cable. A TCP/IP network is a bunch of computers hooked together with cable (or modems or radio waves) using the TCP/IP protocols, which are explained in the next chapter. So a network, for the purposes of this book, is two or more computers which can exchange data with each other and an internetwork is a heap of networks connected to other networks, so that all computers on all the individual networks can exchange data over the large interconnecting network.

It's possible to access the Internet via a modem, but remember that when this happens the user is actually logged into a distant computer, not directly to something called the 'Internet'. It's the remote machine which has the connection to the Internet, not the modem.

Terminal and network connections

Commercial Internet accounts come in several flavours. The only 'real' type is a fully fledged 'network' connection, where your machine at home or in the office becomes a TCP/IP 'client' on a network. 'Client' means that your personal computer is half of a transaction based system – your client needs to see a 'server' at the other end before it can be used. This can happen over a direct Ethernet or modem connection – and a network connection will normally give you full access to all the Internet services such as file transfer with FTP, Usenet, Internet Relay Chat and so on. You will also get the benefit of a full Internet machine name (like **s-sco.demon.co.uk**) and a user ID (**sue**@s-sco.demon.co.uk). Benefits include being able to use the vast range of TCP/IP software, and files transferred to your machine will actually arrive directly on your hard disk.

This isn't the case with a 'terminal' connection. A terminal connection means that you access someone else's Internet computer on a network, usually via a modem. You lose the client–server model (explained in Chapter 3) you'd get on a full network connection, so you can't use TCP/IP software for access.

A terminal connection won't give you a machine name either, but it might give you an Internet mail address. And it won't let you download files direct to your hard disk because terminal connections have to take the files to the remote server and store them in a mailbox area, from where you later download them. (The CIX bulletin board service is a good example of a terminal connection provider.) To get over the problems of users sitting on phone lines downloading files once to the server and then again to the remote machine, some terminal services have introduced a facility called Batch FTP. It gets the files while the user is logged off, for collection at a later time.

There's one other major hassle with terminal connections – not being able to use all that fancy TCP/IP based software with them. Mac and Windows users have software available which graphically displays the directory tree of a remote server, or the

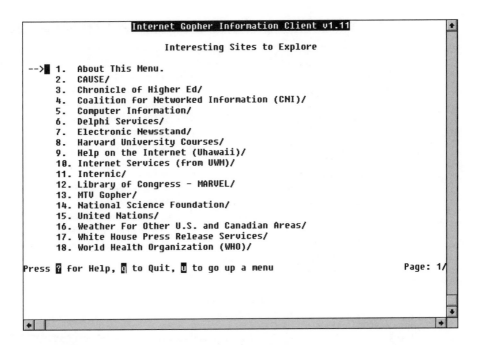

```
          ┌─────────────────────────────────────────────────────────┐
          │         Internet Gopher Information Client v1.11          │
          │                                                           │
          │               Interesting Sites to Explore               │
          │                                                           │
          │  -->█ 1.  About This Menu.                                │
          │       2.  CAUSE/                                          │
          │       3.  Chronicle of Higher Ed/                         │
          │       4.  Coalition for Networked Information (CNI)/       │
          │       5.  Computer Information/                           │
          │       6.  Delphi Services/                                │
          │       7.  Electronic Newsstand/                           │
          │       8.  Harvard University Courses/                     │
          │       9.  Help on the Internet (Uhawaii)/                 │
          │      10.  Internet Services (from UWM)/                   │
          │      11.  Internic/                                       │
          │      12.  Library of Congress - MARVEL/                   │
          │      13.  MTV Gopher/                                     │
          │      14.  National Science Foundation/                    │
          │      15.  United Nations/                                 │
          │      16.  Weather For Other U.S. and Canadian Areas/      │
          │      17.  White House Press Release Services/             │
          │      18.  World Health Organization (WHO)/                │
          │                                                           │
          │  Press ▓ for Help, ▓ to Quit, ▓ to go up a menu   Page: 1/│
          │                                                           │
          └─────────────────────────────────────────────────────────┘
```

Figure 1.1 *Terminal based services can't run TCP/IP based software. This is the view of Gopher through a terminal service.*

result of a Gopher search. A full network connection allows these users to navigate around the Internet with mouse clicks and pretty pictures, and consequently they curse terminal connections which don't allow this to happen.

Because the Internet is so popular many dial-up bulletin boards are implementing terminal connections – so you should be aware of the differences before you part with money. The real feather in the cap of the network connection is that TCP/IP allows multitasking. You can use as much of the available modem or Ethernet bandwidth as you can grab and that means with a fast modem you can send and receive mail while grabbing files from a remote site. Each task you run is called a 'session' and it's common to have multiple sessions open in various windows. Multitasking saves money, or at least it does if you have a personal computer and software capable of doing it.

To sum up – **terminal connections** give you email in and out, some file transfer and telnet facilities. A **network connection** gives you full file transfers, a real machine address

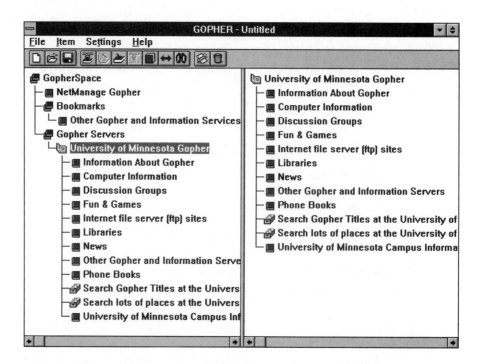

Figure 1.2 Windows Gopher client running with TCP/IP. Navigation is faster and easier than with a terminal service.

(often with multiple user access), and it lets you use TCP/IP based programs.

So – it's make-your-mind-up time. If you only need an electronic mail address then a terminal account with one of the providers already mentioned might meet your needs. On the other hand a full Internet connection brings a lot more functionality – although it's only going to be of real value if you use it – or have the software to exploit it. But think for a moment. Most of the next five years' development in information transfer is going to occur on the Internet. You'll get international voice transfer for the price of a local phone call, the ability to mail multimedia documents (sound and vision) around the world, and eventually, communications such as video on demand, video phone calls and much more. Oh, and there's even something called the Information Superhighway around the corner, but no one yet has decided what it is. If you want to be part of this revolution then go for a full Internet account now. You'll pay less per megabyte of information transferred over a full Internet connection than you will over a terminal service, and you'll be ready for whatever the Internet decides to chuck at you in the next couple of years. You'll also save yourself the nuisance of changing your email address once you do decide to change.

If you are a Windows user, or a Mac user or an Amiga or Archimedes user then it's recommended that you go straight for the throat with a full network account. You'll be able to use all of the wonderful graphical software coming onto the Internet. But if you are a DOS user then things aren't quite so clear-cut. Most of your interaction with the Internet will be via character based terminal emulation and you might find that terminal services are sufficient. But think carefully before you sign up – are you always going to be using DOS? Do you only want occasional Internet mail? Will you be content with a character based command line interface when you see things like the World Wide Web running in full sound and colour over a phone line? If you can unequivocally say yes to these questions then a terminal account may be sufficient, but if you've got any hesitation at all then go for a full network account.

Access points

The other major consideration before you sign up is the relative geographical distance between your location and the Internet provider's access points. These are called Points of Presence (PoPs) which is geek-speak for 'telephone number'. Many of the major Internet providers only have direct dial-up access to London based numbers. This means that users outside London will be paying a fortune in phone charges for access. Some providers make access available to distant subscribers over the packet switch network – but you'll pay extra charges if you use this, and you won't get anything like the full throughput that the latest modems are capable of. Moral – if you live outside London look for a provider with a PoP near you. (If you travel around as part of your job, then look for multiple PoPs.) And don't pay packet switch charges unless you are absolutely sure it's the cheapest option. Remember that file and information transfer takes longer over packet switch than it does over dial-up lines, and it costs more because you have to pay packet switch charges – even if these are reverse-charged to your provider's account, as they often are.

Pricing

The service providers all have different ideas about what constitutes fair pricing. In general you should try to avoid paying hourly charges in addition to phone charges, because the Internet encourages browsing and you'll end up with large bills, especially in the early days when you're finding your way around. Watch out also for fees levied on the amount of data or mail transferred through your account. Look for a provider who charges a single fixed fee for access. It's not recommended that you pay by the minute for access, unless you want to see your service provider get rich, in direct inverse proportion to you getting poor. Charging rates will depend on whether you are using a modem (dial-up) account or whether you want a full-blown corporate installation, but in general you should only pay for rental of the IP address – not for the amount of data you pump through it, or the amount of time you spend using it.

Since this book was first published, many suppliers of terminal based dial-up services have started to advertise their offerings as 'full Internet connections'. This is potentially misleading, or at best ambiguous.

A full Internet service is generally taken to mean one where TCP/IP software is used to provide the connection via TCP/IP access. Readers should therefore be careful about making this distinction – one reader mailed me with a woeful tale of how he'd bought TCP/IP browser software for his terminal account only to find it wouldn't work. For the purposes of definition in this book, services such as CIX, CompuServe, and Delphi offer terminal accounts, not full TCP/IP access, and TCP/IP software will not work with these services at this time.

Summary

The difference between a terminal connection and 'full' network access is large:

Terminal-only access means that:

● You *can* send and receive text mail, and you do get an Internet-savvy mail address.

● You *can* often use Gopher, telnet, FTP and other utilities on your host system to transfer files and log on to remote computers, but you're dependent on the facilities offered by your host service.

● You *cannot* receive files directly to your hard disk – you have to download them from the host, once the host has received them by FTP.

● You *cannot* easily attach binary files to mail messages to users outside your host system, unless your host has compatible 'front end' mail handling software.

● You *cannot* easily extract binary files from mail messages from users outside your host system, unless your host has compatible 'front end' mail handling software.

● You *cannot* easily run multiple sessions on your computer – which means that you can't send mail while you're transferring a file

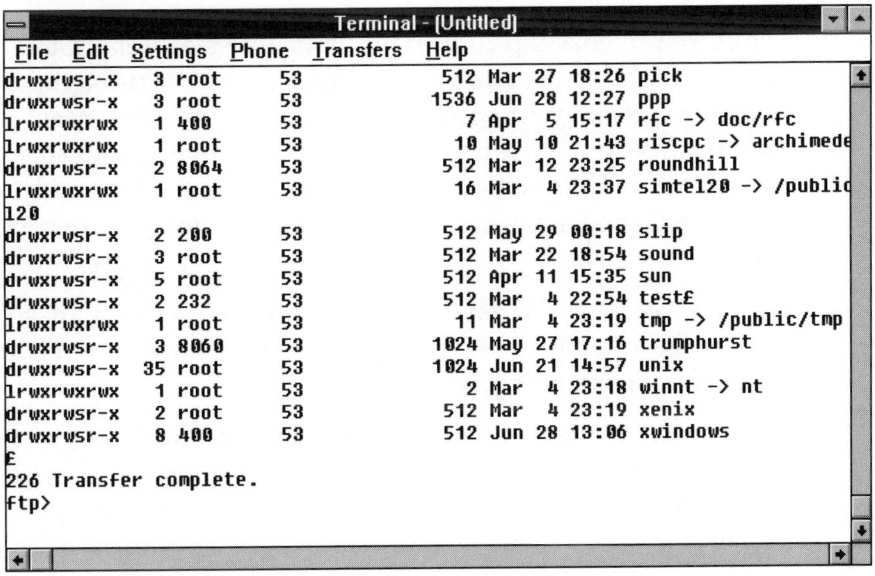

```
┌────────────────────────────── Terminal - (Untitled) ──────────────────▼─▲─┐
│ File  Edit  Settings  Phone  Transfers  Help                               │
│ drwxrwsr-x   3 root     53              512 Mar 27 18:26 pick             ◆│
│ drwxrwsr-x   3 root     53             1536 Jun 28 12:27 ppp               │
│ lrwxrwxrwx   1 400      53                7 Apr  5 15:17 rfc -> doc/rfc     │
│ lrwxrwxrwx   1 root     53               10 May 10 21:43 riscpc -> archimede│
│ drwxrwsr-x   2 8064     53              512 Mar 12 23:25 roundhill         │
│ lrwxrwxrwx   1 root     53               16 Mar  4 23:37 simtel20 -> /publiç│
│ 120                                                                         │
│ drwxrwsr-x   2 200      53              512 May 29 00:18 slip              │
│ drwxrwsr-x   3 root     53              512 Mar 22 18:54 sound             │
│ drwxrwsr-x   5 root     53              512 Apr 11 15:35 sun               │
│ drwxrwsr-x   2 232      53              512 Mar  4 22:54 test£             │
│ lrwxrwxrwx   1 root     53               11 Mar  4 23:19 tmp -> /public/tmp │
│ drwxrwsr-x   3 8060     53             1024 May 27 17:16 trumphurst        │
│ drwxrwsr-x  35 root     53             1024 Jun 21 14:57 unix              │
│ lrwxrwxrwx   1 root     53                2 Mar  4 23:18 winnt -> nt        │
│ drwxrwsr-x   2 root     53              512 Mar  4 23:19 xenix             │
│ drwxrwsr-x   8 400      53              512 Jun 28 13:06 xwindows          │
│ £                                                                          │
│ 226 Transfer complete.                                                     │
│ ftp>                                                                     ▼│
│ ◆                                                                        ▶│
└────────────────────────────────────────────────────────────────────────────┘
```

Figure 1.3   *An FTP server screen from a terminal service.*

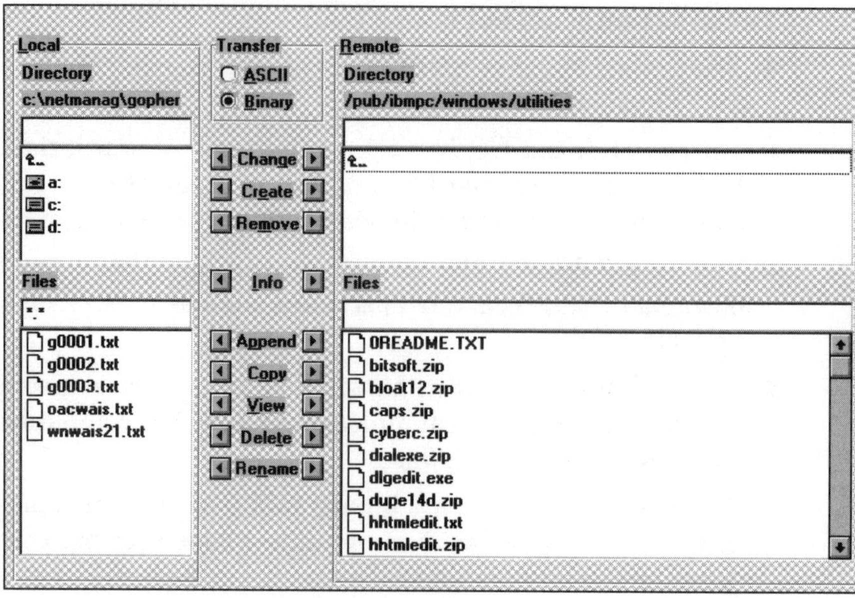

Figure 1.4   *Windows FTP client. Files can be dragged from the remote service to the local hard disk or viewed automatically with Write.*

while you're chatting to a friend with Internet Relay Chat. This is important for modem users – as maximizing your throughput is vital for minimizing your phone bills. However, some Mac systems, notably the First Class client–server system, now permit this, and the CompuServe Information Manager programs for Mac and Windows permit a degree of multitasking over a single modem connection.

● You *cannot* use any of the vast amounts of TCP/IP based mail, FTP, telnet, or Usenet software available (although your host may have made arrangements for these facilities to be provided as part of their 'front end' software.)

● You *cannot* have your own Internet 'domain'. In practice this means that you can't set up a machine of your own and let other people log on to it to transfer files or leave messages. This is perhaps more important to business users than to recreational users – but it can be useful sometimes if you've left a file on your home or work system and you are somewhere else.

Network access means that:

● You *can* receive files directly to your hard disk.

● You *can* easily attach binary files to mail messages to Internet users.

● You *can* easily extract binary files from mail messages from Internet users.

● You *can* run multiple sessions on your computer, thus saving money.

● You *can* use any of the vast amounts of TCP/IP based mail, FTP, telnet, or Usenet software available.

● You *can* have your own Internet 'domain'.

Cons for full network connections:

● You'll have to configure TCP/IP and dial-up software to run on your computer. It's not always easy...

2 Software for Internet use

'There's a huge
amount of
Shareware
available...'

You need a fair amount of computer technology to get started on the Internet. However, almost any personal computer can be used to access the 'Net – as long as it has various bits of Internet-savvy software available for it.

Regardless of computer type you'll need:

- **TCP/IP software**. This provides the basic transport mechanism which handles your data over the 'Net. There are various types, from various sources, but without it you'll have no full access to the 'Net.

You must have TCP/IP software, unless you're running a terminal account.

● **SLIP or PPP** if you're using a modem. These are the 'drivers' which allow TCP/IP to work over serial lines. It's SLIP or PPP which handles the modem dialling and hang-up, as well as providing a text file (called a 'script') which you use to automate the login procedure.

You must have SLIP or PPP software or Windows 'Socket'-type software to access the Internet over a modem, unless you're running a terminal account.

If you have a UNIX machine you'll find that most of the software you need to communicate with the Internet is probably already built in.

Software supplies

You get hold of TCP/IP, SLIP or PPP as *software programs*. It's unlikely that your High Street Washing Machine and Colour Telly supplier will know what you mean when you say you want a Gopher

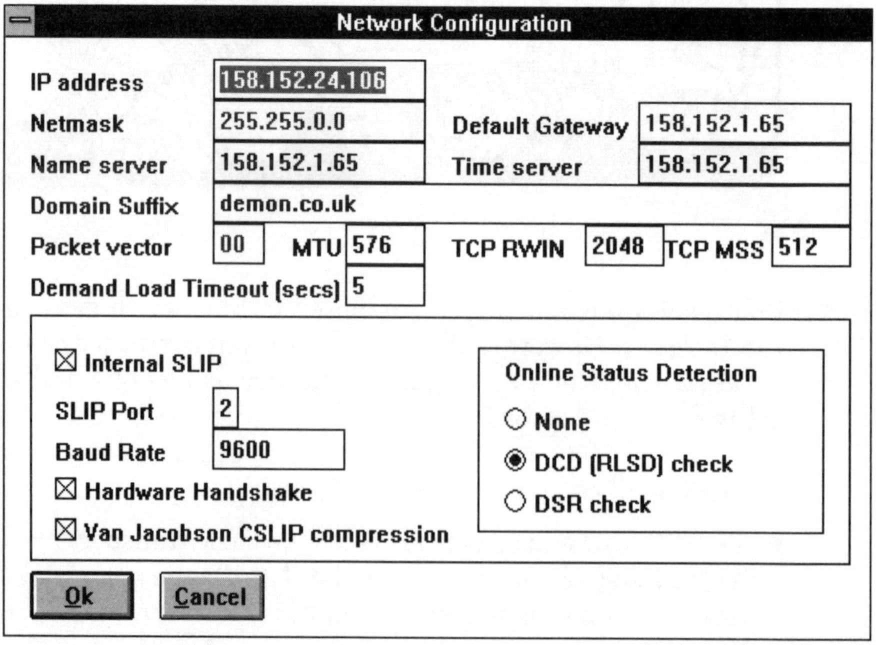

Figure 2.1   *The TCP/IP configuration in Trumpet Winsock for Windows. You need TCP to hook fully up to the Internet.*

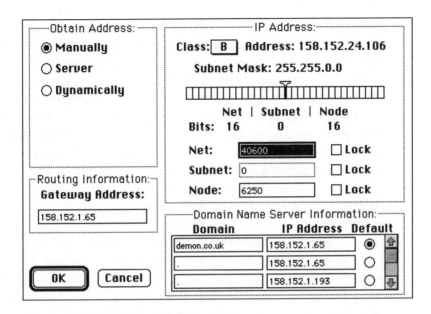

Figure 2.2   *Mac TCP configuration screen. It's very similar to the TCP/IP set-ups for Windows.*

client with SLIP and TCP/IP, so as things stand you will probably rely on an Internet provider to send you the requisite programs. If you already have an account on one of the dial-up systems somewhere, you can often download the programs for free, and of course the Internet itself has dozens of programs available for most computer types. But the most difficult problem for newcomers is getting hold of the software, a problem which will ease as more commercial programs come onto the market.

Shareware or commercial?

You should decide at the outset whether you want to use Shareware programs, or many of the free Public Domain programs available on the Internet. These programs are cheap or free, tend to offer good functionality and are in use on tens of thousands of computers. The downside is that updates and support are sporadic, the programs are not tailored to the services provided by your Internet provider, and there's no guarantee that one program will work alongside another during a multiple session. Most of the Shareware TCP/IP based programs are also designed for use on 'direct' connections – where a computer is connected to the Internet by an Ethernet cable. Few of the Shareware programs take modem users into account by providing offline features, which generally means higher bills for users. Usenet reader programs are a prime example – you can count the number of Shareware Usenet reader programs that allow newsgroups to be read offline (that is, with the modem disconnected and the data saved to disk) on the fingers of one foot.

The alternative is to use commercial programs. These cost real amounts of money, but tend to offer better integration and reliability. You should get telephone support for a commercial program, and you should expect regular updates at a reasonable price. Again, few commercial programs cater for modem users, but at least you should be spared the system crashes and general protection faults that go with using handfuls of Shareware, although not all the commercial programs on the market are perfect. At the moment there are few decent commercial programs that offer good levels of integration for users, although many more will appear on the market as suppliers begin to realize that the Internet isn't a one-day wonder.

Application and client software

Once you have the basic TCP/IP and SLIP or PPP software, you'll need application software to access the various corners of the Internet. For FTP you'll need *FTP software*, for email you'll need *email software* and so on. These are the **client** applications that let you hook into the various application servers you'll find on the Internet. These programs communicate through the TCP/IP link, which is operating through your modem, which is being managed by SLIP or PPP. Does that make sense? You choose client software just as you would choose a word processor or other computer application, that is, you listen to what all the experts tell you, and then go and buy the same program as the guy next door has. In some cases there are no commercial programs available, and you'll have to use the freeware or Shareware options, but once again, it's early days for the Internet in the UK, and there will be more Internet-compliant software available as time passes.

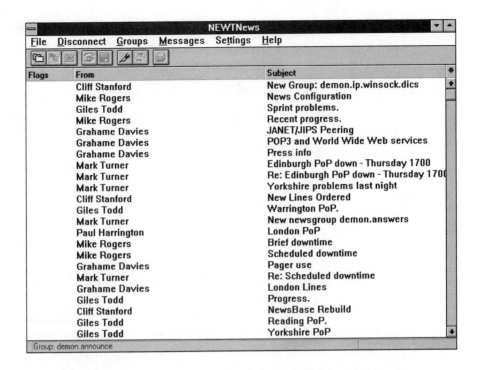

Figure 2.3 *NewtNews, part of Internet Chameleon. It's commercial software, and should therefore be expected to run without problems.*

In practice you will probably end up using the Shareware software distributed by your provider, or by the guy next door, unless you're a business that can afford the services of a consultant or dealer. Early generations of Shareware programs for the Internet were slightly lacking in many respects, but have improved drastically over the last year. There was also a flood of updated software for WAIS, Gopher and the World Wide Web in 1994 and it's now possible to get going for very little outlay.

It's important to remember that whatever software you end up using will be out of date in months rather than years, because the Internet is growing and changing at a phenomenal rate. The basics, SLIP, PPP and telnet, will remain the same, but the other services are evolving rapidly. This may influence your decision as to whether you'll use Shareware or commercial software to get going with the Internet.

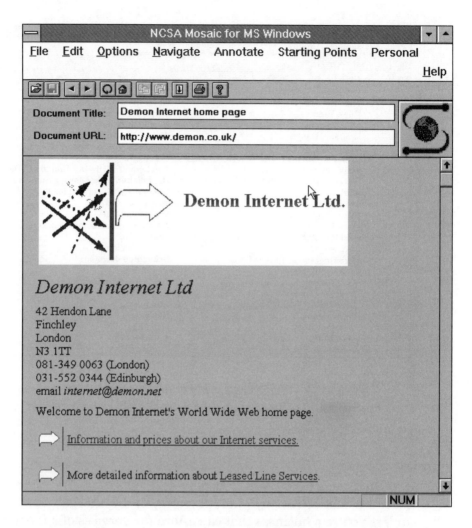

Figure 2.4   *The spectacular NCSA Mosaic client software. Early versions were prone to hangups on some systems.*

Shareware or commercial ware?

The Internet works as a community of sorts, and as it's a computer-centric community many of its denizens are computer programmers or code-dabblers. Consequently there's a huge amount of Shareware on the 'Net, and not a little of it aimed at TCP/IP users. There are two sides to Shareware. On the one hand there's the noble concept of publishing low-cost software which may be of use to others, on the other hand there's the downside of buggy code, untested software and zero support.

A lot of first-generation Shareware falls into the latter category. If it's version 1.0 then it's often full of bugs. But there are exceptions. Some of the Shareware programs offer great functionality and few bugs, so you may want to use them, and this is where the problems start. Much of the Shareware on the Internet originates in the USA, and is aimed at Ethernet users. US Shareware people seem in the main to be based at some educational establishment with a permanent Internet connection thrown in. That's the reason why you don't get many Shareware mail programs with SLIP dialers attached to them or Usenet readers that dump the data to hard disk.

You'll also find it hard to register your favourite American Shareware program, because many of the authors have moved on from their last known email address, or because your bank wants to charge you 25 dollars to raise a registration cheque for half that amount. Getting support or receipts from US Shareware authors is difficult too, and there are few UK corporate accounts departments who will raise a cheque without seeing a pro forma invoice. So in many cases Shareware authors cut their own throats by handling the administration side of their business inefficiently, and UK users are stuck with the dilemma of using unregistered software.

At the moment there is little you can do about this, unless the Shareware author takes credit card orders by mail or fax. Many of them don't because of the huge levies charged on small companies by the credit card authorities. Some Shareware can be registered via CompuServe's SWREG service, but then you need a CompuServe account to use the facility.

But do you need to use Shareware products to get onto the Internet? In most cases the answer is 'yes' unless you are prepared to fork out the large sums required for commercial software. VersaTerm and Internet Chameleon – the two packages used in the preparation of this book – cost around £150.00 each by the time delivery and VAT are taken into account, so you can see why the low-cost Shareware option is so attractive. Alas, if you use Shareware without paying for it for any of the reasons above then you are depriving the author of income, which might just be funding the next whizzo release of your favourite email or News program. Probably the only answer is to lobby your Internet

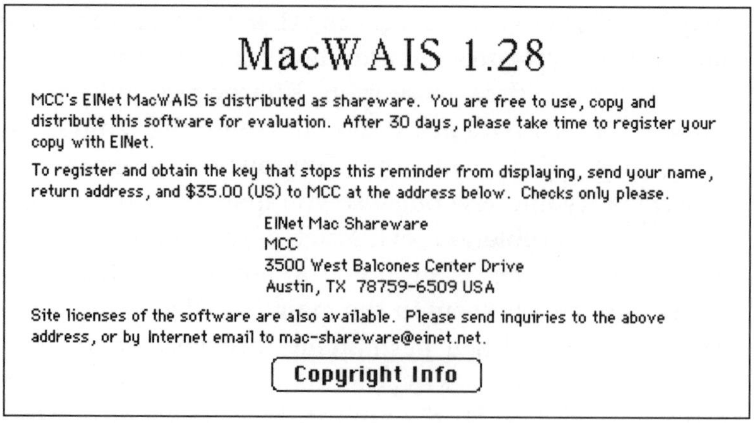

```
┌─────────────────────────────────────────────────────────────┐
│                                                               │
│                   MacWAIS 1.28                                │
│                                                               │
│   MCC's EINet MacWAIS is distributed as shareware. You are free to use, copy and   │
│   distribute this software for evaluation. After 30 days, please take time to register your   │
│   copy with EINet.                                            │
│                                                               │
│   To register and obtain the key that stops this reminder from displaying, send your name,   │
│   return address, and $35.00 (US) to MCC at the address below. Checks only please.   │
│                                                               │
│                EINet Mac Shareware                            │
│                MCC                                            │
│                3500 West Balcones Center Drive                 │
│                Austin, TX  78759-6509 USA                      │
│                                                               │
│   Site licenses of the software are also available. Please send inquiries to the above   │
│   address, or by Internet email to mac-shareware@einet.net.   │
│                                                               │
│                   ┌──────────────────────┐                    │
│                   │   Copyright Info     │                    │
│                   └──────────────────────┘                    │
└─────────────────────────────────────────────────────────────┘
```

Figure 2.5 *Shareware registration screen from MacWais. Most UK corporates are not prepared to use Shareware.*

provider to arrange for site-licensing of the Shareware products with the author(s). This is easier to do *en masse*, and the provider can then license the software to users. But until that happens you are morally obliged to pay your Shareware fees wherever possible, even if the author makes that difficult for UK and European users.

Finally, you may find that you have to use a kludge of ill-matched software to provide the suite of TCP/IP programs you'll need to make use of all the Internet facilities. This is fine in the UNIX world, but not so good for Mac and Windows users where kludges often mean system crashes when two programs are used simultaneously. But it's early days for Internet software for personal computers, and if you are patient you will find more low-priced good software is being written for PCs, Amigas and Macs. When that happens prices of commercial software will fall, giving the user more real choice. Already larger providers such as British Telecom and Cityscape are designing their own access software for the Internet, and it won't be long before providers who offer only Shareware software will start to lose out, especially when easy-to-use custom software becomes freely available. The start of this awakening is already here – Apple have included the MacTCP control panel with the latest release of System 7.5 and Microsoft Window's '95 will include TCP/IP networking too. 1995 will see a large explosion in the number of TCP/IP based software packages available in the UK, and the revised NetManage Chameleon for

Windows is a good example of the way software is evolving to meet market demands.

Watch out too for Internet provision from some unlikely people. Microsoft are about to launch their own global service, with the software to match embedded into Microsoft applications such as Word and Excel. BT, the BBC, IBM and other large organizations are already jumping on the bandwagon and the Internet will be repackaged and sold as a boxed product in high street stores by Christmas 1995. Look out for offers from the national papers as they resell Internet provision to tie in with their own World Wide Web pages...

3 Internet technicalities

'You won't become a Network Guru by reading this chapter...'

SUPER V42

You don't need to read this chapter if you've got all your Internet software up and running and you can get your mail, send messages to 20 million other people, and fight with all the other Internet services you've got at your disposal. You only need to read it if you want a brief indication of how the Network of Networks works, and what all the fuss about TCP/IP is about. This is only the most basic of primers – if you need more information, or are saving up for a beard and sandals so you can become a Network Guru, then you'll find all you need on the 'Net itself – or in your local bookstore. This chapter just points you at some of the buzzwords. You won't become a Network Guru by reading it.

How it all hangs together

Computers on the Internet use something called the Internet Protocol to pass messages around over cables, fibre optic links, or bits of virtual damp string. 'Internet Protocol' is abbreviated to IP for the sake of brevity, and a protocol, in this sense, is a series of conventions that describe how data gets chucked around between computers. IP is a 'packetizing protocol' – that is, it chops data up into small chunks, adds the address of the intended recipient and the address of the sender, and hopes that's enough information for the packet to get to its destination, or back to the sender if it doesn't. The packets are re-assembled (or not) when they get to the destination, to re-create the original data. The actual bit of wire – the connection between the sending computer and the destination – isn't really a bit of wire, but a virtual link which might go over any number of fibre optic cables, satellite links, packet switch networks, dial-up phone lines with modems or whatever comes to hand.

Smart boxes of electronics are used to pass packets between connected networks. **Routers** are boxes that connect different sorts of physical networks together. You might hook up your office Ethernet cable to a router so that the router can convert the Ethernet stuff for use with a modem over a phone link. At the other end you'd have a router and a modem doing the reconversion from phone line signals to Ethernet signals. A **bridge** is a similarly smart box that joins or bridges two similar or dissimilar networks but makes the connection invisible to the user. If you wanted to hook up your network to the one in the next office you'd use a bridge. Bridges are smart enough to work out which computer on the Ethernet should get which packets, but not smart enough to hook straight into modems, which is the job of the router.

Confused? The main thing to remember about all of this is that it doesn't need to be remembered – because if ever you have to fight with a router or a bridge to get your Internet connection going you have a serious problem. But it's handy to know what the techies are talking about when they mention *routing problems*. Most domestic users will never need to get involved to this level – and most commercial users will have a guy with a degree in Altered Consciousness (the Network Guru) to sort all of this out.

All this stuff about routers and bridges is a diversion – IP packets leave one computer and if all's well eventually reach their destination. But IP doesn't always deliver stuff in the right order, or at the same time. Packets arrive depending on all sorts of variables, like the amount of traffic on the net, the amount of network routing that's available, the number of maintenance staff on holiday, and so on. To make some sort of order out of this possible chaos virtually all Internet computers now use a second protocol to control IP. Transmission Control Protocol (abbreviated to TCP) is the controlling protocol which ensures that packets arrive in the order in which they were sent. In fact the use of TCP over an IP link looks for all the world like a direct point-to-point link, although TCP adds a considerable amount of overhead to IP packets. Despite this it's the TCP/IP *pair* of protocols which make the Internet work.

TCP/IP

It's all very well to go around bleating about Internet and Transmission Control Protocols, but you will be saying 'Well heck, this doesn't get me very far'. In fact TCP/IP won't get you very far at all, unless you have a network to talk to, and for most of us that means either using that piece of Ethernet cable you found lying about under the desk, or hooking up to the 'Net via a modem. Out of the two, using a modem is by the far the more difficult, as modems are not designed for use by human beings. And in both cases your TCP/IP software will need to be configured – which means feeding it with the address of the network and workstation, and information about which transport mechanism you're using. Modem users will also need either SLIP or PPP software. These provide methods of getting TCP/IP to work over a serial link, which is what a modem is.

The setting up of a machine for use on the Internet will be done for you in a commercial or university environment – but at home you're on your own. You have to fight with the setting up of TCP/IP, the dialer software in your implementation of SLIP or PPP, and the setting up of addressing and other server based information. This takes about a morning if you've done it before, or a day if you haven't, so allow plenty of time. In TCP/IP no one can hear you scream.

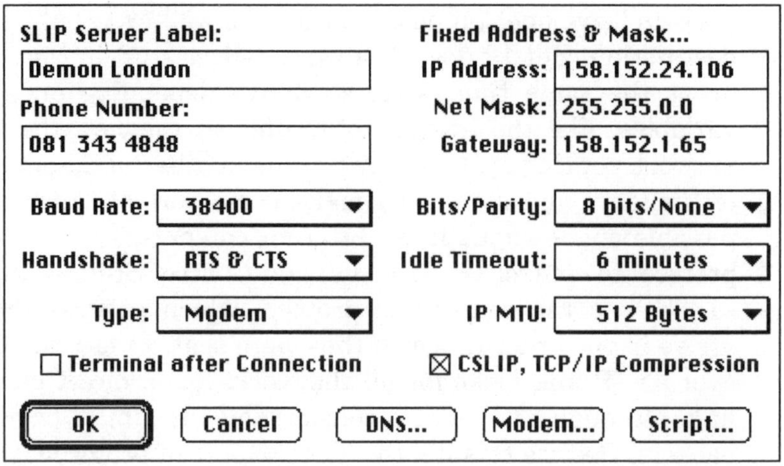

```
┌─────────────────────────────────────────────────────────────────────┐
│  SLIP Server Label:              Fixed Address & Mask...              │
│  ┌─────────────────────┐         IP Address: │158.152.24.106│         │
│  │Demon London         │                                              │
│  └─────────────────────┘         Net Mask: │255.255.0.0│              │
│  Phone Number:                                                        │
│  ┌─────────────────────┐         Gateway: │158.152.1.65│              │
│  │081 343 4848         │                                              │
│  └─────────────────────┘                                              │
│                                                                       │
│    Baud Rate: │   38400    ▼│    Bits/Parity: │ 8 bits/None ▼│        │
│                                                                       │
│    Handshake: │  RTS & CTS ▼│   Idle Timeout: │  6 minutes  ▼│        │
│                                                                       │
│         Type: │   Modem    ▼│          IP MTU: │  512 Bytes  ▼│       │
│                                                                       │
│     ☐ Terminal after Connection    ☒ CSLIP, TCP/IP Compression        │
│                                                                       │
│   ┌──────┐  ┌────────┐  ┌───────┐  ┌─────────┐  ┌─────────┐           │
│   │  OK  │  │ Cancel │  │ DNS...│  │ Modem...│  │ Script...│          │
│   └──────┘  └────────┘  └───────┘  └─────────┘  └─────────┘           │
└─────────────────────────────────────────────────────────────────────┘
```

Figure 3.1 *Typical SLIP set-up from VersaTerm. The IP address is allocated by the Internet provider, as is the gateway address.*

Many a SLIP

Modems were not designed specifically for use with TCP/IP, and to get your Mark Four Whizzbang Wonder to work with it you are going to need either the Serial Line Interface Protocol (SLIP) or the Point-to-Point Protocol (PPP). You buy these as software utilities, or get them for free from the Internet or your Internet provider. Both of these, as far as the user is concerned, sit on top of TCP/IP and make it work over the serial dial-up link that exists while your modem is behaving itself. SLIP and PPP handle things like the telephone number of the service you are calling, the address of the computer at the client end of the link (yours) and whether or not to use compression over the link. Quite often these programs will pick up the address of the remote computer from the TCP/IP controller software you've already installed.

If you are already familiar with standard computer communications programs for personal computers then some of the basic operations of SLIP and PPP might seem familiar to you. With SLIP or PPP managing the TCP/IP link between you and the remote network you don't have to worry about things like downloading

Script Login Configuration...		Script ▼

Send Text:

Wait For:	Timeout:		
			⊠ <CR>
demon login:	90 secs ▼	●●●●●	⊠ <CR>
Password:	90 secs ▼	●●●●●●	⊠ <CR>
Protocol:	90 secs ▼	●●●●	⊠ <CR>
HELLO	90 secs ▼		☐ <CR>
	Ignore ▼		☐ <CR>
	Ignore ▼		☐ <CR>
	Ignore ▼		☐ <CR>

OK	Cancel

Figure 3.2   *Login script for SLIP. A carriage return (CR) is sent at the end of each line if the box is checked.*

files, but you still have to deal with novelties such as parity, handshaking and setting up IP addresses.

Comms geeks will argue the toss about the merits of using SLIP or PPP but to a large extent it depends what your Internet provider has decided to offer you. No PPP? Use SLIP. No SLIP? Use PPP. It's that simple, unless you want to make it difficult. To an extent you'll find that the older SLIP system is widely used in the USA, not so widely in the UK where PPP is often the norm. But if you do have a choice then the word is to use PPP, which is more up to date than SLIP and should be more reliable over modems. It's rumoured to be faster and less error-prone too, but as modems don't provide anything like an optimum link for data transfer this is difficult to quantify. There are concerns amongst technology nerds that PPP takes longer to negotiate its start-up link than SLIP but you're unlikely to notice this in practice. The author uses SLIP on a Mac and PPP on a Windows PC to the same provider with nary a problem, so the real answer must be – if it ain't broke don't swap it for something else that might be, because someone else says so.

You will almost always have to write a script within the SLIP or PPP handler to log you into the remote connection. Internet providers have much fun in changing the prompt at their end of the connection, so that all of the login scripts used by subscribers will suddenly fail to connect until changed. The amusement factor is compounded by the fact that if you cannot log in – you can't find that message telling you the login routine has been changed, and any Internet provider worth their salt will post messages about intended login changes days or weeks in advance.

Both SLIP and PPP utilities need to be configured with all sorts of information, like the phone number of the place you are going to connect to, and your Internet address (we're coming to that in a minute). What you should get from a decent supplier is a modicum of help in setting these things up, because in all truth, fighting with modems, SLIP and IP addresses will tax the brain of even the most enlightened comms guru. This includes the author, who admits to not having a beard, but also to not being a comms guru. This crafty person therefore got Demon Internet Services around on a pretence to fix up the dialling and address routines in exchange for a cup of tea. In fact most UK providers will offer at least a partial get-you-going service, with telephone help if you need it. You might also consider lugging your computer around to the Internet provider to have the software installed, just as you would take your Fiat Uno to the garage to have a radio installed. But phone the provider first, huh? You should expect to pay a fee for this service if it's offered, as it takes longer than you would expect.

Getting the right address

All this stuff about software is going to be of no use to you if you don't have an Internet address. An address is a place where you can normally be found, or at least where your mail will get sent to in the normal run of things. Everybody has an address – you can mail the Queen at Buck House, London, and the letter will get there. You can mail 'That Old Fool, Houses of Parliament, London', and the letter will go to the Prime Minister. For Internet mail, and everything else, you'll need an Internet address.

Internet addresses are peculiar things. They use numbers, because that's how things are with computers. And because there

```
Wait timeout: [40   ]  seconds
                                                        <CR>
○ Out ◉ Wait [ogin:                              ]      □
◉ Out ○ Wait [s-sco                              ]      ☒
○ Out ◉ Wait [word:                              ]      □
◉ Out ○ Wait [password!!|                        ]      ☒
○ Out ◉ Wait [ocol:                              ]      □
◉ Out ○ Wait [ppp                                ]      ☒
○ Out ◉ Wait [HELLO                              ]      □
◉ Out ○ Wait [                                   ]      □

                              ( Cancel )   (   OK   )
```

Figure 3.3   *PPP Login script. It's identical to a SLIP script,*
except for the line that tells the server to use PPP.

are a lot of computers on the Internet you need a lot of numbers to
describe them all. Numbers are allocated to providers on a block
basis and become part of something called the Domain Name
System (DNS). If you set up a TCP/IP network in your back
bedroom and then hook it up to the Internet, you'll find all sorts of
problems if the numbering scheme you've used clashes with the
numbering scheme in the Big Wide World.

Why? Imagine that your long-lost Postal Order has arrived,
and you go and buy 255 computers with the money. When you
finally get out of the asylum you might want to hook them all
together into one quite large network. So you'd give each one an
address, perhaps starting at 1 and finishing at 255. This would be
OK until your friend also got out of the asylum and wanted to hook
his 255 computers up to yours. If his numbering system started at
256 then you'd have no problems – but naturally he's used the same
numbering system as you have, and one of you will have to
renumber a whole set of machines to give each one a unique
address. It's the same with Internet addresses. No two can be the
same, for obvious reasons, and so there's an entire body of people

```
┌─────────────────────────────────────────────────────────────┐
│ Modem Configuration Strings...          ┌──────────┬───┐      │
│                                          │ Modems   │ ▼ │      │
│ Reset Modem:                             └──────────┴───┘      │
│ ┌───────────────────────────────────────────────────────────┐│
│ │ATZ                                                         ││
│ └───────────────────────────────────────────────────────────┘│
│ Initialize Modem:                                             │
│ ┌───────────────────────────────────────────────────────────┐│
│ │AT &F                                                       ││
│ └───────────────────────────────────────────────────────────┘│
│ Configure Modem:                                              │
│ ┌───────────────────────────────────────────────────────────┐│
│ │AT \J0 %C1 \N4 \G0 \Q3 W1                                   ││
│ └───────────────────────────────────────────────────────────┘│
│                                                               │
│  ┌──────────────┐      ┌──────────────┐                       │
│  │      OK      │      │    Cancel    │                       │
│  └──────────────┘      └──────────────┘           ▶           │
└─────────────────────────────────────────────────────────────┘
```

Figure 3.4 *Both SLIP and PPP will configure the modem before dialling. You'll need to be familar with modem set-up strings to configure either program.*

dishing out and managing Internet addressing. You as a punter won't need to worry, because your Internet provider has been allocated a block of addresses, and will let you use one if you pay your bills on time. You'll only have to worry if you've used a private numbering scheme on a non-Internet network, and you suddenly want to hook in. You'll have to change your addressing scheme to suit. Corporates take note!

Letters and figures

The Internet uses 32-bit binary numbers, that is, a series of 1s and 0s, to denote a single address. But because nobody understands binary, that string of digits is broken down into four 8-bit bytes, and then translated into a decimal number. So a decimal Internet address looks like 158.152.24.106, and the more eagle-eyed amongst you will spot that this string of numbers is the Internet address of the author. In fact, all this talk about Internet binary and decimal addresses is a bit spurious because you can use the Internet without stuffing your head full of numbers. Those decimal addresses are actually translated into textual address strings (in fact it happens the other way around) and 158.152.24.106 actually means S-SCO. DEMON.CO.UK. You can use either numbers or text addresses when sending mail or setting up your SLIP or PPP connection, as the text gets translated into the numeric address on the way. It's slightly faster to use the numerical form, although you're not going to notice this over a modem connection.

If you want to impress people in restaurants you can spout the Secret Lore of Internet Addressing. This states that you can tell a lot from a decimal Internet address and bore people to death with the result. In the example my address has a network number of 158.152. There will be loads of other people with 158.152 in their address, because that's the number of the network to which my computer is connected (over a modem or otherwise). My local address is 24.106 – which denotes the host computer on the 158.152 network itself. Networks are also subdivided into Class types but you don't need to know about these unless you're setting up or managing largish networks.

All this stuff about numbers is confusing, so let's forget it. From now on we should use letters, and dip a furtive toe into the Domain Name System. This is a convention which uses a three-letter suffix to the textual address. COM is used for a commercial company, EDU for an educational site, NET for networking sites, INT for international people like NATO, MIL for military (doesn't that include NATO?) and ORG for anything that doesn't fit any of the previous descriptions. There's also GOV for Governmental sites. DNS knows about national demarcations too, and assigns a country code; UK is the UK and CH is Switzerland, not the CHeck Republic, which is CZ – not CK, naturally. Other countries have their own codes.

If you decided to set up your own network, like our friend the loony, you could use LOONY.CO.UK for the domain, and then various machine names at that domain. Machine 1 could be called MARMITE.LOONY.CO.UK, and its user would then add a username: KEVIN@MARMITE.LOONY.CO.UK. Machine 2 could be called BOVRIL.LOONY.CO.UK and its user added as BRIAN@BOVRIL.LOONY.CO.UK. (Now doesn't that just tell you a lot about technology writers?) Oh, and UNIX people like to see addresses in lower case. This is because anything in upper case startles them, and they have to go and lie down in a dark room for a while. So you write address information in lower case as in *kevin@marmite.loony.co.uk*.

Internet addresses are easy to understand and remember – once you decide to stick to alphabetical DNS descriptions instead of numbers. Want to practise? You might mail *president@whitehouse.gov*   or   even   *vice.president*

@whitehouse.gov and you'll receive a reply. This is because Americans know all about computers at birth, and some of their political leaders even have enough brains to be able to use them. Unfortunately mailing *idiot@housecommons.gov* won't get to the Prime Minister or anyone else, because UK Parliamentarians by and large haven't yet got the hang of this tricky computer stuff, although they might do once this book gets published. So if you want to help lever your country into the computer age, write immediately to your MP at the House of Commons, enclosing the ISBN of this book and a handsome letter of endorsement. And copy the same letter to at least 50 other names picked at random from the phone book. Every little helps.

Client–server jargon

There's more jargon in the wacky world of the Internet than in the whole of computerdom. We've already mentioned TCP/IP, domains and addresses, but you'll need to grasp the concept of client–server operations before you step out, blind and naked, onto the 'Net.

Client–server operation is simple. You the client (Wooster) say to the server (Jeeves), 'Go and get me a Martini, or those messages I haven't read, or that file I want'. The server will either have access to Martinis or messages or files, or it won't. If it doesn't you'll get a message saying so. If it does you'll get the result you want. Client–server operation tends to put the bulk of the processing for a computer-happening at the server end, leaving the client (local) end free for other things. In contrast, the file-server model simply lets computers connected to the file server grab files (and save them), which is what you get with a dial-up *terminal* connection. The Internet uses the client–server system, your local dial-up bulletin board probably uses the file-server system.

Finally...

Don't worry about learning any of the jargon in this chapter, until you decide you need it. You can get connected to the Internet without jargon, and indeed it should be the job of Internet providers to make this happen. At least you should know now:

- whether you want a terminal connection or a full network connection;

- that you need TCP/IP for a full connection, and SLIP or PPP (or a Windows Socket) if you want to use a modem;

- that you need a recognized Internet address to make everything work over TCP/IP links;

- that you don't need more jargon than this to get going.

Part 2

Internet tools

4 Electronic mail (email)

'As yet you can't contact the Prime Minister by email...'

Electronic mail is one of mankind's greatest inventions, second only to the tin opener in terms of usefulness. With electronic mail (email) you can exchange messages with people you've never met, swap data files, pictures, or spreadsheets with friends, or mail commercial information and data around the world for the cost of a phone call to your local Internet provider. It's email that makes the world go round, and it's email at which the Internet is particularly good.

Email has several advantages over other forms of electronic communication. It's better than fax (for straight text) because it's cheaper, and you don't need to chop down trees to receive a message. It's also more flexible – it's much cheaper to electronically 'cc' a message to ten people than to fax to ten different numbers, because you don't need to send ten messages. One message goes to your email service, and the mail handler there distributes it. And email is automatic – if a message comes into your mailbox you can generally access it from any telephone in the world, whereas a paper fax needs to be manually redirected. And email gets past those bad-tempered secretaries who 'edit' faxes to their boss. Email the Head of British Telecom and he will get the message, not some top-heavy bint brought in to decorate the place for a day.

From a corporate point of view email saves money, and Bill Gates, the richest PC owner in the world, says, 'I couldn't run my business without email'. So if you want to communicate with 20 million Internet users, 2 million CompuServe users, and Bill Gates – get yourself a computer equipped with a modem, and an Internet email address.

Internal/external mail

Email comes in various flavours. **Internal** mail is what you get if you set up a system in your company. Even if you have links with your regional offices you still have an internal mail system – because people who have an account somewhere on your system can't send mail to external users on other systems, unless there's provision for external users to get mail via a gateway. The great majority of corporate mail systems in the UK are internal. Things are different in the States, where the majority of mail systems operated by companies have **external** links into the wide world. External mail means that corporate users can both send and receive email from any user in the world with an Internet-savvy account.

Do you need external mail on your system? Many company directors in the UK think that there might be a security problem, or that their employees might spend time mailing Virtual Valerie, or that external mail might just be a time-waster, but if you're in the business of selling any sort of product then you need an Internet-savvy mail system. If you don't have one, the competition, especially in the States, certainly has.

Email brings huge benefits to individual users too. This book, for instance, couldn't have been written without it. Quite often it was common for the book, or matters relating directly to it, to generate ten or more messages a day. Email brings communication, and communication generally brings benefits, and Internet email is so far the most cost-efficient method of long-distance text communication yet invented.

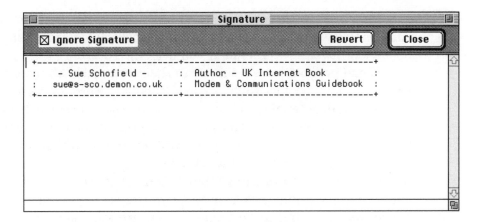

Figure 4.1   *Automatic signature generation in VersaTerm.*

All about email

Email works in the same way as ordinary postal mail, except the carrier is the Internet, not the Royal Mail. You construct a message by putting the address of the recipient at the top, followed by the main text. Your email program takes care of adding your own address, and a heap of other things too, like adding your signature automatically to the bottom of files, sorting out binary (data) files from plain text, and so on. Email programs vary in their capabilities from platform to platform, but their basic function is to make the construction, sending and receiving of email as painless as possible.

If your computer is already hooked up to the Internet, or you have a dial-up terminal or network connection, then the chances are you are the possessor of an Internet-savvy mail address. It's important to know whether this is the case or not, because if you don't have an Internet mail address then you can't receive mail from external Internet users. Many of the bulletin board systems in the UK have cottoned onto the fact that they can make money by selling email addresses and most of the larger systems now offer you this facility. Even smaller services are catching up. It's likely that most of the commercial dial-up services of any size will eventually provide Internet email and if you are thinking of signing up with a dial-up service provider, large or small, then you shouldn't part with real money unless you get an Internet mail address thrown in. Otherwise you'll feel a complete nerd when your boss/client/lover says 'I'll email you over the Internet'.

Email programs are a subject in their own right. Many of them will append binary files such as spreadsheets or word processor data to your mail as enclosures, not a few of them provide basic or complex text encryption, and some of the really good ones actually work. Your choice of mail program will depend on which computer platform you are using, and what level of service is provided at the server (remote) end of things, but by and large you shouldn't pay out money for a mail program until you've seen it work with the service you're going to be using. If you are still using DOS or a similar line editor to read and write your mail messages then you're missing out a little – because there are some good mail programs around for Windows users. The cost of email programs isn't really an issue, because there is a lot of free and nearly free email software around for all platforms.

Tricky bits – the mechanics of email

How email gets to and from your machine is a source of wonder and frustration. You'd think that something like a straightforward ASCII message would be easy to ship around a network, but like all things to do with computers, and especially to do with UNIX, email seems to be a particularly complex subject to master. But the basics are, well, basic.

Remember all that stuff about domains earlier on? Email addresses contain domain information, plus a little bit about the user. At its most basic, the first part of a mail address is the username. The second part (after the @ symbol) is the descriptor of the machine that's handling the collation and storage of your incoming mail. After the address comes the body text of the message, and the last bit is the signature. Dial-up users have their mail stored by their service provider, who then sends it to them when they log in. If you have a direct Internet connection you generally don't have to do anything to get your mail, other than

```
┌──────────────────────────────────────────────────────────┐
│ ☒ Use Router                      Time Zone:               │
│   ┌──────────────────────────┐    ┌──────┐                 │
│   │ post.demon.co.uk         │    │ gmt  │                 │
│   └──────────────────────────┘    └──────┘                 │
│                                                            │
│   Your return name:               ☒ Hide windows when in background │
│   ┌──────────────────────────┐                             │
│   │ sue@s-sco.demon.co.uk    │    ☐ Autoquote when replying │
│   └──────────────────────────┘                             │
│   Your return user ID:            ☒ Warn when deleting mail │
│   ┌──────────────────────────┐                             │
│   │ sue@s-sco.demon.co.uk    │    ☒ Play sound when mail arrives │
│   └──────────────────────────┘                             │
│   Your return machine name:       ☒ Enable ⌘Q              │
│   ┌──────────────────────────┐                             │
│   │ sue@s-sco.demon.co.uk    │    ☐ CC to self             │
│   └──────────────────────────┘                             │
│                                                            │
│   ┌───────────────┐              ┌──────────┐  ┌────────┐  │
│   │ Signature...  │              │ Cancel   │  │   OK   │  │
│   └───────────────┘              └──────────┘  └────────┘  │
└──────────────────────────────────────────────────────────┘
```

Figure 4.2   *Setting up mail gateways in Leemail, a Mac mail program.*

start your local mail handling program and perhaps type in a password.

There are different ways in which mail is handled at remote servers, and differences in methods of getting mail to the recipient, but the essentials are straightforward. Look at the email system as being an infinitely long river into which people can chuck parcels. The river eventually goes over a weir upon which stands your butler armed with a long stick. You've told your butler that every time he sees a parcel with your name on it he is to fish it out of the river and give it to you when you next turn up for lunch. If you're not in, Jeeves will put the mail in a mailbox so that you can pop in and collect it at your convenience.

In this analogy your butler is working as a mail handler. So if you want to send mail to the author via this method you would address it to sue@s-sco.demon.co.uk, but it would actually be held by a server called post.demon.co.uk. It's the mail handling server which looks at all incoming mail to demon.co.uk, slices out mail addressed to its users and forwards mail on when users log in. In fact all you have to remember is that, for modem users, your mail has to be stored somewhere on a server, so that it's there the next time you log in.

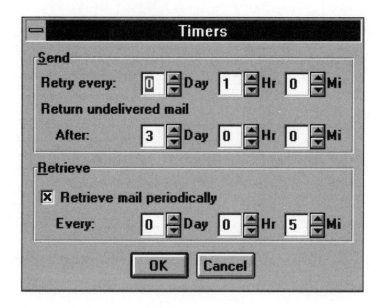

Figure 4.3 *The smart mail timer feature in Internet Chameleon.*

The politics of mail provision

Some UK Internetters will often be presented with a choice when they ask their service providers about mail provision. Your service provider will offer something called SMTP mail or POP mail, occasionally both, and sometimes something called UUCP.

SMTP is the Simple Mail Transfer Protocol, so called because it isn't. The other common offering is POP mail, currently in a third reincarnation and called POP3 mail. UUCP is UNIX to UNIX Copy Program – which on the face of it doesn't look much like the name of a proper mail program. It still doesn't look like a proper mail program when you get close up to it, and UUCP mail is best avoided, unless you have no real alternative. You won't find much UUCP stuff unless you work in a UNIX house, and even then you'll notice that most people have found something better. UUCP mail addresses are different to most other forms of email addressing, and if you see something with exclamation marks dividing up the address then it's UUCP.

But back to SMTP, which works by loitering with intent

outside your mailbox back at the service provider's office. When mail comes in SMTP tries to forward it to the destination machine. If that machine isn't available SMTP will keep trying for about three days. If it still can't deliver after that time SMTP will often give up. Moral: make a habit of getting your mail daily.

The other common mail handling system is POP3 (which stands for Post Office Protocol, third attempt) and is a deal more complex. You run a POP3 client on your machine, and tell it to go and get the mail, rather than wait for it to be sent. POP3 is also a bit more flexible than SMTP – you can tell the POP3 server to deliver your mail to another address, which might come in handy if you are going to work in a different office – and it has the advantage of being supported by a large number of email programs.

One important thing to watch out for is that some of the Shareware mail client programs (the ones that run on your personal computer) will use SMTP to send mail and POP3 to receive it. If your service provider only provides SMTP and the mail program you have needs POP3, you'll have to use two programs to handle your mail – one to send stuff out, one to retrieve it. Provision of SMTP mail only is less common than it once was, especially as Windows and Mac users tend to prefer POP3 mail because most of the Shareware email programs for those two platforms support it. However, there's a catch with the implementation of POP3 from some suppliers such as Demon. In the case of Demon, if you have their POP3 mail server sending your mail, you won't be able to have multiple mail addresses at your sub-domain – or rather, all mail for any user at your domain will be sent to anyone who logs in to the domain with POP3 software and the password for the POP3 server. In the USA most users won't worry about having two or more users at the same account for the same fee – they simply open a second account.

On the other hand, most UK users will not have access to POP3 mail from that supplier – which means they'll need to use a commercial SMTP program such as NetManage Chameleon for Windows – or if they're Mac users, they'll need either AddMail and Eudora, or LeeMail and Eudora to both send and receive mail. They will not be able to use otherwise widespread mail programs such as PC Eudora because of the lack of POP3 provision. (Chameleon can handle both SMTP and POP3 mail.)

This SMTP send and POP3 receive issue is going to be a big

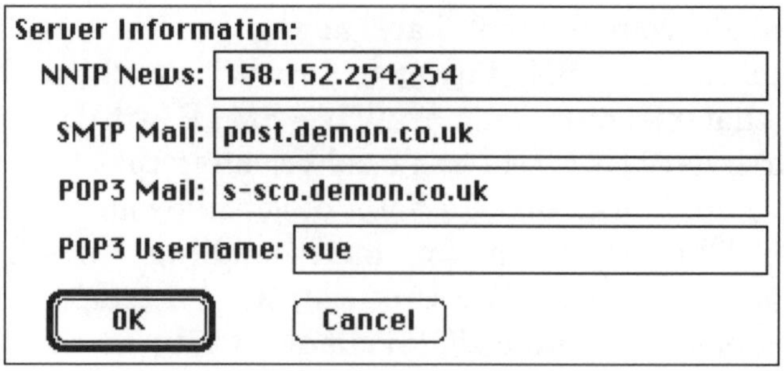

```
┌─────────────────────────────────────────────────┐
│ Server Information:                              │
│   NNTP News: ┌──────────────────────────────┐   │
│              │ 158.152.254.254              │   │
│              └──────────────────────────────┘   │
│   SMTP Mail: ┌──────────────────────────────┐   │
│              │ post.demon.co.uk             │   │
│              └──────────────────────────────┘   │
│   POP3 Mail: ┌──────────────────────────────┐   │
│              │ s-sco.demon.co.uk            │   │
│              └──────────────────────────────┘   │
│ POP3 Username: ┌────────────────────────────┐   │
│                │ sue                        │   │
│                └────────────────────────────┘   │
│   ┌──────────────┐    ┌──────────────┐          │
│   │     OK       │    │   Cancel     │          │
│   └──────────────┘    └──────────────┘          │
└─────────────────────────────────────────────────┘
```

Figure 4.4   *Setting SMTP and POP3 mail options.*

one in 1995 because, regardless of what some UK suppliers decide to implement, the largest provision of email software is going to come from the USA. Already there are new commercial versions of the fine Eudora program for Macs and Windows machines, and as we've seen, standard programs such as Eudora need a 'standard' combination of SMTP and POP3 mail to work at all.

If you are opening an account for your Windows machine and your Internet provider doesn't provide a choice of POP3 or SMTP (or both) – ask them what the alternative options are. If you're stuck with SMTP only mail and you want to use Windows or Mac Shareware mail programs you'll have to use two or more of those programs to get the most from your email. This is a ludicrous proposition when computers are supposed to be getting easier to use. As an example, the finest all round integrated Mail/Usenet/ FTP and telnet program for any platform is VersaTerm Link for the Mac, yet it can't be used with the standard Demon Internet service (at the time of writing) because of their lack of POP3 provision. Demon's POP3 service will cost you £180.00 net per year extra, if you decide that you want to use Eudora software with your machine. Other suppliers take note.

If you are using a terminal Internet connection such as any of the many BBS based mail hook-ups, then you can dismiss all this stuff about POP3 and SMTP. Your service provider will simply put all your mail into your standard mailbox. You'll get it when you log in and ask for it. In some ways this is an ideal situation if you just want quick and easy access to your mail, and in fact the majority of UK journalists still use this method for sending electronic text around. The disadvantage is that a terminal connection cannot generally provide you with direct hooks into the Internet, and binary files sent this way will need a separate decoder routine. You won't be able to use a mail program with a built-in UUdecode or BinHex ASCII descrambler in fully automatic mode to turn those messages back into spreadsheets or files.

Mail program facilities

So what do you look out for when buying, borrowing or stealing a mail program for Internet use? You'll need basic text editing features, such as backspace, delete, plus cursor movements, and cut & paste will also be invaluable. Spelling checkers are useful, but if you are going to mail a message of more than a few lines, presumably you'll create it in a word processor and then paste it into a mail program. An address book is vital, as is the ability to copy mail (cc) to more than one person. Group addressing is also handy for corporates, or mail freaks who have to tell everyone about everything. Group addressing lets you create a set of addressees with a single title, in the address book, and the entire set of addressees will get the message if it's sent to the group as a whole. But one of the most useful facilities is a reply generator. You click a button marked 'reply' – and the software creates the reply message header and dumps part or the whole of the message to which you are replying into the text editor, preceded by > marks. You then dive in and edit the pertinent bits of what the sender said, appending your own replies. Sounds complex? Look at this:

> and furthermore you'll be hearing from my solicitors anon (line from original message preceded by >)

I've never heard of a solicitor called anon. Is this a joke? (reply text)

---

sue

Both lines of text get sent back in the message, and the signature is added automatically.

Things to do with email

You've got the account set up, mastered the software and even maybe thought that personal computers can actually be used for something useful. So what do you do with your new email service? Well, you can mail the author for a start, as at least that way you'll be able to tell if your mail is working. You'll get a reply of sorts as the author has a stock of ill-mannered mail messages she keeps for replying to people who buy her books. Then you can practise your Smiley skills. Smileys, or 'emoticons' as the Americans like to call them, are ASCII characters used to make a picture. 'Picture' in this context is stretching things a bit, but a colon, a hyphen, and a close-bracket sign placed together thus :-) and viewed sideways make a Smiley face. Other nonsensical trivia abound. There are sad faces, faces with glasses, pictures of the Pope, pictures of the Pope with glasses on, pictures of the Pope on the loo, and more. All you have to do is to look at them from the right angle. Of course, if you're a wizard wordsmith you won't ever need to use a Smiley, because people will know from your lucid text whether you are being humorous, or just your normal obnoxious self. You might even send your boss an email which says 'You're a snivelling exploitative git' and put a Smiley after it to show you're only joking. You're sure to be excused and given a pay rise for being so inventive.

The author actually hates emoticons because they are slowly replacing the English language in the real world and even the national newspapers have started to use them. That way they don't have to pay for proper writers. But when you're young, or a newcomer to the Internet, or 'write' for a newspaper, being obnoxious hardly matters. :-)

By the way, the Internet contains heaps of other ASCII images. The Usenet group *alt.ascii.art* is full of pictures laboriously created out of ASCII characters in much the same way one might create a model of the Eiffel Tower out of matchsticks. It's art, Jim, but not as we know it.

Things to do with email, Part II

This section is for those readers who didn't believe me and have signed up with a terminal service provider such as CIX,

CompuServe, or any one of the burgeoning numbers of UK based bulletin boards attached to the Internet by way of their Internet-savvy mail addressing.

In English that means that you can do an awful lot with just an email account – without access to FTP or Archie or any other of those complicated bits of TCP/IP based software. You can do an awful lot more *with* them, but that info is in the following chapters.

There are a couple of caveats; most terminal accounts charge by the minute or second for your time on line, and not a few charge per Internet message received, or the amount of storage space taken up by your incoming mail. As always, check the small print carefully before you go requesting megabytes of data to be sent to your mail account – it could cost you a lot of money.

Here's a small summary of what's available to you if you only have an email account. It may be more than enough for many readers:

● *Archie file searches*: Want to know where to find recipes for Mississippi Mud Pie or that file containing the Windows screen saver with Santa on it? Archie can interact with emailers – see Chapter 7.

● *Mail-lists*: Your email software becomes a library of incoming information – everything from Aardvarks to Xenophobes is covered in the LISTSERV system. See this chapter and Chapter 5 for more info.

● *Electronic magazines (Zines)*: These are often available by email direct from the compiler. LISTSERV has most of the details, the new batch of UK Internet magazines will carry the rest.

● *Electronic shopping*: A number of suppliers now sell mail order by electronic mail. Details are now published on the World Wide Web, along with pictures of the products – the email addresses of suppliers can often be found in the technology pages of the national papers.

● *Electronic file transfer*: You can get files from Internet sites equipped with FTPMAIL which does what you'd imagine – it sends you files by mail. It's a bit like fishing by remote control from the moon, but briefly you send mail to a FTPMAIL server, ask for an index, and then use that to select the files you want. Before you get hot under the collar with the thought of having all those files mailed to you for free, remember that you may be paying a charge to your service provider for downloading the subsequent huge mail message, the FTP directory command system you'll have to battle with will be in UNIX, and you'll have to use UUdecode or BinHeX to turn the file into an executable. And each time you want a list of a directory you'll have to send a new message. FTPMAIL is time consuming. If these difficulties only add spice to your Internet pudding then full details of FTPMAIL are in Chapter 8. Start saving for the subsequent phone and divorce bills now.

There's a lot more for email users but you should at least get a flavour of what you can do with email from the above. In most cases email is by far the most important aspect of Internet use for many people, and if you are prepared to lose out a little on TCP/IP access then a terminal account with an Internet-savvy email address is the next best thing.

In the UK many corporate email accounts are now Internet savvy – that is, they can send and receive from other Internet addresses and if that's the case with your email account at work then you should have access to all of the above. Some corporates limit access to incoming mail but this is rare. Send a message to the Author at sue@s-sco.demon.co.uk if you want to try out your external mail. If you don't get a reply the chances are that she's emigrated with the winner of the National Lottery, or more likely, your corporate mail system doesn't permit external mail.

Mail-lists

Email lists are slightly further up the ladder of human endeavour. A mail-list is something you join, and in the course of a few hours or days, you receive endless messages covering the sphere of interest you enquired about. Mail-lists seem like quite a Good Idea when you're a techno-tyro, but their novelty wears off the day your first phone bill arrives. Some of the mail-lists are quite informative. You can have the White House mail you with the President's agenda for the day and then wonder just what the heck he does on his days off, which seem to occur about once every three days. Other lists cover national or regional issues, or aspects of human

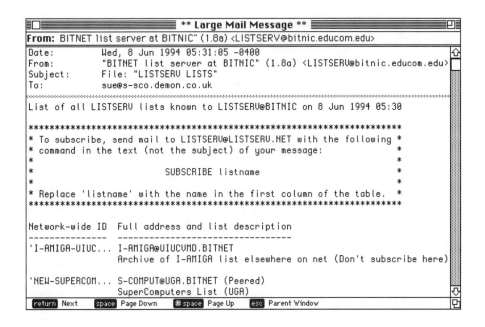

```
≡□≡≡≡≡≡≡≡≡≡≡≡≡≡≡ ** Large Mail Message ** ≡≡≡≡≡≡≡≡≡≡≡≡≡≡□≡
From: BITNET list server at BITNIC" (1.8a) <LISTSERV@bitnic.educom.edu>
Date:        Wed, 8 Jun 1994 05:31:05 -0400                            ⇧
From:        "BITNET list server at BITNIC" (1.8a) <LISTSERV@bitnic.educom.edu>
Subject:     File: "LISTSERV LISTS"
To:          sue@s-sco.demon.co.uk
List of all LISTSERV lists known to LISTSERV@BITNIC on 8 Jun 1994 05:30

************************************************************************
* To subscribe, send mail to LISTSERV@LISTSERV.NET with the following *
* command in the text (not the subject) of your message:              *
*                                                                     *
*                    SUBSCRIBE listname                               *
*                                                                     *
* Replace 'listname' with the name in the first column of the table.  *
************************************************************************

Network-wide ID  Full address and list description
---------------  ---------------------------------
'I-AMIGA-UIUC...  I-AMIGA@UIUCVMD.BITNET
                  Archive of I-AMIGA list elsewhere on net (Don't subscribe here)

'NEW-SUPERCOM...  S-COMPUT@UGA.BITNET (Peered)                         ⇩
                  SuperComputers List (UGA)                           ╝
 return Next    space Page Down   # space Page Up    esc Parent Window
```

Figure 4.5   *Listservs can generate large amounts of incoming mail.*
This is a list of mailing lists...

sexuality, or what to do with that model of the Eiffel Tower you
made out of matchsticks.

Mail-lists vary in content and interest. Many mail-lists contain
stuff other people have mailed in. You post a message to the list
server, and everyone else on the list gets a copy, whether they like
it or not. They are called *reflector* lists. Other mail-lists are
assembled by the list owner, who then sends out single-topic mail.
Mail-List Digests are simply large files containing all the stuff
mailed to the server by members. You get a huge mail-message or
file containing hundreds of messages at a time. In both cases mail-
lists can be moderated, that is, have offensive or off-topic stuff
edited out by the list moderator. While moderating mail (and
Usenet groups) might seem like censorship, many aspects of
Internet mail and messaging benefit from a small amount of
control. On the other hand, too much control makes the moderator
seem like a totalitarian ogre to his victims, and there's often a very
fine line between the two extremes.

Mail-lists can be fun, especially if you can find one which hits
your particular interest spot on, but it's often harder to get off one

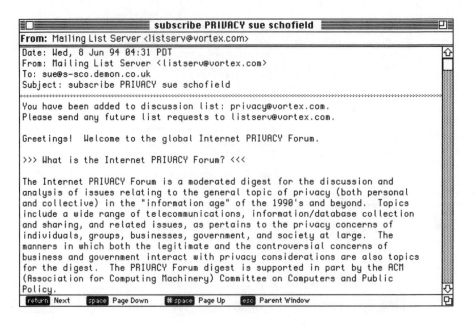

Figure 4.6 *Mail from the Privacy Listserv.*

than to get on. To sign on to many lists you simply send a mail message saying 'Subscribe me' or some such, and you'll be on the list. To leave, you send a message saying 'Resign' or 'Unsubscribe' or similar. Often it gets ignored. Many mail-lists now have 'intelligent' software that lets you pick and choose which topics you want to receive from the lists, and in what order or format, and the White House system is a good example.

Nerds, geeks and mail-bombing

The Internet being what it is, someday you are going to upset someone. You'll post an inoffensive message in a Usenet group, and sure as eggs is eggs you'll get mail back, public or otherwise, casting aspersions upon your parentage. In truth there's not much in the way of offensive private mail most of the time, and you're unlikely to be waylaid by other Internet users, but if you do post something contentious you are going to upset someone. And if it's a really badly placed message you'll be mail-bombed – a scenario where revengeful Internet geeks mail you with huge files which clog up

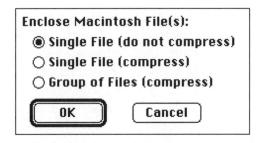

Enclose Macintosh File(s):
- ◉ Single File (do not compress)
- ○ Single File (compress)
- ○ Group of Files (compress)

[OK]   [Cancel]

Figure 4.7   *Mailing files with email. Decent mail programs let you attach files to the message. Binary files are automatically encoded into ASCII, with a button marked Enclosures, or File Attachments.*

your mailbox. This doesn't happen a lot, but there have been some cases where particularly offensive (or famous) people have been mail-bombed. In any case it makes sense to set a limit on the size of mail messages you can receive, especially if you're using a list server to mail you. The NATO list server is particularly fond of mailing out messages of 30–40 kilobytes, which can be expensive to download over a modem. Most decent mail programs have a facility to let you set the size limit. Some have options which change long email messages into files, which are then copied to your hard disk as text files. This works well for binary files sent to you as email (mail attachments).

If you are getting obscene or threatening mail then your first port of call is your Internet provider to ask for this mail to be intercepted. But be aware that many of the terminals and workstations connected to the Internet in universities can be operated anonymously, and often there's little chance of tracking down the origins of *ad hoc* obscene or threatening mail.

Mail attachments

A mail attachment is something you attach to an email message. It takes the form of a binary file which is embedded into the text of the message (usually just below the main body of text) and it's a great way of sending real data around the world. A binary file can be a spreadsheet file, a graphic file or digitized photograph, or a complete software application, and you can send binary files over the Internet to anyone who is equipped to collect them. Binary files are sent over the Internet by a process called ASCII Representation. It might not be called that in any other book on the Internet, but that's a good description of how it works. In fact the Internet can't handle 8-bit binary files as produced by these new-fangled personal computer thingies because it's a 7-bit system and personal computers use 8 bits. So binary 8-bit data files are encoded into a 7-bit representation of their hexadecimal codes, and then fired over the Internet as email. At the receiving end the ASCII text is decoded back into binary, and the result is a reconstruction of the original file.

The actual program tool you need to achieve this small miracle varies depending on which computer and which mail software you are using. PC and Amiga owners can use variants of UUencode and UUdecode, whilst Mac users need BinHex, a single utility which provides both coding and decoding functions. However, most of the better commercial mail programs will handle code/decode functions automatically for you, and at both ends too. All you have to do is set up a document with the address of the recipient in it, add a few lines of text to say what's happening, and click on the 'attachment' or 'enclosure' button. The program then picks up the data file and does the rest. Alas, in the world of DOS, where things just haven't caught up with clicky-button technology, attaching a file can mean an awkward process of encoding the file and sending it with two different programs. But Mac and Windows users will find all of the hard work done for them – if they get a half-decent mail program.

Once you get the hang of the need for converting files for transfer you can use this method for transferring data files from DOS to Macs, and vice versa. You might, for instance, want to transfer Word for Mac files into Word for Windows. You just code them into ASCII, ship them over the net as email, and your Windows-owning colleague on the other side of the world can load them straight into his PC.

There are some emergent 'standards' for attaching binary files to mail. One of them is MIME – Multipurpose Internet Mail Extension – and there are others fighting for dominance. MIME is perhaps the one you'll hear most about, as the business community are now paying lots of money for MIME-compliant email systems.

Internet-hostile mail systems

Once word gets around that you have an Internet account you'll probably be asked to send binary mail files to people. While you can certainly send ordinary ASCII text to anyone else in the world who has an Internet-savvy mail address, life gets complicated when you need to send or receive binary files. Things are more complicated than they should be in the UK especially, mainly because there are thousands of bulletin board systems in this country which sprang into being before Internet usage became widespread. In the UK the subculture of modem and electronic communication users revolves, not around the Internet as it does in the States, but around large dial-up systems such as CIX and CompuServe. Both of these systems use mutually exclusive methods to transfer files between subscribers, and you cannot (at the time of writing) use your newly found Internet mail skills to directly send a binary file to either of these two systems – except as a binary-coded ASCII mail message. CompuServe looks like being the first to break the deadlock and is revising its Internet interface to provide a more usable front-end for users. This might, or might not, provide an easy way for Internet users to send files to CompuServe users. At the very least CompuServe could release a new version of their Mac and Windows based front-end systems (called MacCim and WinCim respectively), which will automatically handle the transfer of ASCII-encoded binary files. However, CompuServe users pay an extra fee for using Internet mail, so this option isn't likely to gather much support if it ever comes about.

There's a problem too for CIX users. CIX uses an internal method for binary file transfer called BINMAIL. BINMAIL doesn't work outside CIX, so you need a CIX account to be able to use it. If you need to transfer binary files to a CIX user you can only UUencode them and send them as mail.

Luckily, many corporates can send binary mail to CompuServe via a variety of electronic mail hubs, and if your company uses external electronic mail there's every chance that you can get binary files routed to CompuServe in this manner. You won't be able to do this with CIX and the hundreds of other UK-centric dial-up systems which use their own internal mail 'standards', so you'll have to use UUencode or its equivalent.

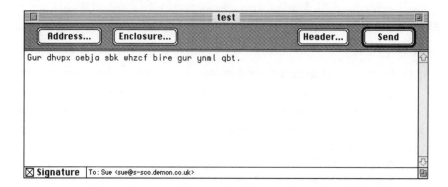

Figure 4.8 *A ROT13 message. The text says: The quick brown fox jumps over the lazy dog.*

Anonymous mail

If you are an observer of how complicated human beings are capable of making their, and other people's lives, one day you'll come across the phenomenon of anonymous mail. Unlike anonymous FTP, where the remote service pretends that it doesn't know or care who you are, (despite the fact it can read your domain address in each packet) anonymous mail is altogether more sinister.

Anonymous mail servers take a message from anyone, strip out all addressing information from the originating message, and then forward the rest of the message on to its destination. If the recipient has a sufficient lack of wit to reply, the anonymous server will pick up the reply, check the originator's address in a look-up table and mail the reply to him/her. Anonymous mail thus serves to bolster the poor image that the Internet has, and appears to be mainly used for sending abuse to Usenet Groups and celebrities.

It's real use, (if anything on the Internet was ever going to serve mankind with a useful purpose) is for contact with assistance groups such as AIDS and other help organizations. But anonymous mail often serves no real purpose, except to waste the lives of people who have it inflicted upon them.

Anonymous mail also comes from 'open' terminals in many US campuses, and the upcoming 'cybercafes' – where you pay real money for a virtual good time. Campus based open terminals often

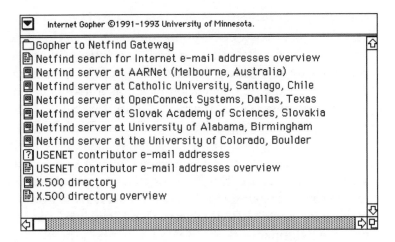

```
┌─────────────────────────────────────────────────────────────┐
│ ▼  Internet Gopher ©1991-1993 University of Minnesota.        │
├─────────────────────────────────────────────────────────────┤
│ 🗀 Gopher to Netfind Gateway                               ⇧ │
│ 📄 Netfind search for Internet e-mail addresses overview     │
│ 🖳 Netfind server at AARNet (Melbourne, Australia)           │
│ 🖳 Netfind server at Catholic University, Santiago, Chile     │
│ 🖳 Netfind server at OpenConnect Systems, Dallas, Texas       │
│ 🖳 Netfind server at Slovak Academy of Sciences, Slovakia     │
│ 🖳 Netfind server at University of Alabama, Birmingham        │
│ 🖳 Netfind server at the University of Colorado, Boulder      │
│ ❓ USENET contributor e-mail addresses                        │
│ 📄 USENET contributor e-mail addresses overview              │
│ 🖳 X.500 directory                                            │
│ 📄 X.500 directory overview                               ⇩ │
├─────────────────────────────────────────────────────────────┤
│ ⇦ ▏▒▒▒▒▒▒▒▒▒▒▒▒▒▒▒▒▒▒▒▒▒▒▒▒▒▒▒▒▒▒▒▒▒▒▒▒▒▒▒▒▒▒▒▒▒▒▒▒ ⇨▫      │
└─────────────────────────────────────────────────────────────┘
```

Figure 4.9   *Finding email addresses with Gopher.*

have a generic address, which will indicate the originating site in the message, but not the name of the originator who will use a nom-de-junk. Some campus based open terminals now automatically add a disclaimer to these messages, which in effect says that the obscene message you just got is being paid for by the US taxpayer as part of some mother's son's educational process.

Many Internet providers will automatically filter out messages from anonymous mail servers, and many commercial mail products have a feature which can be set up to reject mail from these sites. But if anonymous mail blights your phone bill then send the message, together with a reasonable and calm request to the Postmaster at the anonymous mail server concerned. Many of these are real people, and would not like to see full details of abuse of their service splashed across US or UK national papers, especially if they are inhabiting a site paid for by tax dollars, or pounds sterling.

Encrypt/decrypt

Mail over the Internet isn't as private as you might think. There have been numerous instances of mail being intercepted, and there are endless rumours that the FBI, the Inland Revenue, the CIA, and Jeremy Beadle all have secret hooks into private mail. To get over these fears many mail programs now provide encryption of text. The most basic encryption routine is something called ROT13. ROT stands for Rotation, and all the letters of the alphabet are rotated thirteen places forward in a ROT13 message. ROT13 is therefore hardly an encryption at all, as a five-year-old can decrypt ROT13 messages in a matter of minutes. So ROT13 is used to protect the endings of jokes in public mailings, or to keep sexually explicit material from the eyes of those who don't want to read it.

There are other more serious encryption schemes around. VersaTerm Link for the Mac provides a good one – but publishes the key as an appendix in the manual. At least it would baffle *ad hoc* lurkers for a while. PGP (Pretty Good Privacy) is another, as is the proposed Clipper system. But do you really need to encrypt your mail messages? The first thing to realize is that few people use encryption so you have to make sure that the recipient uses the same scheme. At the moment this is difficult if you use an Amiga and the recipient uses a BBC Micro or a NeXT Workstation.

If you do have commercially sensitive information to send over the Internet then you should look at some method of password-protecting it, at least. One easy way is to password-protect word processor or spreadsheet files in the application program, or to bundle files through a compressor program such as PKZip for the PC, Stuffit for the Mac, or LHA for the Amiga. These programs will produce a collection of files (called an archive) which can be password-protected and sent over the 'Net after being converted to ASCII in the normal way. Similarly you shouldn't mail your credit card details around, nor post messages which say 'I live at such and such address and my hobby is collecting rare diamonds' (or Macintosh computers) otherwise you'll be receiving mail from burglars asking you when you're going on your holidays. Unfortunately, they don't always ask.

The subject of mailing credit card numbers around is a thorny one. As the Internet continues to lean more towards Mammon than Academia there will be more commercial transactions carried out. At the moment many of the transactions between vendors and customers will require a credit card number, and generally speaking the Internet is not a safe place to leave credit card details suspended in Cyberspace. Many commercial vendors will dispute this (they would, wouldn't they), but there are an increasing number of programs around called Packet Sniffers. The sole purpose of these is to track IP packets travelling over a network, and log their contents to disk. Packet Sniffers generate huge amounts of logged data, and it takes a while to write algorithms to sort that data into human-readable form, but it can be done, and the format of credit card data is easy to distinguish from plain text traffic. So the answer is – at least be wary when mailing your credit card number around. There is a slim chance that it might be intercepted and misused, as happened to one William Gibson. Gibson is a cult Cyberspace guru and fiction scribbler, who found his credit card details being hunted down and then published on the 'Net by self-styled Cyberpunks. But then if you write a cult book called *Neuromancer*, what do you expect?

Finally, if you're female, you are going to have to face up to the fact that the Internet is a male-dominated phenomenon, and that it's used for everything from adolescent tribal posing to the distribution of material you wouldn't want your dog to see. General rule number one is that there are no general rules, general rule number two is not to give out your private address or phone number without good reason. There are documented cases of hairy psychopaths getting hold of email addresses and then selling subscriptions for Internet newsletters to the unfortunate recipients.

Sending mail to other addresses

It's all very well having all of this mail stuff at your fingertips, but there's a snag. How do you know who to send mail to? It would help if everyone who bought a modem was given an email address and had it tattooed on their forehead, but until this notion gets passed at the next Conservative Party conference we'll have to find another method. If you have an email address then at least publish it on your business card or letterhead, and stick it on the Christmas cards this year. It all helps make the electronic world go round.

If you want to send mail to other people you'll sometimes come across an address which makes little sense to you, or to the mail handling facilities you're using. Unfortunately there are few conventions for mail addressing outside the Internet, despite pro-testations from UNIX geeks that it's all perfectly straightforward. Want to send mail to user number 100113,2132 at CompuServe? You'll need to address it to 100113.2132@compuserve.com. Note that the comma in the address has been changed to a full stop, and the suffix 'com' has been added. Other mail services, such as those operated by IBM, are equally quirky, and the easiest way to get over this is to ask for an Internet-compliant mail address from your intended addressee. There are numerous lists of addressing conventions on commercial systems, and one notable one is published by Scott Yanoff on the 'Net. You can't read it here because Scott wanted 500 dollars cash before giving permission to publish on paper, despite his own protestations that the 'Net shouldn't be misused for profit motives. Funny old world, the Internet.

Bounced mail

Sending mail to addresses other than those on your own system is pretty much of an *ad hoc* affair, although most of the mail gets through most of the time. But it can take anything up to two days for mail to arrive, although the vast majority is delivered worldwide in a few hours. The biggest problems are caused by faulty addresses, and much mail is bounced (returned to sender if possible) because of this.

Bounced mail will be returned to you with a message in the header telling you why. Reasons vary from 'Host Unknown', where routing services can't find the part of the address after the @ sign, to 'User Unknown', where routing finds the bit of the address after the @ sign but can't find the user there. 'Service Unavailable' occurs where both user and host are found but the host computer there is not accepting mail because someone spilt Old El Paso Extra Hot Taco sauce into the hard disk. And 'Can't Send' happens because of network, or 'administrative' problems, where the recipient hasn't been paying his or her Internet provider's bills.

Fingering the pie

There are no real user-directory services on the Internet, so if some smart Alec in a shiny suit offers to sell you one, turn him away with a smile. Besides, any such directory of email addresses would be out of date before it was written. However, there are a couple of ways you can sometimes track down a mail address. One of them is through a UNIX command called Finger. You get onto the net, find yourself a command line interface, and type <finger address>. (You might try 'finger sue@s-sco.demon.co.uk'.) What you get back depends on what Finger finds as it rummages around the network routing looking for the address. You might get a 'Not Found' message or a 'Last Logged in' message. You might even get a text message back telling you all about the guy you have fingered, as some UNIX people like to put a small resumé in a text file (called a plan file) which gets sent to people who finger them. You might even get back the first line of something called the Project file, but this will be a rare occurrence, as UNIX users are too busy with political infighting about the superiority of one version of UNIX over another to get any real work done.

Finger often doesn't work as it's not always implemented on all systems for a variety of reasons, security being one of them, bad-tempered and paranoid network administrators being another. Some compilers of lists on the Internet put details of those lists into the plan file, so you get them when you finger the person's address. But don't depend on Finger to work all the time.

FAX gateways

Many email services offer a FAX gateway. This is a facility where you send electronic text to your Internet provider in the normal way, it's converted to a fax and then faxed. Fax gateways have their pros and cons. They don't (generally) operate for free – so you'll pay a premium on top of the call charge to the destination. To counter that, they can be useful for sending the odd fax when you're away from home, but the advent of the cheap fax modem makes most Fax-send gateways a little obsolete.

What is useful is a fax-to-email gateway. Your Auntie Flo, who knows nothing about modems, sends you a paper fax. It arrives in your mailbox and you call in and get it as electronically mailed text. Alas, fax-to-email gateways are still rare, as faxes aren't sent as text but as images. The conversion routine from fax to text is thus cumbersome and expensive to implement, and the character recognition software needed isn't 100% accurate. However, there are a number of companies selling virtual fax mailboxes. You take out a subscription and are given a fax number for the mailbox. Faxes arrive in the normal manner, and are stored until you call in and ask for them to be sent to you. You then set your computer's fax modem to receive mode, and wait for the fax to arrive.

Virtual fax mail is still a bit advanced, and not yet considered a part of the Internet email scene. Neither is it cheap enough for mass appeal. But it's extremely useful for the travelling salesman, or book author, and like all things electronic, will become more common as prices fall and Internet providers catch on. A London company called Business Space offers non-Internet Virtual Fax Mail. Talk to Jane Kirkham on 0171 917 9917 for details.

Finding the unfindable

You can often track down Internet users with WHOIS. You send email to mailserv@internic.net or any of the other whois servers with the command *whois xxx*. Here's part of the help file you'll get back when you send out a search message with the wrong syntax. But it's often better to get hold of email addresses by phoning the people concerned or by sending them a fax.

<OVERVIEW>

WHOIS is used to look up records in the main database. Each record has a "handle" (a unique identifier assigned to it), a name, a record type, and various other fields depending on the type of record.

To use WHOIS, simply type in your target string. The default action, unless directed otherwise with a keyword (e.g. "domain root"), is to do a very broad search, looking for matches to your target in many fields: handle, name, nicknames, hostname, net address, etc., and finding all record types.

WHOIS keywords fall into four categories: those that specify a FIELD to be searched, those that specify the TYPE of record to be found, those that modify the interpretation of the input or tell the type of output to produce, and those that are commands, such as HELP, QUIT, and so forth.

To tell WHOIS to restrict its search to ONLY a certain field in the database, there are the following three keywords (shown with their minimum abbreviation in all CAPS):

Examples:

HAndle or '!'	!sb65 or HA sb65
NAme or leading '.'	.borinski or NA borinski
Mailbox or contains '@'	stanb@host

Searching for X500 users

X500 is a global directory system defined by the International Standards Organization. It's used mainly by corporate bodies who have installed office automation systems with email systems, and provides the external directory system for those users. There's a utility on the 'Net called FRED which allows you to search X500 directories for a particular name, but it has to be said, as it's said in every other book about the Internet, that the best way of finding out someone's email address is to pick up the phone and ask them. If for some reason you can't do that, and you think the person concerned might be in an X500 directory, you can telnet to a fred server and enquire there. Alas, fred servers tend to be regional – despite X500 being a 'global' directory server – so telnetting to a USA based server may not always yield the correct results for a UK based user. Many Gopher servers are now carrying X500 directories, and using Gopher is an easier way of doing things. Fred servers are at wp.psi.com and wp2.psi.com, amongst other places, and you can telnet to them and log in as 'fred'. Type 'help' for a list of commands.

Favourite places

Some interesting email addresses from Seth Godin's book *Email Addresses of the Rich and Famous* – ISBN 0-201-40893-7 – reproduced with kind permission:

Al Gore – Vice President, USA
vice-president@whitehouse.gov

Anne McCaffrey, author
72007.1473@compuserve.com

Bill Clinton
president@whitehouse.gov

Bill Gates
billg@microsoft.com

Billy Idol, 'musician'
idol@phantom.com

Bob Hoskins, actor
75300.1313@compuserve.com

James Randi, magician
72740.456@compuserve.com

Santa Claus
santa@north.pole.org

Santa's elves
elves@north.pole.org

Terry Pratchett, 'writer'
tpratchett@unseen.demon.co.uk

The Clinton Administration
75300.3115@compuserve.com

Tom Clancy, author
tomclancy@aol.com

Most UK national newpapers, technical and computer magazines can now be contacted by email – their addresses are normally published in the small print alongside the publisher's address or under the byline for particular journalists. As yet you cannot contact most Members of Parliament or the Prime Minister by email, but there are rumours that this might happen 'soon'. The Queen doesn't have an email account, either, but is reputed to be saving up for one.

Favourite places – list servers (listservs)

You can get a complete listing of listservs by emailing **listserv@bitnic.bitnet** with the words 'list global' in the text.

Here's a tiny sample of what's available. Listservs come and go, so don't be disappointed if your favourite list is no longer working.

Animal rights
animal-rights-request@xanth.cs.odu.edu

Artificial life
alife-request@iuvax.cs.indiana.edu

British cars
british-cars-request@encore.com

Chaucer
listserv2siucvmb.siu.edu
(send: SUB CHAUCER <your real name here>)

Kites
kites-request@harvard.harvard.edu

More lists of mailing lists
mail-men-request@attunic.att.com

'Net stuff (ftp servers, lists and so on)
listserv%vmtecmex.bitnet@cunyvm.cuny.edu
(send: SUB NETSCOUT <your real name here>)

United Nations
listserv@indycms.iupui.edu

Vegetarian
listserv%gitvml.bitnet@cunyvm.cuny.edu
(send: SUB GRANOLA <your real name here>)

5 Network news

'Newsgroups
contain all of the
world's knowledge...'

As well as getting textual information from the 'Net via email and mail-lists you can also fill up your hard disk with information from Usenet. Usenet is really a large virtual bulletin board onto which any Tom, Dick and Harriet can post a message and Usenet therefore provides a wonderful global view of just what a complete waste of time man's endeavours on this planet really are. Messages may cover any topic and be posted onto any message base, but generally speaking messages in any given newsgroup will follow a particular topic. At least that's the theory, although there's much within Usenet topics which is decidedly 'off-topic'. Any message posted into a topic will be trundled around the world in a couple of days, or in some cases, hours.

Most Internet providers provide access to most Usenet groups, although many commercial sites remove access to groups containing material likely to be regarded as offensive. Many local bulletin board services now carry access to the Usenet too, but in

some cases you're likely to find that you only have read-access –
that is, you can't post messages or replies to messages, especially if
you have a terminal-only connection.

Getting hold of Usenet

If your Internet provider supplies access to Usenet then you'll need
a Usenet reader program to get at the information. These programs
vary in their ability to make life difficult for the user. Many of them
don't cater for capturing news to disk for perusal at a later date
(thus saving on costs of running a dial-up line while you download,
sort and read your news). Others have a clunky batch-driven
system which attempts to provide offline facilities of some sort. The
reason for this is simple. Until very recently the Internet was only
for those who had a direct Ethernet connection, where you can
spend as much time as you like plugged into the 'Net without
running up phone charges. It's a problem which many American

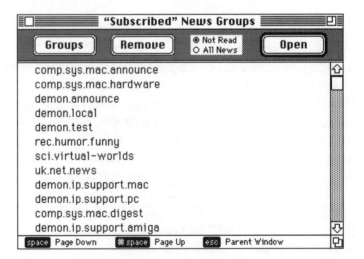

Figure 5.1 *Subscribed newsgroups. These are manually
selected from a large list of all newsgroups in many news
programs.*

software authors (and authors of American Internet books) haven't addressed, because dial-up access is still a minority sport in the Land of Plenty.

The best Usenet readers are hooked into your email facilities, so you can reply to a message either within the Usenet group or by personal email. Nearly all network news is delivered using a scheme called NNTP – Network News Transfer Protocol, and consequently you'll need an NNTP-savvy program to collect it from your provider. If you are using a terminal session, instead of a full TCP/IP connection, you can often get your news mailed to you as email. On some terminal systems you specify the groups you are interested in, and then go back in a couple of hours to collect the data which has been collected for you and saved into your mailbox. Again this is a clunky way of doing it, although better than nothing, and you do get the opportunity of reading your news with the phone disconnected – that is, offline.

Newsgroup contents

Newsgroups contain all of the world's knowledge. The great disadvantage is that this knowledge is filtered down through the minds of geeks, know-it-alls, journalists, computer-bigots, religious fundamentalists and techno-wibblers, and you have to do a lot of panning to find just a little gold.

Newsgroups are divided into hierarchies and their title is thus supposed to be descriptive of their contents. Anything beginning with SCI should contain topics bearing some resemblance to scientific matters, REC is recreational, SOC is social, and so on. There are also a lot of regional groups, where Germans can speak German, or at least write messages to each other in German, Finns can write in Finnish, and Americans can have a stab at English. You'll also find Russian newsgroups full of what appears to be random gibberish, for which you will need a program capable of decoding Cyrillic characters. The result is random Russian gibberish. Similar sentiments may be expressed about Japanese newsgroups.

There are any numbers of ALT newsgroups too, where ALT stands for 'alternative'. Here you can pick up all sorts of things, many of which will not respond either to medical treatment or to

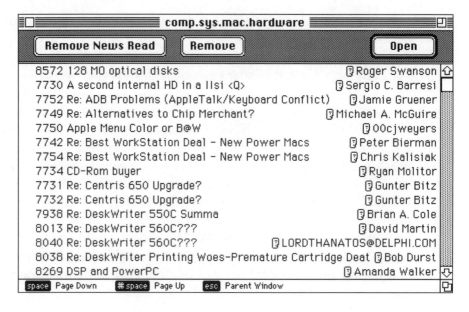

Figure 5.2 *Contents of a newsgroup. Each line is an individual message.*

localized anti-pornography legislation. You get hold of image files from Usenet groups by using the UUdecode or BinHex decoders mentioned in Chapter 4.

It's the 'uninhibited' nature of the Internet in general, and Usenet in particular, which is causing the hairs on the necks of UK Government ministers to stand up. Already the media has latched on to the fact that there are images and messages in many of the ALT Usenet groups which are deemed unsuitable for public consumption in this country, and it's very likely that the next few years will bring in some sort of knee-jerk legislation to limit access to these feeds in the UK. The only real way that this can be done is to threaten Internet providers with the crime of distributing pornography, which will result in many of the Usenet groups being pulled from general distribution. When that happens it will be a sad day for the anti-censorship brigade, and a bonus for the Thought Police. In the meantime you can gain access to most of the Usenet groups, most of the time, through most of the Internet providers in this country.

Getting your hands dirty with Usenet

The actuality of Usenet is simple – you join a newsgroup and download or read online the messages it contains. If you feel sufficiently moved you hit a key, and your computer presents you with a text editor into which you compose your message and then hit the send key. Your witty and brilliant reply then appears in the newsgroup and is there the next time you log on. (The actual mechanism of Usenet programs varies, so don't worry too much if you are using a different editor to compose your Usenet replies to the one you would use for your email.)

Many Usenet messages seem to be entirely constructed of the text from the previous message, preceded by a > sign. This is a function of some text editor programs, where you click an on-screen button marked 'Reply' and the editor constructs the reply message headers but adds in the complete text of the message to which are replying. This makes it very convenient for you, but a pain in the butt for everyone else who has to read the complete text of a message dozens of times over. The problem gets worse when Internet geeks, intent on making some facile point, will not only copy the entire message, but the ten-line signature of the guy who sent it in the first place. This makes sure that out of the 30 megabytes of Usenet stuff you've downloaded at great cost, only ten bits of it is of any real interest. The rest is repeats of messages and signatures. So, use your editor with care and sense, and watch for that copying facility. It can get out of hand. And keep your signature (called a 'sig' in geek-speak) to three lines or less. It all helps keep the tedium of free speech to a minimum.

Some newsgroups are 'moderated', which means that you can't post to them directly. A 'moderator' is someone who is egocentric enough to believe they should operate a closed newsgroup, and limit or control what appears in it. To send mail to a moderated news group you mail the moderator directly, who then decides whether what you have to say carries any virtue and includes it if it doesn't.

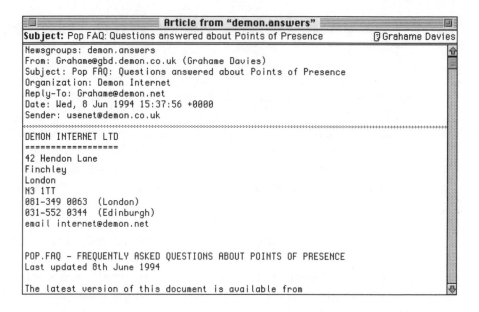

Figure 5.3   *Contents of a message. You can respond either by mail, or directly to the newsgroup with many news/email packages.*

Net etiquette

There is a spurious form of fascist control on the Internet, imposed by cyber-idealists and regulated by its denizens. 'Netiquette' demands that you use lower case for all public mail (upper case is translated as SHOUTING!) and that you shouldn't use more than three lines for your signature as it 'uses up disk space'. These rules (and others) seem extremely petty once you're plugged into the Internet, especially when you see some of the blasphemous and obscene messages posted by users, and mind-blowingly inconsequential stuff posted by religious evangelists. It seems that while you can inform the world that Elvis Presley is not only God, but is alive and well and will be signing books at MacDonuts on Thursday, you can't use upper case for the text of a message.

Strange also, that the Internet community which prides itself so much on its supposed freedom should choose to impose any limits at all, but then anarchy can only work properly if it's correctly controlled. Whether you subscribe to Netiquette is up to you. But use upper case incautiously and all of the spotty dog's-breath students sitting with their feet up at the American taxpayers' expense will send you mail grumbling about your wild excursion into the unknown.

Other Netiquette inconsequences include sniffy comments about the Internet being used for 'commerce', and wildly out-of-order comments by UK based administrators of the JANET system (Joint Academic Network). One of these chaps recently posted a message complaining of recreational use of JANET by British people, mentioning that while it's OK for American students to use JANET, we Brits aren't allowed access other than for research. Seems reasonable, when you consider it's we Brits who are paying for it.

Newsgroup distribution

Remember that whatever you send to a Usenet group is splashed all over the world in a matter of hours, and can be and often is reproduced without permission or payment, so be careful of what you say. However, there are ways you can limit distribution of your postings. If you put a line in your message header thus, you'll limit distribution to the USA only:

Distribution: usa

There are huge numbers of distribution limiters, so most people don't bother with them, mainly because they don't always work. But you can limit your postings to just the UK with the UK suffix, so try that if you don't want the whole world to comment on your writing abilities. If you have a half-decent editor on your system you'll find that there's a 'distribution' box which pops up with a pick list of all the distribution limiters. If you're using DOS then you'll do it manually, at the moment. And if you are using one of the American based Shareware Usenet programs you'll find it difficult to set distribution parameters automatically, as all Americans believe that all communication should go worldwide. 'Communication is Knowledge', they say, in much the same way as they sold us chewing gum and hula hoops.

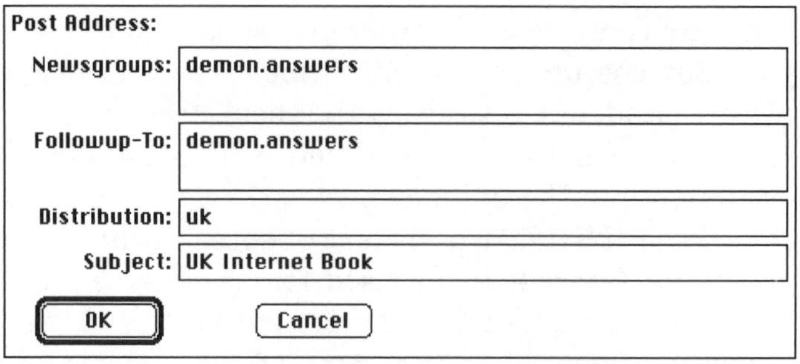

```
┌────────────────────────────────────────────────────┐
│ Post Address:                                        │
│  Newsgroups: │ demon.answers                       │ │
│                                                      │
│ Followup-To: │ demon.answers                       │ │
│                                                      │
│ Distribution: │ uk                                 │ │
│       Subject: │ UK Internet Book                  │ │
│  ┌────────┐            ┌──────────┐                  │
│  │   OK   │            │  Cancel  │                  │
│  └────────┘            └──────────┘                  │
└────────────────────────────────────────────────────┘
```

Figure 5.4 *You should be able to set the distribution of your newsgroup postings. This one will only appear in UK newsgroups.*

New newsgroups

New groups appear on Usenet almost by the hour. Many of them will have little or no consequence to you (or anyone else) and you won't want them eating up space on your computer. Your NNTP news program will either tell you that a new group has been created, or will provide a clicky-button which you can press to show all the new groups which have sprung up since you last checked. Many DOS based news programs run a check for new groups either on demand or when you start up your connection. In every case you'll have a command which lets you join, or ignore, each new group.

Every so often, say once a month for newsgroup freaks, you'll want to grab a complete list of all newsgroups, and then spend a week formatting it up as a nice text document which you can pin on the bathroom wall. You've then got a huge list of newsgroups which you can browse through at leisure, selecting target groups to add to your personal list.

If you're a modem user and you want to try this then make sure you do it a time when you can afford the resultant phone bill. Many news programs not only download the complete list of newsgroups but sort them alphabetically too, and they will quite happily do this while your modem is sitting on the line eating up your non-disposable income. Despite this warning, most Internet freaks have huge and complete lists of newsgroups lying around like confetti, which shows just why the telecomms providers are

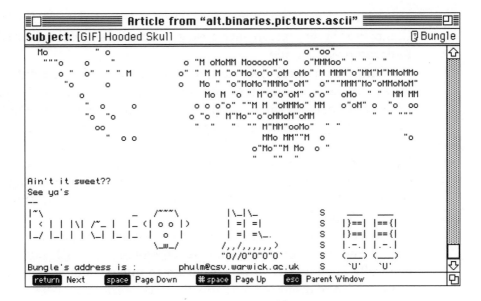

Figure 5.5   *An exotic 'sig' made of ASCII characters.*

starting to get interested in the Internet. In principle you can join and leave newsgroups at will; in reality your ability to do this will be limited or enhanced by the software you're using to provide access. Some providers keep an up-to-date list which can be downloaded very quickly but you may or may not be able to use this with your news reader directly.

Yes, but is it Art?

Many newsgroups provide binary files of images, artistic or otherwise, and there are a number of techniques used over the Internet to get these files into standard messages. The most common is to encode a binary file such as an image file into an ASCII representation of itself with a program called UUencode, and to use UUdecode to bring the file back to binary. It can then be decompressed if need be, and run on your computer. Quite often these files turn out to be compressed archives, which for PC users means that they will be compressed using PKZip or a similar alternative. For Macs they will be archives created using Stuffit or Compactor or similar. In each case you'll need the relevant software to decompress the file.

After they have been decoded some files will turn out to be 'self-extracting compressed archives'. These need no external program to expand them – you just run them if they are DOS EXE files, or click on an icon if they are Mac or Amiga files. In many cases you'll already have a battery of file decompressors if you've been using a computer for any length of time, and in all cases all decompressors can be downloaded from almost any computer-centric FTP site. (If you don't understand what that means, read Chapter 8 on FTP.)

Back to those images. Many of the image files on the Internet are stored in GIF (Graphics Interchange Format) and you'll generally need a GIF viewer program to make them visible. There are a wealth of other formats too, but GIF is the most used and you can always find a GIF viewer for your particular computer on the Internet.

Listserv

Listserv groups are slightly different to Usenet groups. You send a mail message to the group's email address, and your message gets sent to everyone on the list, if it's set up that way. Everyone else's mail gets sent to you in return. (On some systems mail only gets sent between originating and replying authors, and consenting adults.)

Listserv is a great way of generating mail to yourself, but beware the cost of downloading a hundred mail messages over a dial-up link. Watch out too if you're a CompuServe user. Harry Gard, the man who invented CompuServe in 1969, decreed that users of that service would pay an extra fee for receiving Internet mail. Consequently you'll go bankrupt the day that 4000 messages concerning Life, the Universe, and KY Jelly come flooding into your CompuServe mailbox. (You can get a complete list of listserv servers by sending 'list global' to listserv@bitnic.educom.edu. Don't send your ten-line signature, and don't expect a rapid reply.)

When you find a listserv which you think is worthy of your razor-sharp intellect, you send a subscribe message:

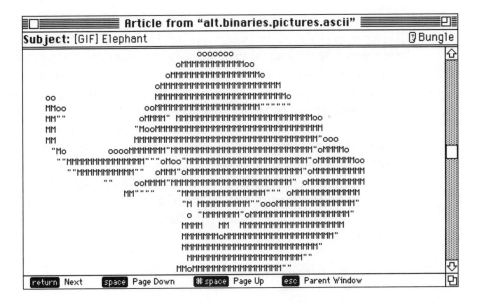

Figure 5.6   *ASCII elephant, from the alt.binaries.ascii news-group.*

mail to: listserv@ames.arc.nasa.gov

---

subscribe frequent-flyer name

Don't send <name> – it won't bring you any large cheques. And use your own real name, not your email address. (The listserv picks up your email address from your mail header.) You can abbreviate 'subscribe' to 'sub' if you like beaming non-human-readable messages around the world.

The listserv address is actually 'frequent-flyer@ames. arc.nasa.gov' but you are sending your request for mail to the listserv computer. You now wait until you get your first 5000 mail messages, or you start sending mail to the group:

Mail to: frequent-flyer@ames.arc.nasa.gov

Hi Guys,

Did you hear the one about the Sopwith Camel and the Fokker?

– but it might be better to get a few messages first so you can judge the tone of things. In fact, one of the least benign aspects of 'Netiquette' is that some newsgroup contributors like to jump down the throats of new users who post messages, especially if they post messages which say 'Hi – I'm a new user'. These benign and literate people (who are only fascists in their spare time) tend to put first-time users off as part of some obscure power struggle, so previous remarks about sitting around for a while and watching what the Grown-ups do should be noted.

When subscribing to listservs your mail should always be addressed to the group, not to the listserv, although when you've had enough you can mail the listserv with an 'unsubscribe' message:

mail to: listserv@ames.arc.nasa.gov

---

signoff frequent-flyer

You can also mail the listserv with a demand for help, and if you send 'info ?' you should get a list of available documentation back. 'Help' will bring you the help files.

Look out for the SET commands available on your favourite listserv. 'SET frequent-flyer digest' will bundle all your replies up into a daily report. Not all SET commands are available on all listservs, so check out the help files.

Other useful commands are:

SET xxx NOACK, which stops the blessed thing returning your own mail to you as an acknowledgement.

SET xxx NOMAIL, which stops mail temporarily.

SET xxx MAIL starts it again.

The listserv system shows up the pitfalls of trying to communicate with three million people from your back bedroom. Listserv is quite a dumb process, and you'll get lots of messages from some servers saying that such-and-such people who were once on the list are no longer reachable. You might also fall unsuspecting into a moderated list, where the moderator used to be a Personnel Manager, and doesn't let your messages into the list until you've been a subscriber for a year, just so you know your place. And some moderators are Network Nazis, and won't let you into the list unless you agree entirely with what they have to say, and sign a Non Disclosure Agreement (NDA).

To complicate matters some apparently private lists are mirrored in Usenet groups. You then find that, where you mistakenly believed you were replying to just a couple of hundred people, your mother/boss/publisher finds you plastered publicly all over Alt.Hamster.Eating, or worse. Quite often it's the newsgroups which find themselves targets of outraged moral stances taken up by journalists paid to be outraged, and it's not rare to see out-of-context Usenet messages plastered all over the US tabloids. So if eating hamsters is your bag, at least use an alias. Don't use sue@s-sco.demon.co.uk – it's already taken.

The one thing to remember about both listserv and newsgroups is not to open your electronic mouth unless you have something worth communicating. If everyone on the Internet followed that credo then two-thirds of mail-lists and newsgroups would dry up overnight and there would be dancing in the middle lane of the Digital Superhighway, when it finally arrives.

The curse of ROT13

What you want to read on an Internet newsgroup or mail-list is up to you. There is no censorship on the 'Net, other than at a local level, because there's no single governing body. As mentioned previously, the ROT13 encryption scheme is used to protect more sensitive individuals from the content of some of the newsgroups, but in practice all this serves to do is to flag the message as being especially suitable for the sexually curious or hamster-vores. In the UK we are much less open about sexual matters than in other countries and you may decide that you don't want your 13-year-old daughter (or son) getting hold of some of the material that's available. This is a real problem for many parents and at the moment there is no solution, other than to try to be reasonable. The general reaction to computer based communication of sexual matters is to ban it, which simply serves to push it underground, where it reappears covertly in school playgrounds. It's far better to talk it through with your children before making Draconian rules about what they can and can't access on Daddy's computer.

Some half-decent Usenet groups

Most of the stuff on Usenet is of limited interest to UK users, simply because the vast part of it originates in the USA, where different value systems apply. You'll doubtless find your own level in these groups but for newcomers there's news.announce. newusers. News.answers is worth looking at (allegedly) although rec.humor.funny, which is mentioned in all the other Internet books as being riotously amusing, is about as funny as a heap of dingo's kidneys, as far as this scribbler is concerned. If you want real humour (with two u's) then join alt.zen where there are often bizarre clashes between materialistic Zen Masters armed with computers, and nerds who have met someone whose best friend knows a guy who once read *Zen and the Art of Motorcycle Maintenance* – over someone else's shoulder.

Favourite places – Usenet

Here's a list of selected newsgroups, which might, or might not, be of some interest. If not there's 40,000 more available, at the last count. You can get lists of groups from various places, including news.announce.newusers. Look out too, for the Clarinet (clari) newsgroups, which contain real news from around the world. Your Internet provider may not provide them as there's a cost implication, although you can subscribe to them personally with a credit card.

Newsgroups

comp.society.cu.digest
A moderated group – The underground Computer Digest.

misc.misc
A miscellany of miscellany. Contains much of little interest.

misc.kids.computer
Sprogs and pooters come away...

misc.consumers
Consumer topics of an American kind.

rec.scuba
Think or thwim.

cern.ski.club
Off-piste particle physics from the Swiss Atom-Smashers.

soc.women
Non-male topics.

talk.bizarre
Aliens from the planet Thrarg meet Marks & Spencer Man.

alt.paranormal
Things that go BMP in the night.

alt.sex
Sex is what the middle class put their coal in.

alt.ascii.art
Pictures made of letters, intriguingly daft.

alt.comedy.british
Comments on us, by foreigners.

demon.adverts
Sell your grannie at half price.

(Demon also carry many useful UK computer support groups. Grab a full list from your News server for details.)

6 Telnet

'You can log into
NASA databases
and pickup info on
Shuttle launches...'

Do you remember those old Star Trek movies, where Captain Kirk would beam down to another planet, blast a few harmless life-forms, and then be back home in time to nibble Uhuru's communicator? Telnet is a bit like that – it enables you to pop 'into' the computer of your choice, perform a few miracles, and then pop back home with only minimum damage to your dilithium crystals. Telnet is yet another bit of client software which you can use to log on to remote computers, and perform tasks as though you are sitting at the remote computer itself.

There are a few conditions though. You'd find it difficult to run a Windows program over telnet, because telnet doesn't understand the new-fangled personal computer thingies, although you could telnet into the computer used to control the Hubble space telescope – because you don't need anything as complicated as Windows to run multi-billion-dollar space projects. So telnet is a bit like all the other bits of the Internet: it's OK if you can find a use for it, a waste

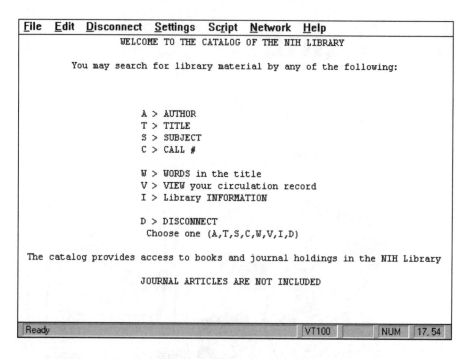

File	Edit	Disconnect	Settings	Script	Network	Help

```
                    WELCOME TO THE CATALOG OF THE NIH LIBRARY

          You may search for library material by any of the following:




                    A > AUTHOR
                    T > TITLE
                    S > SUBJECT
                    C > CALL #

                    W > WORDS in the title
                    V > VIEW your circulation record
                    I > Library INFORMATION

                    D > DISCONNECT
                     Choose one (A,T,S,C,W,V,I,D)

     The catalog provides access to books and journal holdings in the NIH Library

                    JOURNAL ARTICLES ARE NOT INCLUDED
```

Ready		VT100		NUM	17, 54

Figure 6.1 *Telnetting to the National Institutes of Health Library in the USA.*

of hard disk space if you can't.

Fortunately there's no shortage of places on the Internet you can telnet into. Want to order a book (this one maybe)? Telnet to books.com and you can search book titles for the one you want. The commercial company (remember the 'com' suffix) that runs the service will also take your order for the book and mail it to you the same day. Want to rummage around NASA's database of extra-galactic objects? The same applies, although you can't as yet order black holes on your credit card. There are too many telnet sites to list in this section of the book, and you'll have to trust me when I say that telnet is remarkably useful, once you get the hang of all the nerdy stuff you need to get it going. It's telnet which gives you basic access to many of the Internet's secrets, such as Archie, Gopher, Internet Relay Chat and live backgammon sessions.

It pays to get the hang of telnet, because having the ability to run programs on other people's computers is a great asset, and the joke about controlling space telescopes from that heap of tin you are pleased to call a computer is in fact a reality.

What you need for telnet

You need a telnet client installed on your computer, that's what. If you use the services of an Internet provider, you might be able to use the telnet client installed on his computer. But in either case you'll also need a 'terminal emulator' – which is a long word for a piece of software which makes your exotic personal computer look like a boring old character based terminal. Yes folks, UNIX systems still talk to users via dumb terminals, so please don't snigger through the rest of this chapter. But which terminal software? And just what is a terminal anyway?

A terminal is something which, in its most basic form, takes in and spits out computer information and displays it on a screen or printout. In its most advanced form a terminal can also take in human input and convert it into something computers understand. The earliest terminals were simple solenoid-operated printers, and as electric keyboards became available they were tagged onto printers to give them an input/output capability. Old-timers will remember the 'TeleType' printers which used to print up the BBC's football results on screen. If you're under 25 you won't have a clue what I'm talking about.

Despite being old technology, terminals are still used in the UNIX world because UNIX was developed to talk to human beings through dumb character based interfaces. Terminals also happen to be cheaper than personal computers, which is why there are still vast numbers of them around in the commercial and academic world.

Like everything else in the computer world, there are various standards for terminals – a standard in this case being something that one manufacturer hopes to foist upon all the others, and the most common standards are Digital Equipment's DEC VT100/VT102 emulations, and TeleType (TTY). TTY terminal emulation is exceedingly simple, and is the preferred method of getting around, but most UNIX boxes expect to see a slightly more exotic terminal emulation. VT100/102, or derivatives VT220 and VT320, are all used somewhere on the Internet, and you'll need a program on your computer that can provide these emulations. If you trip over a remote system running on a large IBM system, you'll probably find you need IBM 3101 emulation or even 3270, although it's surprising what you can get away with if you try VT100 on everything.

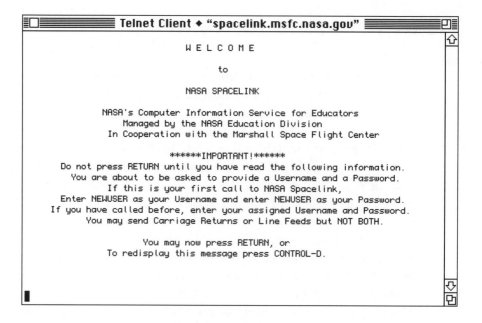

Figure 6.2   *The Nasa Spacelink Service via telnet.*

Don't forget that your terminal emulation program needs to sit on top of all the other stuff you need for Internet working. You still need your transport system (TCP/IP), your modem handler (SLIP or PPP) and your telnet client software. You can't just use a terminal emulator on its own to hook into the Internet, unless you are going through a third-party gateway such as a dial-up bulletin board.

Once you've grasped this annoying fact, you can set up your terminal emulator and get hooked up to the Internet. Unfortunately there are no hard and fast rules about setting up your terminal software, but a good place to start is with VT100 emulation, which will get you into most places. The rule is – if in doubt revert to either TTY or VT100.

Telnet commands

Telnet servers have their own series of commands. Once you're into one you'll need to get out, and the best way to do that is to type 'quit'. If this doesn't terminate your connection to the server then try sending CTRL] (hold down the CTRL key and then press the

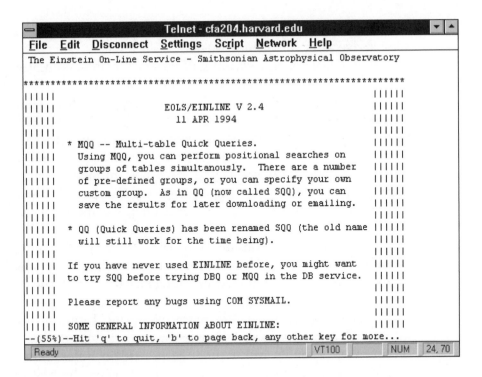

Figure 6.3   *The Smithsonian Astrophysical Laboratory (login as einline).*

square bracket sign). This is the telnet escape sequence, and it should drop you back to the telnet> prompt, where you can then type 'quit'. If it doesn't, try CTRL D, or CTRL C. Other logout sequences exist, and the best way to discover them is at first hand. If your terminal has a 'log to disk' facility or a 'scroll-back buffer' then you can use these to grab the data on the screen from the remote service and save it for later perusal.

Other telnet secrets

Telnet seems impenetrable to users of modern personal computers. This is because it *is* impenetrable, and no amount of reading books will be a substitute for telnetting around and making a nuisance of yourself. The trick is to log in to your Internet provider and type telnet <sitename>, or fire up your telnet client. A good basic telnet site to start with is books.com. Order a book while you're in there – they arrive after about four weeks.

If you're using any sort of half-decent terminal emulator you'll find that it lets you connect to different ports on the remote machine. Again there's no widely accepted regime about which port connects you to what, but in many cases logging into one port gives you access to the public service, whilst logging into another gives you access to the most secret inner workings of the System Manager's personal diary. If you see a port number mentioned in listings of telnet addresses then always try that port first – because you will in all probability get thrown off the remote server if you don't.

Finally there's a rather more complex way of logging in to remote servers. It's called rlogin, and tends not be available on public servers, although like everything else to do with the Internet there are exceptions to that statement. If you need to use help with rlogin then you'll need the services of an Internet guru, as information about you and your password are kept on the remote server. You probably won't come across rlogin unless you have a corporate account on a server, and if you do then the best place to go for advice about how to use it is the System Manager's office.

Slow servers

Like all Internet processes telnet can seem extremely slow at times. You type in a command, the screen starts to display text ... and suddenly stops. The only advice, especially if you're paying online or telephone charges, is to log out from slow telnet sessions, and try again later. It's often the case that telnet servers slow down drastically when under load from the other 655 000 users logged in, and your only recourse is to disconnect. The speed of telnet sessions also depends on the load placed on all the various bits of the routers, cables and other bits of elec-trickery which make up the Internet, so the best advice for maximizing throughput on telnet or FTP sessions is to use the Internet during off-peak hours, as far as possible. You can get a fast session to most USA servers from the UK between 7:00–12:00 hrs GMT, as the USA is six or more hours behind us. Some UK Internet users also claim faster results after midnight, UK time.

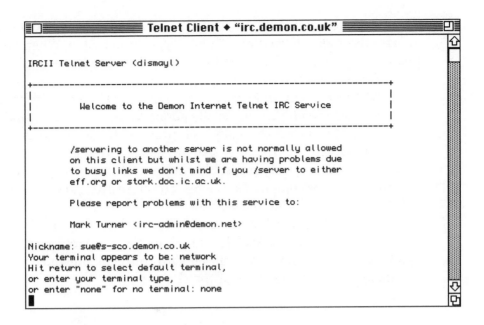

Figure 6.4   *An Internet Relay Chat server via telnet. This is the only screen we could find suitable for family viewing...*

Go to the talkies

Telnet opens up lots of avenues to the Internet rummager. One of the most futile is Internet Relay Chat, a sort of electronic river of garbage into which you empty the trashcan of your own personality. IRC is the place to find nerds, geeks, blasphemers, neonazis, rebels without a cause, causes without rebels – and computer journalists. In short it's an uncontrolled moving ribbon of human detritus. Consequently it's much loved by adolescents with terminal acne (a joke there somewhere) or by older folk with hairs growing on the palms of their hands. No, don't check – it's the first sign of madness. IRC was designed by a Finn, presumably because there's nothing to do in Finland during the long winters. It's a bit like Iceland, which has the highest rate of computer literacy in the world because it's too cold to do anything except breed and muck about with computers. There's a similar joke about Norway, where family trees apparently don't have any forks in them.

You get into IRC by telnetting to an IRC server. A good UK one is irc.demon.co.uk. You'll be asked for a nickname, and when that's been accepted type /LIST. This will scroll up a list of available topics currently under discussion. To join type /join #topic. When you've had enough, type /QUIT to get out, fast. But read the help file first, as IRC is not for novices.

IRC is a great money spinner for the telecomms providers, where users spend an hour on the phone to say something that can be handled by speech in a couple of minutes. If you're a parent and you're reading this, then the best way to recoup some of the money that your 12-year-old son is blowing on IRC is to buy shares in communications companies. Usenet group Alt.IRC serves the needs of the well-heeled and hairy-palmed.

One of the great triumphs for IRC (perhaps its only triumph) was to act as a news feed for the Gulf War. A transcript of the happenings is on the disk enclosed with this book, in which you can judge for yourself the value of the IRC system.

Telnet file transfers

There are any number of terminal based telnet services around. If you have a CompuServe account you can telnet to **compuserve. com**. You can also use your normal ZMODEM, XMODEM and other file transfer protocols at some telnet sites, because all telnet is doing is providing the link service between you and the remote system. And you can generally use your dedicated front end software over telnet – for instance, you can use CompuServe's WinCim software over telnet, instead of going in via a dial-up line. However, your ordinary terminal software may not be able to communicate over TCP/IP, which is the transport protocol going on underneath telnet. This is because most UK based communications programs like to talk over modems and you'll need a TCP/IP, compliant terminal program to make ZMODEM (or other asynchronous file transfer protocols) work over telnet.

Hytelnet

Hytelnet is an attempt to bring the Graphical User Interface to boring old character based terminals. It's also a neat way to find out about telnet and telnet sites. You log in to a Hytelnet site and follow the prompts. Use the cursor arrows to move up to the <highlighted> options and press Enter. Hytelnet will bring up the page with the information on it. The place to start your search for interesting sites is a Hytelnet server such *access.usask.ca*. Hytelnet has been overshadowed by recent developments such as the World Wide Web, but is mentioned here for old time's sake.

Telnet services

Telnet is an important part of the Internet, because it lets you do real work. You can log into the Library of Congress and check out almost any book or author, you can log into the NASA databases and pickup info on Shuttle launches. More than a thousand other databases are available for browsing.

You can also play Backgammon or GO in realtime against a human opponent by telnetting to a server and getting stuck in, and playing games over the Internet is a favourite way for American students to spend taxpayers' money on an 'education'. The most notorious sapper of tax-dollars is the Multi-User Domain, or MUD. MUD is a game where you solve problems – such as how to pick up the jewels without waking up your tutor. You can also meet other telnetters inside the domain, pretending to be wizards, or dwarves – hence the multi-user tag. MUDs are such attractive places to be that there is now real concern about students junking their academic career in favour of typing:

```
<go left>
<pick up>
<put down>
<vaporize>
```

and so on.

There are vast numbers of online games available at *lambda.parc.xerox.com* (port 8888), including online chess games. You can find out more by loitering around the *rec.games* newsgroups, which carry crazed messages from gamesters stuck at the first post.

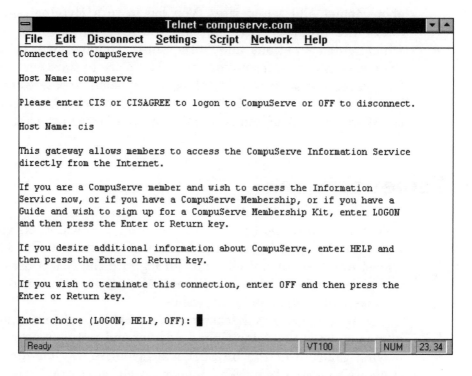

Figure 6.5 *Accessing CompuServe via telnet. Most of the larger online services now support telnet access.*

Favourite places – telnet

access.usask.ca
Login as hytelnet. Site contains details of many telnet resources.

Books.com
Search for authors or book titles. Shipping to the UK takes about four weeks and costs less than four dollars.

Colorada Alliance of Research Libraries (CARL)
pac.carl.org, login as pac.

eve.assumption.edu port 5000
Takes you to dragon.mud, the text based adventure game. Watch those phone bills.

Internet Relay Chat
The UK server is at irc.demon.co.uk. Another lives at prof.jpl.nasa.gov, which is based at the Jet Propulsion Lab in California.

Library of Congress
locis.loc.gov
Catalogue to the biggest library in the world. Access is often limited for non-USA calls, but it is possible to get in, from 9 a.m. to 9 p.m. Eastern time.

Library at Dartford College
library.dartford.edu.
Includes lots of Shakespeare. Busy site when we tried it.

Merit Network
hermes.merit.edu
Gateway to Michigan's regional net. Lets you into many US online services, including SprintNet and CompuServe. Useful if you're travelling out of the UK and need to get your CompuServe mail from an Internet workstation. Other good gateways for rummaging include Washington University at wugate.wustl.edu.

Nasa News
spacelink.msfc.nasa.gov
You'll need to leave your name (register) to get access to lots of NASA info, including details of Shuttle schedules. Other good space places are ersin.esa.it for details of European Space Agency doings.

Scrabble
next2.cas.muohio.edu port 777
Online Scrabble.

gopher.netsys.com – login as enews for Electronic NewsStand.

bbs.noplace.com – No Place Like Home BBS.

liberty.uc.wlu.ed – login: lawlib.

ds.internic.net – login: wais, for InterNIC Directory of Directories.

archie.doc.ic.ac.uk – login: archie for Archie use via telnet.

7   Uncle Archie

'Results can take up
to three days to
arrive...'

After six chapters of getting slowly used to fighting with UNIX,
you're probably ready for Archie. Archie is a tool that helps you find
information on the Internet, and like all tools on the Internet its
usefulness depends on the ability of human beings to order data
into neat and tidy piles. (If it's not in the tidy pile, then Archie can't
find it.)

Archie has been described as a card index of Internet files,
which is a bit of a misnomer. Archie is more like that deaf old bat
you employed 20 years ago as a secretary, and haven't yet had the
heart to fire. You tell Archie to go and find a file, and then it comes
back with lots of not quite the right information. Archie is only one
of the search methods available on the Internet, and like most
character based interfaces, it's looking more shabby with each day
that passes. If you prefer to use Gopher to search for your data then
you can bypass Archie for much of your rummaging, but it's
included here to prevent book reviewers from shooting me down in

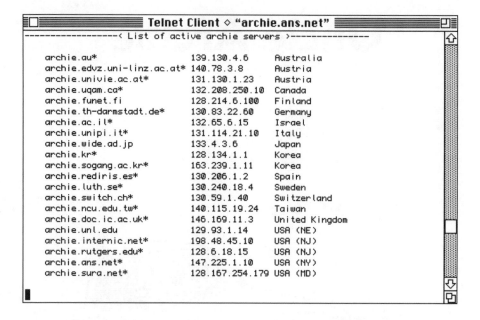

```
┌──────────────────────────────────────────────────────────────┐
│▐□▐▐▐▐▐▐▐▐▐   Telnet Client ◇ "archie.ans.net" ▐▐▐▐▐▐▐▐▐▐  [▓]│
│---------------< List of active archie servers >---------------  ⇧│
│   archie.au*                139.130.4.6      Australia           │
│   archie.edvz.uni-linz.ac.at* 140.78.3.8     Austria            │
│   archie.univie.ac.at*       131.130.1.23    Austria            │
│   archie.uqam.ca*            132.208.250.10  Canada             │
│   archie.funet.fi           128.214.6.100   Finland            │
│   archie.th-darmstadt.de*    130.83.22.60    Germany            │
│   archie.ac.il*             132.65.6.15     Israel             │
│   archie.unipi.it*           131.114.21.10   Italy              │
│   archie.wide.ad.jp         133.4.3.6       Japan              │
│   archie.kr*                128.134.1.1     Korea              │
│   archie.sogang.ac.kr*       163.239.1.11    Korea              │
│   archie.rediris.es*         130.206.1.2     Spain              │
│   archie.luth.se*            130.240.18.4    Sweden             │
│   archie.switch.ch*          130.59.1.40     Switzerland        │
│   archie.ncu.edu.tw*         140.115.19.24   Taiwan             ▓│
│   archie.doc.ic.ac.uk*       146.169.11.3    United Kingdom     │
│   archie.unl.edu            129.93.1.14     USA (NE)           │
│   archie.internic.net*       198.48.45.10    USA (NJ)           │
│   archie.rutgers.edu*        128.6.18.15     USA (NJ)           │
│   archie.ans.net*            147.225.1.10    USA (NY)           │
│   archie.sura.net*           128.167.254.179 USA (MD)          ⇩│
│▐                                                              [▣]│
└──────────────────────────────────────────────────────────────┘
```

Figure 7.1   *Of all the servers in all the world, you had to walk into Archie's.*

flames: 'Schofield carn't (sic) write Internet books because she hates Archie' – or some such.

Are you being Servered?

Archie servers can be accessed in two ways: conventionally by telnetting into an Archie server, or by sending search requests to the server by email. The first method is marginally faster than waiting two days or more for an email reply.

To get into an Archie server you telnet to the Archie server of your choice, and a good start is ***archie.doc.ic.ac.uk***. It's at Imperial College in London, and is fairly fast, if you catch it on a good day when it's working and the guy with the beard is back from Majorca. A number of Archie clients are also starting to appear for Windows and Macintosh computers.

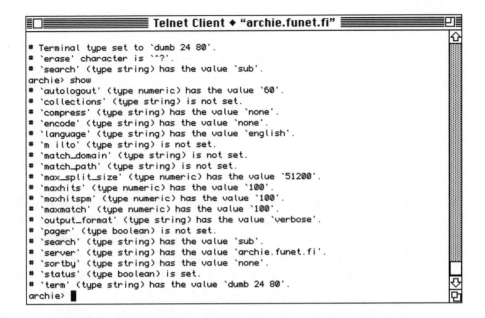

Figure 7.2   *Archie command line settings. Should searching for information be so difficult?*

Search me

Archie uses several search methods to locate the data you want, and all of them are command line driven and come in various guises of complexity. You set up which search method you want after login.

The search methods are:

exact
sub
subcase
regex

You should try the *exact* method first, as long as you know what you're looking for. It's faster, allegedly. However, most people start with *sub*.

You set the search method up with:

set search exact (or *sub* etc.)

and then type in whatever it is you want to search for:

set search sub
prog amiga

The Archie server will then do its stuff and rummage around the world's databases until it finds a match. In this case Archie will come up with a list of all of the sites which provide Amiga files, as a scrolling list. In fact it's such a long list that the information will scroll off your screen. You should therefore at least be using a terminal emulator with a scroll-back buffer, which lets you call back the data for display. DOS people, who know little of scroll-back, will find benefit in a terminal emulation package that logs data to disk. In both cases you'll need to investigate whatever Archie sends you, as you'll get a lot of information back, not all of which will be relevant. But you can use the mail commands to mail the output to yourself.

Archie search methods

The *exact* method looks for an exact match to the search string you've typed in – but there are other choices. Here they are:

Sub matches the search string anywhere in the text. If you typed:

set search sub
prog amigastuff

Archie should find:

amigastuff.lzh
Amigastuff.faq
amigastuff.txt

Subcase matches the search string for case. If you typed:

> *set search subcase*
> *prog Amiga.stuff*

Archie should find:

> **Amigastuff.faq**

It won't find:

> **amigastuff.txt**
> **amigastuff.lzh**

Regex stands for 'regular expression' and is a method of using wildcards to limit search matching. Not many PC or Mac users bother with it, because it's about as intuitive as discovering Relativity. Consequently many personal computer users are happy to do *sub* matching. If you want to get to grips with *regex* searching then you're recommended to pick up a book on UNIX – because typing long search strings hooked together by *regex* expressions leads to more errors than success.

Other Archie commands

You should limit Archie's searching, to provide you with a reasonable number of matches. Archie will look for up to 1000 matches before it gives up, which takes time. You can change this limit with the *maxhits* command:

> *set maxhits 50*

will ensure that you only get the results of 50 matches. A good number is somewhere between 100 and 200.

The *pager* sets up the number of lines displayed on a page, which is normally 24. You can check with the *show* command, and reset the pagination with:

> *set pager 18* (or some such)

Autologout will set the time allowed before throwing you off. Again, check with *show* before you alter it.

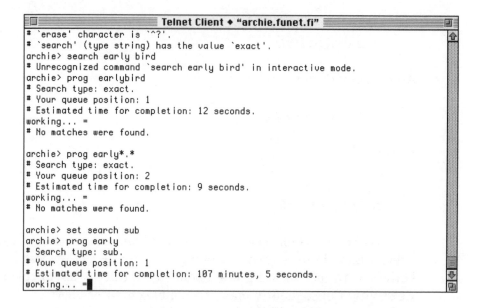

Figure 7.3   *Archie estimates 107 minutes for a search. It's not so good for modem users, unless you use Archie by email.*

Status (on/off) gets Archie to show you the status of the ongoing search, and *sortby* sets the way Archie displays the results. You can set *sortby* to:

hostname/rhostname – which displays the results by alphabetical list of the host on which the search string is found. *Rhostname* gives a reverse alphabetical search.

time/rtime – newest or oldest modification date.

filename/rfilename – alphabetical filename or reverse alphabetical filename.

The availability of commands can vary, so check before you configure Archie to send you nothing, after a long wait.

Archie also has a *whatis* function, which is used instead of the *prog* command. If you type *whatis filename* you might get a list of descriptions of available files. The *whatis* command searches these description lists for matches, and is a slightly more intuitive method of fighting with Archie. But don't forget that Archie doesn't do any file transfers for you – you will still have to FTP to the indicated site and directory to get the data. Progressive it ain't. However, some Archie clients can now do this. They remove all the command line stuff and display the results nicely. You then double click on the file to be FTP'd and it's sent to you directly.

Mailing Archie

You can email search requests to Archie, which makes more sense than hanging around an Archie server consuming telephone time and patience. All the functions mentioned so far will work, and you may find it useful to make up an Archie mail template in your mailer program. You simply send an email to the Archie server of your choice, containing the search requirements, and if you've done everything correctly, you should get a reasonable response. Remember not to send your automatically generated signature to Archie, as it won't appreciate it.

Here's an Archie email request:

Email to archie@archie.doc.ic.ac.uk

---

set mailto sue@s-sco.demon.co.uk
(makes sure you get the response mailed to you)

servers
(returns a list of archie servers)

help
(returns the help file for that server)

set search subcase
pro
Amiga

set maxhits 100

quit
(ends the request.)

And that's it.

If you've done everything properly you should get a reply, usually within a few hours, although it can take longer, like three days, to arrive ... .

Other search methods

Archie is, well, kind of quaint. It's a bit like those stodgy computerized indexes they've now put into municipal libraries. It's quicker to search through the shelves by hand than it is to learn the archaic user interface. There's several more forms of search mechanism on the Internet including Gopher, Veronica and World Wide Web. So if Archie doesn't suit you then look at those other ways of finding what you're after.

Favourite Archie sites

None. But check out the screen shot showing Archie sites.

8 FTP

'FTP works
exceptionally well,
most of the time...'

You're going to like FTP. Everyone does. FTP stands for File
Transfer Protocol, and it's the single most popular hobby on the
'Net, if the fact that it takes up 48 per cent of all network traffic is
anything to go by. FTP is simply the art of transferring files from
one place to another, using the 'file transfer protocol', which gives
its name to the process.

FTP comes in two flavours. There's the sort of FTP where you
use a terminal emulator and a set of gormless and odd-ball UNIX
commands, and the sort of clicky-button FTP which happens on
Windows, Macintosh and Amiga machines. In the first case you're
back to the character based interface of UNIX, but the newer
graphical environments make navigating around remote servers
very easy, and you don't have to learn commands such as CD or
Grep, or CTRL]. But in both cases you'll need to learn about
hierarchical file structures, how to fight with compressed archives,
and the mysteries of Anonymous FTP.

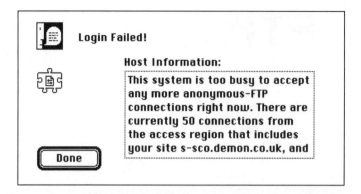

Figure 8.1　*FTP is the single most popular thing on the 'Net. Consequently there might be a few queues.*

Starting up

You'll need an FTP client installed on your machine to use FTP – unless your service provider has got one on his system which you can access via terminal emulation. To get into an FTP site you either type:

ftp sitename

or you fill in an on-screen form containing the information required. Once you get to the log-in screen you'll be asked for a username and password. Here's your first problem. Unless you work at the site, or have bought large amounts of beer for the guy who runs the network, you won't have a login identity. So you use 'anonymous' if you can spell it, and 'ftp' if you can't. Most sites accept either, but for those that don't you'll have to learn to spell, anonymously. For a password you should type your full username and an @ symbol – which makes anonymous FTP rather less anonymous than it would otherwise be. You should then be logged into the system.

However, you'll often find that many FTP sites don't like hordes of people logging in during office hours, or that the number of anonymous users is limited for various reasons. The convention is that anonymous users should keep their FTP usage to a

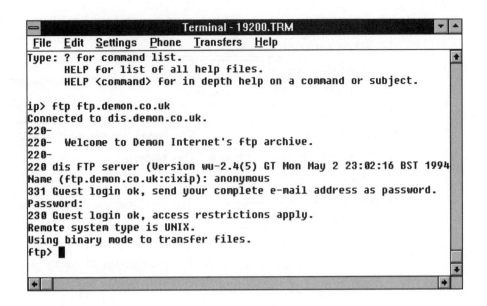

```
─                     Terminal - 19200.TRM                   ▼ ▲
 File  Edit  Settings  Phone  Transfers  Help
Type: ? for command list.                                          ▲
      HELP for list of all help files.
      HELP <command> for in depth help on a command or subject.

ip> ftp ftp.demon.co.uk
Connected to dis.demon.co.uk.
220-
220-  Welcome to Demon Internet's ftp archive.
220-
220 dis FTP server (Version wu-2.4(5) GT Mon May 2 23:02:16 BST 1994
Name (ftp.demon.co.uk:cixip): anonymous
331 Guest login ok, send your complete e-mail address as password.
Password:
230 Guest login ok, access restrictions apply.
Remote system type is UNIX.
Using binary mode to transfer files.
ftp> █                                                              ▼
◄                                                               ►
```

Figure 8.2 *Anonymous login to an ftp server. Use your username as the password.*

minimum during office hours, but that's going to be difficult as it's always office hours somewhere on the Internet. Correspondingly you'll find that many of the more popular ftp sites are constantly busy and you won't be able to get in. But if this is your first ftp experience then try ***ftp.demon.co.uk***. Despite the name you'll still have to type ftp as a command – before typing ftp.demon.co.uk. GUI users will just use ftp.demon.co.uk as the site name.

Once you're in you'll be presented with a directory listing of the files on the server, or at least the files in the first directory of the server. If you're familiar with DOS then you'll know of hierarchical directories, which are a bit like nested Russian dolls. You navigate from the top directory downwards, and have to come back up to the top to go down another branch.

The CD command means change directory, and is used to move around the system. DIR shows the files in the current directory, and GET gets a file. Simple so far? Maybe – but then you have to remember to get your files as either ASCII or binary. ASCII means that you get a plain text file back at the receiving end of things. Binary means you'll receive your file as an executable, or a spreadsheet, or a graphics file – in short as the sort of data your computer doesn't expect you to read with a plain text editor. You

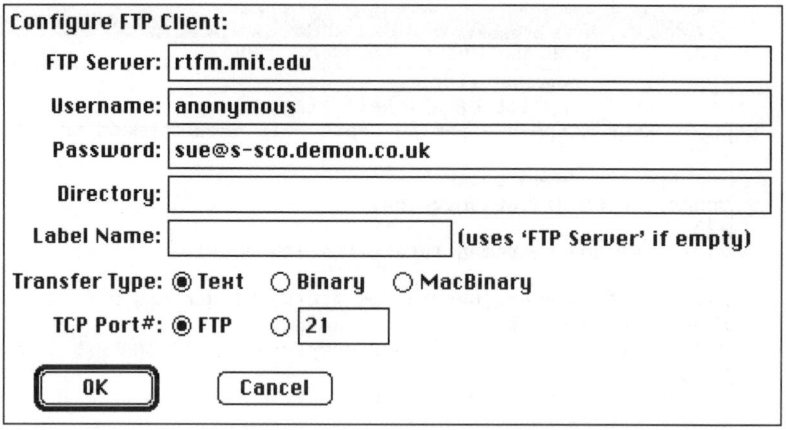

```
┌────────────────────────────────────────────────────────┐
│ Configure FTP Client:                                    │
│   FTP Server: │rtfm.mit.edu                           │  │
│    Username:  │anonymous                              │  │
│    Password:  │sue@s-sco.demon.co.uk                  │  │
│   Directory:  │                                       │  │
│  Label Name:  │                          │ (uses 'FTP Server' if empty) │
│ Transfer Type: ◉ Text   ○ Binary   ○ MacBinary          │
│    TCP Port#: ◉ FTP    ○ │21    │                       │
│  ┌──────────┐      ┌──────────┐                          │
│  │    OK    │      │  Cancel  │                          │
│  └──────────┘      └──────────┘                          │
└────────────────────────────────────────────────────────┘
```

Figure 8.3 *Setting up a GUI for anonymous login. Windows programs need the same parameters.*

tell the remote server which type of transfer you want before you start, by typing in ASCII or binary before the GET command. If you're in any doubt then try binary – except for files which are obviously text files, such as Read Me files, or LS–LR files which contain the directory listings of the server you're on. Binary is sometimes called Image mode – as it sends a binary image of the file on the server, bit by bit. In ASCII mode it just sends the characters of the ASCII alphabet, so what you get on your computer can be read by a text editor. You can get multiple files with the MGET instruction and if you have write access to the remote server you can leave files on it with the PUT command. Most anonymous users will never bother with either of these instructions.

Generally speaking, all of these commands are used only on servers connected to your computer by terminal emulation – you will have a series of button options to navigate and collect files if you're using Windows, Mac or Amiga software. What you may lose with such GUI-based software is the ability to see just how big the remote file is before you start downloading it over a modem link. This can be important, as file transfer speeds over even V32 bis modems can be extremely low due to loading or system usage, and spending half an hour downloading a large file over a modem is quite common. The trick is to look for a file listing the directory details of the ftp server. This will let you see just how big that file is before you try to download it, and directory listings are often kept in a file called 'Index', or READ.ME or LS LR. To complicate matters those directory listings themselves can be quite large (the one on ftp.demon.co.uk is over two megabytes long) so you'll still have an expensive download just to pick up the directory listing. Other GUI clients have a Get Info button which hops off to the server and grabs the file size and directory information. GUI clients tend not to download this sort of stuff by default, as it takes up even more modem time to get data which you may not be interested in.

What you will also realize when using ftp is that modem connections of any flavour just don't make it as far as economical file transfer is concerned, a theme which will become more apparent as we move on to other Internet based services. But as the only alternative at the moment is an ISDN or leased line we must wait for the Information Superhighway to become a reality, say in ten or twelve years' time. In the meantime you can buy CD-ROMs containing many of the more popular Internet ftp archives. There's SIMTEL for DOS, CICA archives for Windows – and any number of Info-Mac clones for the Mac. These cost between £12 and £50 in the UK, less in the USA, and are, at the moment, the most cost-effective methods of distributing software normally found on the Internet. You can order them by email from the USA. Mail Joe@config.sys for a list.

FTP arcanery

If you're using a terminal to hook into ftp you'll see that each command you type in to the server results in some sort of output, preceded by a three-number digit. This is put there, not so that the guy with the beard and sandals who is looking after the remote site can suss out these diagnostic codes, but so your ftp program can take appropriate action if there's an error. Most ftp programs don't bother with these numbers, because if they did, writers would have to fill up needless pages in books with long and sordid explanations of what they mean.

And what about those codes you see before a file, like -rw- -rw- r- -? These are the attribute settings for the file or directory, and are called 'permission masks'. You only need to know that if you need to know more you should be buying UNIX books, and that 'r' stands for 'read only'. You shouldn't be able to overwrite a read-

```
┌─────────────────────────────── ls-lR ───────────────────────────────┐
│ total 1080                                                            ⇧
│ drwxrwsr-x  4 root        512 Mar  4 23:23 4.3                        │
│ drwxrwsr-x  2 peter       512 Mar  4 23:18 BSD                        │
│ -rw-rw-r--  1 root       3398 Apr 21 15:24 FTPVIEW.TXT                │
│ drwxrwsr-x  2 root        512 Mar  4 22:14 NeXT                       │
│ drwxrwsr-x  7 root    |   512 Mar  4 23:23 SCO                        │
│ drwxr-sr-x  3 root        512 Apr  7 16:40 VAX                        │
│ lrwxrwxrwx  1 root          8 Mar  4 23:38 accu -> /pub/cug           │
│ drwxrwsr-x 21 oliver     1024 May 11 20:35 amiga                      │
│ drwxrwsr-x 15 ubik        512 Apr  6 01:05 antivirus                  │
│ drwxrwsr-x  4 arcturus   1024 May 11 06:15 archimedes                 │
│ drwxrwsr-x  7 root        512 Apr  7 16:54 archives                   │
│ drwxrwsr-x  5 chaos       512 Apr 16 23:52 atari                      │
│ drwxrwsr-x  5 peter       512 May  6 11:49 books                      │
│ drwxrwsr-x  2 root        512 Mar  4 23:24 commercial-demos           │
│ drwxrwsr-x  2 root       1024 May  1 18:04 cpm                        │
│ drwxrwsr-x 12 root        512 May  8 14:46 cug                        ⇩
└──────────────────────────────────────────────────────────────────────┘
```

Figure 8.4   *Permission masks on an FTP server.*

only file or change its name or do any of those things which, in the UK, will put you in breach of the Computer Misuse Act. And you won't see those masks under many of the GUI based programs, which is yet another blessing, although a Show File Information or Get Info button should bring them up.

Here are some useful terminal commands for ftp:

cd fred	– changes to directory 'fred'
cdup	– goes up one directory
cd /	– go to top of tree
cd ..	– go up one subdirectory
asc	– sets file transfers to ASCII
bin	– sets file transfer as binary
mget	– use for multiple file receives (not with GUIs)
cd / nextdir	– changes to a new directory.

Don't forget to leave a space between the / and everything else as you need a space after the first word. And don't forget that these commands may differ from server to server. And ... UNIX file and directory names are case sensitive. FREd is different from FReD, just to make life as difficult as possible.

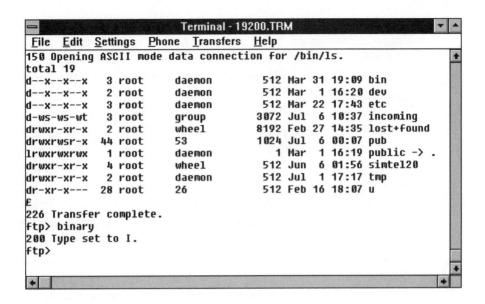

Figure 8.5   *Set binary mode before downloading executables or compressed files. 'Type set to I' means Image mode, that is, binary.*

File compression

Users of bulletin boards, dial-up services and the Internet will be well aware that most computer files can be compressed down into around a half of their original size or less, by the use of file compression programs such as PKZip, Stuffit, Compact Pro and the like.

There are many reasons for compressing files, the most obvious being the need to fit more files in a given area – be that a local hard disk or a network server. File compression utilities are also useful for adding two or more files into a single bundle for transmission over modems or for adding encryption or password protection to files. Some compression programs also allow compressed files to be filed to disk in segments for reconstitution at a later date (multi-disk segmenting). And most compression programs also have an option to create self-extracting archives. These let users decompress files without access to the original program (but can add about ten per cent or more to the size of the compressed archive.)

The most common format for compressed PC files is PKZip. These compressed files have a suffix of ZIP and you'll need PKUnzip (or a PKUnzip-compliant clone utility) to decompress these files. You'll find such an animal on almost all ftp servers that distribute PC files.

Mac users will come across several compression utilities. Probably the most common is Stuffit, which produces files with a suffix of SIT. Slightly less common, but in use on many dial-up sites, is Compactor (suffix is cpt), and many sites are starting to carry files with an LZH suffix, which means they are compressed with the Mac version of LHA, titled MacLHA. A Mac program called Zipit produces some compatibility with ZIP files generated on PCs. Self-extracting Mac Archives often have a suffix of SEA.

Many Mac sites carry files in 'disk image' form. This is a scheme where a bit image of a floppy disk is compressed into a single file, and the corresponding decompressor is used to re-create the disk image. This process either creates a floppy disk with the original information on it, or mounts an image of the virtual floppy onto the desktop. DiskCopy is the utility to do the former, MountImage to do the latter and disk image files often carry the suffix 'image'. MountImage is sometimes the more useful of the two, as it allows users of pre-SuperDrive Macs to mount an image of a 1.44 megabyte disk on the desktop of a Mac which can only read 800 kB floppies. You'll find image files used to carry copies of Apple installer disks, for instance.

Let's go one step further and consider what happens to files when you load them up to the Internet. As mentioned previously, your file has to be translated to coexist with the antiquated file structure of the Internet, and a utility called BinHex effects this transmutation on Macs, and UUencode does the same on PCs. BinHex or UUencode translates your neat and tidy binary file into an ASCII representation of its hex code. This can then be squirted around the Internet with impunity as a text file and restored to binary on reception. (BinHex files have a .HQX suffix.) FTP handles PC binary files as bit images, so they come and go as binary files, but you will have to tell your FTP client that you want a binary transfer in almost every case. It's a common mistake to download binary files as ASCII, in which case they don't work when you get them.

As if that wasn't enough, the UNIX fraternity often decide

that an additional compression process is needed to compress compressed files while they live on the server, and many Internet servers now use a GNU-ZIP variant to do this. The result is that you'll need yet another process to unlock your data. These files have a gz suffix and you'll need Gzip to turn the file into binary, Binhex or UUencode format. Some sites purport to do this for you automatically if you put a + sign before your password, and Imperial College, London runs just such a scheme. But despite some correspondence between the author and the comms guru at src.doc.ic.ac.uk this scheme wouldn't work for this writer and a number of other correspondents.

There are a number of other compression schemes around. LHA is used on both Amiga and PC files, and is creeping across to the Mac platform, and ZOO files are starting to catch on, although the older ARC utility is slowly fading away. You can find decompression utilities for all of these files in a number of places, so getting hold of them should not be a problem.

Graphics stuff

Graphics files are stored on ftp servers in various formats, the most common being GIF files, the most uncommon being Mac 'picts'. Other formats abound, and you'll generally need the right sort of file viewer on your computer to view and manipulate graphics files. GIF files will go straight into most graphics programs on most types of computer, and GIF files are consequently the lingua franca of ftp and dial-up comms users. TIFF files, on the other hand, come in a dozen different types and are not guaranteed to cross computer boundaries smoothly. There are also JPEG files, and TGA files (targa). TARGA files are slowly being replaced by JPEG files. As mentioned, you'll need a graphics viewer of some sort to see these files on your PC or Mac (the Amiga comes with one built in, of course). Graphics Workshop is a good all-rounder for the PC, and Graphics Convertor is arguably the best all-round Shareware graphics program for the Mac, or any other platform. Both are readily available on the Internet from many ftp sites.

Graphics file transfers

Once you've grabbed the file from an FTP server you may want to share it around a little. Your friends will all have their own ideas about what constitutes a computer so you'll need to learn ways of sharing graphics files around. The trick is to bring the file into a common disk format, and then convert it into a common file format. Mac, Amiga and Atari machines have utilities that let them save files in MS-DOS formats – but if all else fails (and you have a modem) you can upload the file from the alien computer to your favourite email service, and then download it to your computer for conversion. Other tricks include using null modem cables between serial ports.

Most of the Mac's graphics translator programs will work with most graphics files on MS-DOS disks – for instance, if you have a Windows BMP file on a PC floppy disk then Apple File Exchange will read it into the Mac without error. It can then be translated with Graphic Convertor or similar. But Mac users often run into problems with TIFF and EPS files. TIFF files have many inherent formatting differences, including black and white, grey scale, 24-bit, 4-bit and 8-bit images. TIFF also supports the use of multiple types of data compression – and to complicate matters further, two byte-ordering schemes are supported (Intel and Motorola), as indicated by the internal TIFF file header. So don't be surprised if you have problems loading ftp'd TIFFs into your computer.

PC based Encapsulated PostScript Files on the PC come as either plain ASCII files, or binary files with a header that describes both the PostScript commands and the preview (TIFF or Metafile) section of the file. Again, not all EPS files will translate between computers or platforms, so if you have a choice, go for GIF.

Getting the best from FTP

FTP works exceptionally well, most of the time. It runs slowly if the remote server is busy or the route your TCP/IP packets take is busy, or if you don't have the correct form of 'handshaking' on the modem link. You can multitask FTP sessions if you have the right

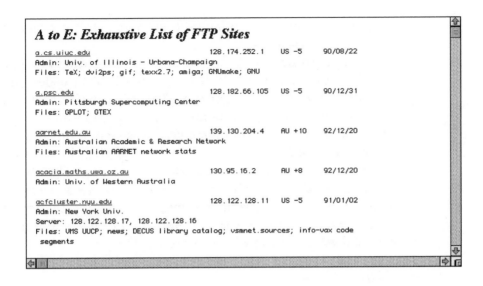

Figure 8.6 *More FTP sites than you can shake a modem at. Use World Wide Web to find them.*

sort of client software – that is, you can log into two or more sites and download files concurrently, which is a good way of economizing on modem use. But if you open too many sessions you'll slow things down considerably.

One tip (for V32 bis and faster modems) is to watch the RD (receive data) light on your modem. If it's not continuously lit then your modem isn't constantly occupied. Try opening another FTP session and starting a second download. You may find that you can take advantage of spare bandwidth on your dial-up link. Alas, if your computer has an internal modem you won't have any lights to look at but you might have an on-screen indicator which shows how much data is arriving in a given time. Other tips for achieving low-cost transfers include using FTP at 3 a.m. – Eastern Standard Time, and buying CD-ROMs with the files already on them.

FTP by mail

With commendable foresight, and the magic of the word processor, Chapter 4 mentioned that you could get files by email from any site so equipped to do that. FTPMAIL will test your patience to the full as it entails programming command-line based UNIX systems from four thousand miles away.

The first thing to do is to find a site which supports FTPMAIL. One such lives at the notoriously overloaded *mail-server@rtfm.mit.edu*, another is at *ftpmail.sunsite.unc.edu*.

Both of these sites provide an ftp-by-mail gateway to most of the other ftp servers. The command syntax is similar on both. Start by sending an email message to the site with Help in the subject line, and in the body of the text. Don't send your signature, or anything else in the body of the message or it will be interpreted as a command. At the same time you might as well get the top-level index so add a second line with the word Index on it and finish off in true code-warrior style with the word Quit:

> *help*
> *index*
> *quit*

Then wait for the result. On Boxing Day 1994, mail went full circle in about 20 minutes. In the middle of a US semester it might take a lot longer. The help file you'll get will look like the following, which is a truncated version:

> *From: File Transfer by Mail <ftpmail@sunsite.unc.edu>*
> *Date: Mon, 26 Dec 1994 07:38:01 -0500*
> *To: sue@s-sco.demon.co.uk*
> *Subject: <FTP EMAIL> response*
>
> *<FTP EMAIL> response*
> *ftpmail@sunsite.unc.edu – ftp's files and sends them back via electronic mail.*
>
> *If you have problems please email ftpkeeper@sunsite.unc.edu and quote the following line:*
> *$Revision: 1.23 $*
>
> *Valid commands to the ftpmail gateway are:*
>
> *reply-to email-address*
> *Who to send the response to. This is optional and defaults to the users email address –*
>
> *followed by one of:*

help	Just send back help
delete jobid	Delete the given job
open [site [user [pass]]]	Site to ftp to. Defaults are sunsite.unc.edu anonymous reply-to-address.

If there was an open then it can be followed by up to 100 of the following commands:

cd pathname	Change directory.
ls [pathname]	Short listing of pathname. Default pathname is current directory.
dir [pathname]	Long listing of pathname. Default pathname is current directory.
get pathname	Get a file and email it back.
compress	Compress files/dir-listings before emailing back
gzip	Gzip files/dir-listings before emailing back
mode binary mode ascii	Change the mode selected for the get command. Defaults to binary.
quit	End of input – ignore any following lines.

Example scripts are:

open
dir
quit

(Connect to sunsite.unc.edu and send back the contents of the top level directory)

reply-to lmjm@doc.ic.ac.uk
open
cd unix
get buffer.shar
quit

> *(Connect to sunsite.unc.edu and send back the file buffer.shar to lmjm@doc.ic.ac.uk)*
>
> *open src.doc.ic.ac.uk*
> *cd graphics/X11/X.V11R5*
> *get ls-lR.Z*
> *cd ../contrib*
> *compress*
> *ls -ltra*
> *quit*
>
> *(Connect to src.doc.ic.ac.uk, send back the file ls-lR.Z in graphics/X11/X.V11R5. As this is a binary file it has to be transferred in binary mode. Because it is binary it will automatically be uuencoded (the default binary encoder). Then change to ../contrib and mail back a compressed directory listing. Although compressing ls output makes it binary, which then has to be encoded, it still ends up smaller than the original.)*

As you'll see from the examples it's possible to use FTPMAIL effectively, as long as you're prepared to learn the scripting. However it's a far cry from using a graphical FTP client on a direct TCP/IP connection, although as you'll agree, it's much better than nothing.

Favourite FTP sites

FTP sites are too numerous to list, but a good way to get to them is with Gopher or World Wide Web. That way you can find a site which carries the information you need. Rather than list more than a handful of sites it's suggested you read the Gopher chapter and start from there. Here are a few sites to whet your appetite.

ftp.demon.co.uk is a good UK site. It carries almost all of the software you need to get going, plus lists of FAQs (Frequently Asked Questions) and lists of other lists.

mrcnext.cso.uiuc.edu has the Project Gutenberg files. Project

Gutenberg was set up to carry non-copyright works of literature in electronic form, and has much of interest.

toybox.gsfc.nasa.gov carries space images, but the site can be slow during the rush hour. Modem users beware.

wiretap.spies.com carries electronic books, stuff on privacy issues and much electronic bric-a-brac, and is almost always available.

ftp.uu.net

Internet Talk Radio in

/usenet/news.answers/internet-talk-radio/anonymous-ftp-list.Z.

These are monster (20–30 Mbyte) files containing the Internet Talk Radio files, a sort of Radio Internet. Features include 'Geek of the Week'.

titan.ksc.nasa.gov for the WinVN NNTP Newsreader.

sseop.jsc.nasa.gov for yet more shuttle images.

ames.arc.nasa.gov in pub/GIF for yet more space images, ds.internic.net for InterNIC Directory of directories.

csd4.csd.uwm.edu for inet.services.txt (Yanoff's Services List).

nic.merit.edu (documents/fyi/ and documents/rfc) – For Your Information and Requests For Comments files.

gorgon.tft.tele.no – Yellow Pages in pub/groupware. But the USA version, not the UK one.

gopher.netsys.com on port 2100 for Electronic News4Stand.

merlot.welch.jhu.edu – biology info.

gopher.msen.com – jobs in US.

marvel.loc.gov – Library of Congress Machine Assisted Realization of the Virtual Electronic Library.

fatty.law.cornell.edu – Cornell Law School Information.

9   Gopher

'You could get to
like gopher-ing with
Veronica...'

Gopher is either a dreadful misuse of the English language ('go fer
it') or a burrowing rodent of the family Geomyidae. And if we are
being tautological in a zoological sense we might quibble that
Gopherus, the burrowing tortoise of North America, bears more
resemblance to the electronic variety than Geomyidae, as neither is
particularly fast when it comes to modems. So Gopher is an
information search tool, which originally came from the University
of Minnesota, which has a Gopher of the Geomyidae variety as a
mascot. You use Gopher to search for things on the 'Net – but
unlike Archie, Gopher is menu driven. You could get to like
Gophering, whereas the same cannot always be said for Archie-ing.
     To set about Gophering you need a Gopher client on your
computer at best – or the use of a telnet client over a terminal link
at worst. You open your Gopher client (you have already connected
to the 'Net by modem or Ethernet) and start clicking on menus, or
fighting with typed-in commands. Gopher is client-dependent –

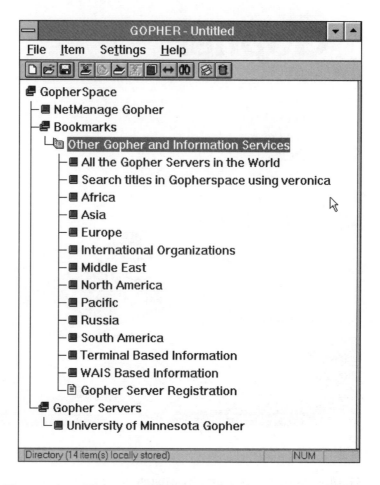

Figure 9.1   *This is the Gopher client from Internet Chameleon.*
Navigation is by point and click.

that is, some Gopher clients are pretty poor, some are just pretty, and some are just poor. Windows users get a good Gopher client in Internet Chameleon, and in the Shareware HGopher software. Mac users will love TurboGopher, which is also Shareware and as fast as they come.

The speed of the Gopher client you are using is fairly important, especially so over phone lines where you're paying money not to receive data. And Gopher likes to pull pictures off the 'Net and show them to you, so a speedy user interface is vital. You can get most of the latest releases of Gopher software from the ftp site at ***boombox.micro.umn.edu*** but alas the site is often busy.

Most service providers can also get you the software so ask there if in doubt.

I know I want it – but what does it do?

Gopher pulls information off the 'Net. It's a 'document delivery service' which can get you text files, binaries, images, executable and plain old lists. Gopher was originally developed in April 1991 by the University of Minnesota and consequently you'll find that many Gopher clients default to the University of Minnesota on start-up.

Gopher in actuality is a bunch of dedicated computers called Gopher servers. Each Gopher server knows about all the other servers (most of the time), so if a Gopher server doesn't have the info you want it should go and look it up elsewhere at another Gopher server. It presents these searches as a series of menus from which you pick the next item you want. You navigate around between Gopher servers, or you search either a particular server for information, or all of the servers, or just all the menu titles on all the servers (menu titles contain preset pointers to major services like Electronic Books). The All Servers approach means that you have discovered GopherSpace – that hypothetical realm inhabited by those stupid boxes of silicon we are pleased to call computers.

Using GopherSpace

You can access a Gopher server either by using the Gopher client stored on the computer at your Internet provider's end, or more commonly by using your very own Gopher client software. You can also telnet into a Gopher server and do it that way, but running your own client software is faster, and you get a say in what the interface looks like. Most Gopher client software comes ready configured with a 'home' server. This is usually the University of Minnesota, as previously mentioned.

If you've got your client software from an Internet provider then the home page might reflect his interest in selling you connect time, but generally speaking, the University of Minnesota is where Gopher tyros end up. Once you're connected you will be presented

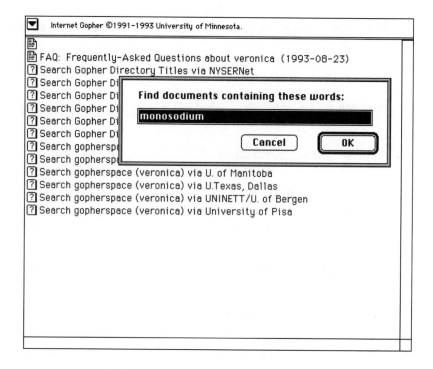

Figure 9.2 *Gopher searches GopherSpace (other Gopher servers). Veronica lets you search multiple sites for keywords.*

with a menu of places to go, things to do, and it's up to you to start exploring. You do this by actioning menu requests and following menu items until you get to where you want to be. This is easier than it sounds but in the early days of your Gophering you will neither know where you want to go, nor recognize where you are once you get there. But it doesn't take long to navigate around the system, and after a while you'll really get the feeling that GopherSpace is a rather good term for the virtual environment you're in whilst Gophering.

Veronica

After a couple of hours of floating around in GopherSpace you are going to ask how to find specific items in such a sea of menus? The answer is the 'Very Easy Rodent-Oriented Net-wide Index to Computerized Archives', or Veronica. Of course it is.

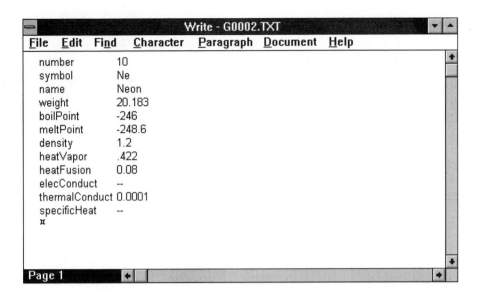

Figure 9.3   *If you use a GUI Gopher client, it will hook into other programs to display the result. Text files from Gopher can be automatically displayed in Windows Write, for instance.*

You get to Veronica by following Gopher menus to **Search topics in GopherSpace using Veronica**. You'll get to a further set of menus from where you choose a Gopher server (pick the one nearest to you). Picking one site then lets you type in a search string, and off it goes to get the data. You'll get a response in seconds, or more probably you'll get a message saying that the Gopher you chose as a gateway for searching is too busy to handle your request. You can either try again, or go to another server. If you search 'Gopher directory titles' you'll just be searching the menus available on the Gopher servers, which is useful for those common searches like Lists of Gopher Servers (search on Lists). If you search 'GopherSpace' you'll be looking at all of the indexes, and you'll find many more files that match your search criteria.

If you know where the information you want is you can usually go straight to that server and type in your request. This saves network bandwidth and should speed things up a tad, although many Gopher servers seem to be permanently busy these days. In both cases you'll be rewarded with screens full of information which matches the keyword typed in, and your heart will surge with joy. Or you'll be cross and bitter because the server is busy or it cannot find what you want and then your heart will be dour and grey. It's worthwhile remembering that Gopher gets about the Internet by telnet and that if you do find a site you're interested in and want to return to you can telnet there yourself. But it's often quicker to Gopher around, especially if you have a GUI Gopher client, because you don't have to muck around with UNIX's demands for login codes and so forth.

You may also run into the phenomenon of The De-Clienting of GopherSpace – where network administrators remove telnet clients from their Gopher servers on the basis that it's better if you use your own. This is also a great move towards the Coming GUI-ness of GopherSpace and the day may come when you'll never see a command line interface ever again.

Bookmarks

Once you discover bookmarks you'll wonder why the Internet is reputed to be so difficult. The Gopher client lets you navigate back to places you've already been by way of bookmarks. You find a Gopher server which contains, say, the entire text of 'The Big Dummy's Guide to the Hitch-Hikers Guide to the Art of Derivative Book Titles', and you want to go back there when Kevin arrives with the brown ale and the modem. You set a Gopher bookmark (methods vary depending on the access method) which will take you back to the site or archive you were at when you set it. On a Mac or a PC those bookmarks will still be there the next time you use your Gopher client – but alas, if you telnet to a Gopher site you'll lose your bookmarks as soon as you disconnect. But at least it's a great way of justifying an upgrade to a Mac or Windows computer.

Getting files with Gopher

Gopher is user friendly, despite that fact that the server side of things runs under UNIX. The latest Mac and Windows versions of the client software (using something called HGopher) can do as many things at once as you've got the memory for, which rather makes you wonder how DOS ever got to be so popular. You can kick off a search in one window, navigate in another, and download a file

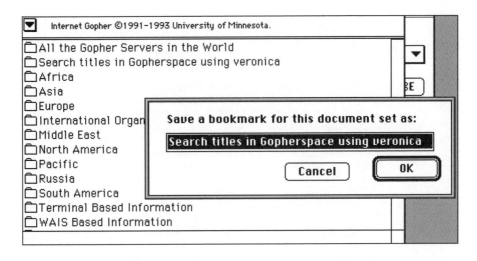

Figure 9.4 *Bookmarks let you save navigation points or pointers to entire documents in your client software. If you use bookmarks on a terminal service you'll lose them when you log off.*

in a third – as long as your modem, your service provider and your personal computer can take the strain. Gopher can then download the file to you via FTP or, if you're using a terminal, via one of the asynchronous file transfer protocols like Zmodem or Xmodem.

GUI Gopher software can also be hooked into other programs you've got sitting on your computer, and will display GIF files online if it can find a GIF viewer, or pick up and play sound files if you have the matching software and hardware installed. In fact Gopher is the single most really neat way of finding files and data on the 'Net, and one can only wonder why it's such a comparatively recent introduction. If you're confused about why you should be using Gopher servers instead of Archie to locate files and data – remember that Archie provides pointers to FTP sites, while Gopher is an archive indexing system in its own right. In many cases you'll be able to find what you need with Gopher – but in some cases you still need Archie. And the astute Internetter will use both methods to find files, and perhaps use Gopher for a bit of recreation.

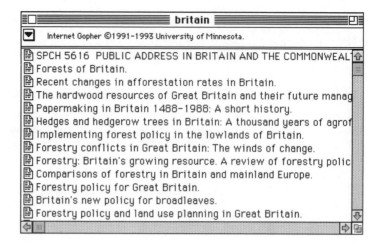

Figure 9.5   *Any of these documents can be pulled down as files to your hard disk. Gopher also knows about FTP so you can get executables via Gopher, too.*

WAIS

WAIS is Wide Area Information Server, and it normally gets a chapter to itself in yer average Internet book. It doesn't get one here because the WAIS servers themselves are in a constant state of being rehashed – which means that any examples given may not work – and you may find that you can get all the information you need from the Internet using Gopher. (Gopher can pick up WAIS servers as part of its ferreting.)

The main advantage of WAIS over Gopher is that it will search multiple WAIS servers at one swoop, whereas Gopher takes a peek inside one at a time. WAIS servers also tend to carry a lot of academic files, and it's consequently of great use for scientific or academic research.

You get to a WAIS server by telnetting to one, or by using the WAIS client you almost certainly don't have on your machine. Or you can get to WAIS via the World Wide Web, which is getting to be the grandaddy of all Internet search mechanisms. Try telnetting to quake.think.com as your first attempt – it was running as this book went to press. Type WAIS at the login prompt, to get to the WAIS front end.

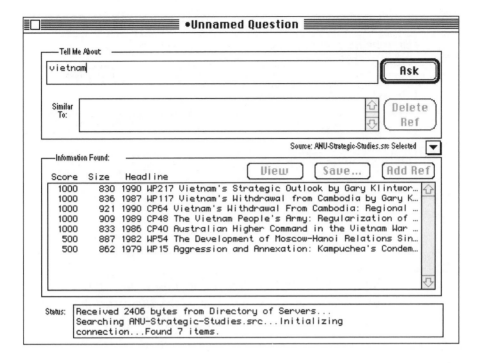

Figure 9.6 *Searching WAIS servers can be quick – but you can get them with both Gopher and World Wide Web. You don't need a dedicated WAIS client to get involved.*

WAIS servers used to present the user with a list of other WAIS servers but had to stop when the list started to edge up to several hundred sites. So WAIS (at quake.think.com) now presents only the top directory, which might not mean much if you've not WAISed before.

You search through WAIS-space by entering a keyword – you'll be given a prompt – and then picking from a list of databases which contain the keyword you entered. With some WAIS clients you can point the search at a single server or the whole list of WAIS servers, which will provide more results, quantitatively speaking.

Telnet WAIS screens are a bit picky about the sort of terminal emulation you have – you need to be able to select an item from the list by moving up and down, which means your terminal emulation has to work well. If it doesn't work like that then try typing in the number in brackets you'll see at the end of each search item.

The Boolean search mechanism is simple – if you want to refine the search you can use AND, OR, NOT as separators – but

Figure 9.7 *WAIS tends to point to available academic resources, as well as real files. Here, the result of a search points towards a record available from Australia.*

not all WAIS servers will work with them.

As an example, if you want to search on 'arabic' and 'grammar' you enter the two keywords separated by a space:

    arabic AND grammar

(Don't use 'and' in lower case.) You'll get a list of search results back, with the number of 'hits' per search (out of 1000) indicated in the Score Column. Pick up the document with the space bar and if it's what you want you can mail it to yourself by hitting the M key, or by following the prompt.

If you find WAIS useful then try the Gopher method of accessing it, which might be quicker. And if you get really hooked on WAIS then you can get WAIS client software for your machine from several sites, notably by FTPing to wais.com and looking in /pub/freeware. Some of the WAIS clients are much easier to use than the character based interface you get with telnet, and the MacWAIS client in particular is a joy to behold. As always, the client software varies in its usability, so if you have a choice, shop around.

Which one when?

It's crunch time. You've worked through this book, and come across several methods for locating files on the Internet. Which one should you use?

Despite protestations from Internet geeks armed with Ethernet terminals and UNIX, the best method of searching the Internet is the one you're happiest with. Archie is slow and command line based – which means you can use it from almost any dial-up provider via a terminal connection; WAIS works best with a GUI client and provides a direct link to many academic databases. But Gopher is the easiest of the lot, and the fastest over modem links. It can also hook into those WAIS servers, and so it perhaps offers the best compromise. It's worth spending a little time exploring Gopher client programs too, as they differ in their ability to present information in a coherent manner. And you may have to configure your Gopher client to bring up various file viewers; as an example the Windows Gopher programs tend to bring up 'Write' for text files, Paintbrush for BMP files and so on. You'll need to spend some time fine-tuning this aspect of your Gophering to get the best from it.

Finally, Gophering is one of the nicest ways of giving money to your telecomms provider – it provides a key to many of the doors on the Internet. Go for Gopher.

Clever Gopher stuff (1)

Gopher provides labels which tell you what sort of file you're looking at. You won't see these 'file identifiers' if you're using a graphic Gopher client (which will show them as icons) but you will see them with a character based client:

0   Item is a file.
1   Item is a directory.
2   Item is a CSO (qi) phone-book server.
3   Error.
4   Item is a BinHexed Macintosh file.
5   Item is a DOS binary archive of some sort.

6   Item is a UNIX UUencoded file.

7   Item is an Index-Search server.

8   Item points to a text-based telnet session.

9   Item is a binary file! Your client must read it fully (until the connection closes). This could take a while on a large file.

T   TN3270 connection.

Experimental IDs:

s   Sound type.

g   GIF type.

M   MIME type. Item contains MIME data.

h   html type.

I   Image type.

i   'inline' text type.

Clever Gopher stuff (2) – enhanced Veronica searching

When you select a query type, your Gopher client will present a dialog box. The search is not case-sensitive.

You may get better results by entering a multi-word query rather than a single word. Multi-word queries will find only those items whose titles contain all of the specified words. For instance, 'book' might find 4000 items, but 'Apple PowerBook' will find 2000.

By default, the Veronica servers will deliver only the first 200 items that match your query. You can request any number of items by including the '-mx' command phrase in your query. X is the number of items you wish.

'book -m' will provide all available matching items.

'book -m1000' will provide 1000 items.

You may find a message at the end of your Veronica results menu:

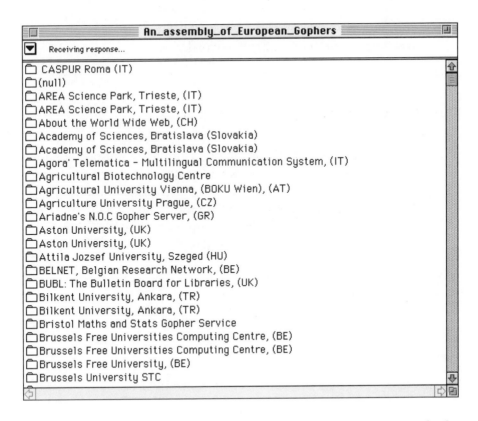

Figure 9.8   *A warren of EuroGophers. Pick servers outside the USA for faster searches.*

"*** There are 59173 more items matching your query ****"

Use ' book -m' to rerun the search and get all the items.

Boolean Veronica searches

The search understands the logical operators AND, NOT, OR.

If you use a simple multi-word query, such as 'mammal whale', it is the same as using AND between the words. For instance 'book electronic' is the same query as 'electronic and book'. An asterisk ('*') at the end of a query will match anything, so use it as a limited form of wildcard search. The asterisk character may be used only at the end of words as the search will fail if a '*' is placed within a word or at the beginning of a word.

Favourite Gopher sites

They're all wonderful. Check out Gopher menu options for 'all the Gopher servers in the world' and start rummaging. Some interesting places are the Electronic Frontier Foundation, set up by Lotus 1-2-3 salesman Mitch Kapoor, The Economist Magazine, Islamic resources, Schoolnet, Long Term Ecological Research, and Papyrus. After that, take your pick.

10 World Wide Web

'Necessity is the
smotherer of convention'
Lambert Jeffries

Sit back a minute, and think about personal computers. You might
dwell on just how poorly designed they are, or why this year's model
always costs a thousand pounds but has a second-hand value of
three hundred, or why, after the tens of billions of dollars spent on
research, we still don't have a decent user interface. Then congratu-
late yourself. You've turned into a computer visionary, and if you
should put your thoughts to word processor, you will certainly
become a millionaire.

Computer visionaries were around long before personal
computers were invented. Babbage was one, Clive Sinclair another.
Some of the later visionaries even had the benefit of technology.
They put their thoughts into deeds and invented graphical user
interfaces, Internet Relay Chat, Doom and Visicalc, in no particular
order. Others invented concepts which seemed odd at the time, but
now are starting to bring real benefits to computer users as the
technology to make them feasible becomes available.

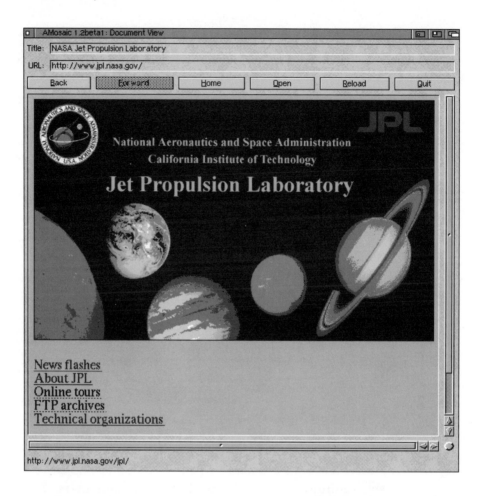

Figure 10.1 *NCSA Mosaic is available for most GUI computers, including the Amiga. This shot was taken with an Amiga 1200.*

If you go back through some of the early hobbyist computer magazines you'll find that a lot of journalists were getting very hot under the collar about something called Hypertext, as long ago as the early 1980s. Hypertext was going to revolutionize the way that computer users were presented with information – because a single document could provide links to other documents and services. If this chapter were a Hypertext document you would be able to click on 'Doom', either to pick up a brief description of what Doom is, or to go on to shoot up aliens (or whatever they are) with a shotgun. If it were a good implementation of the Hypertext concept, you'd be able to leave Doom running in a window and go on to knock up a few sales figures in Visicalc, or spread abuse on IRC, all at the same time. Your Hypertext browser would leave the links to the original document in place so you could pop back at a moment's notice without having to reload the images or the text.

The technology to make Hypertext hum along didn't really start to become available until the end of the 1980s, by which time Visicalc was just a fond memory. (Many of today's Internetters and personal computer users won't know what part Visicalc played in the history of personal computer-ing.) But Hypertext has found its place as a navigation and search tool for the Internet, and the World Wide Web is flavour of the month, mainly because it uses a decidedly handsome piece of client software to let users wander around the Internet.

W3 – the World Wide Web (WWW)

Development on what was to become the WWW was started in 1980 by a guy called Tim Berners-Lee working at the CERN complex. His Hypertext system was designed in isolation from other budding Hypertext software, but became the focus of a system designed to ship information around between particle physics scientists. Early client software for WWW was character based but the National Center for Supercomputing Applications (NCSA) stepped in and designed GUI based WWW browser clients for Mac, Windows and X-Windows. These browser clients are probably one of the main reasons that WWW is so popular. Today it's reported that there's a new WWW server appearing on the 'Net every day.

WWW uses the Hypertext metaphor to present information. You access it through a GUI client like NCSA's Mosaic, or Cello, or you can get at it via telnet and one of the character based clients such as Lynx. The character based clients aren't of much interest to the current generation of Amiga, Mac or Windows users, because WWW provides a rich feed of graphics and sounds in addition to text based information. You click on an icon and a picture (eventually) appears, or a sound erupts. The graphics and sound handling is provided by the graphics and sound handling programs you have on your computer; the WWW client serves only to hook information into your machine's software support routines and

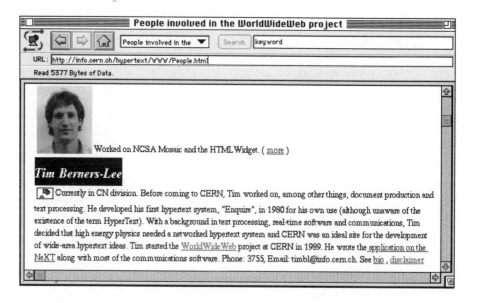

Figure 10.2 *Tim Berners-Lee, father of the World Wide Web. You get his biography, including photo, from the Web itself.*

display hardware. If you use telnet to get to WWW pages you won't be able to get the graphics files, which is yet another major reason to go for a full Internet connection, especially if you think that you'll ever want to get sound and vision from the 'Net.

NCSA Mosaic

Mosaic is currently one of the most widely used WWW browsers, probably because it's free, and probably because it works. You use Mosaic to navigate around Internet resources by point-and-clicking on links or pointers to other services. These have HTTP addresses (Hypertext Transport Protocol) which are resolved by the TCP/IP connection to take you straight to the site containing the relevant data. This method of navigation supersedes all other methods of rummaging around the Internet – it provides a seamless way of getting from server to server, and country to country, without the technology of navigation or the complexities of UNIX getting in the way. You'll see the HTTP addresses appear in the status bar of Mosaic, if you have this option turned on.

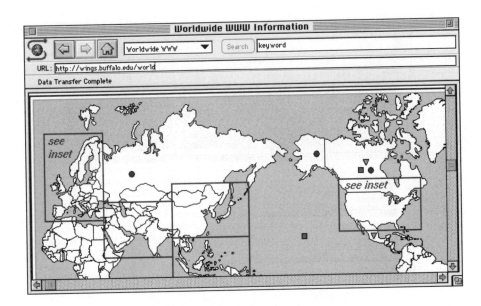

Figure 10.3   *A lesson on the death of the UNIX command line interface. Clicking on a region brings up a list of countries as fast as your modem can shift the data.*

Mosaic lets you select a 'home page' to which you'll always be taken when you start the software up, although you can change this to any other page you wish. (The home page is a bit like the default Gopher server you are taken to when you start up a Gopher client.) You start to navigate by clicking on text links, which appear in blue, or underlined, or both. Once you've been to that link, the text for the link turns red and may be cached in your computer's memory to speed up access if you return. You can click on picture icons to see graphics files displayed on screen – like a colour magazine page. Pages already received are cached into memory or to disk, which means that Mosaic can run adequately over a fast modem link. ('Fast' in this case means a modem to V32 bis standards.) You can also grab pages and save them to disk, either as text files or as Mosaic native files. The latest versions of Mosaic are commonly available on the 'Net, especially from the NCSA server at ***ftp.ncsa.uiuc.edu***.

As we've seen with Gopher and Veronica, and with WAIS, your ability to navigate around the Internet is limited by the capability of the client programs or server based utilities that you use to find data. Just as Gopher supersedes Archie, so WWW supersedes

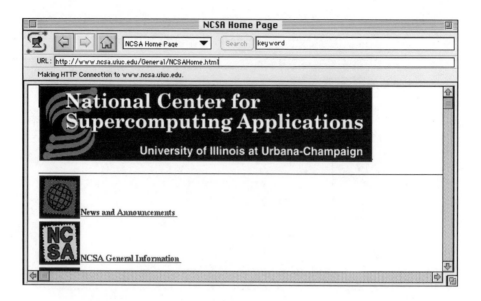

Figure 10.4   *The NCSA home page. It tells you where to get*
the latest browser software for your computer. Mosaic's built-in
FTP client lets you download them off the page.

Gopher and Veronica because it will hook seamlessly into Gopher
or WAIS servers if the link appears to take you there. You don't
have to know about the technicalities of the Internet to make use of
it, which is why WWW is so important to non-technical users. It's
the first real tool (or maybe the second after the GUI Gopher
clients) for traipsing around the Internet which doesn't demand a
grounding in UNIX before it can be used.

The best way to find out about the World Wide Web is to jump
straight onto it. You'll need a WWW browser such as Mosaic (for
Mac, Windows, Amiga) or Cello (Windows). You then log in to your
Internet provider as usual and fire up the browser. Mosaic needs no
pre-configuration. You'll be able to navigate around the menus with
ease. If you are running a slow modem then look for a menu option
to 'Display URLs' (uniform resource locators). Deselect this before
you start and the graphic images will not be sent to you unless you
click on the icons.

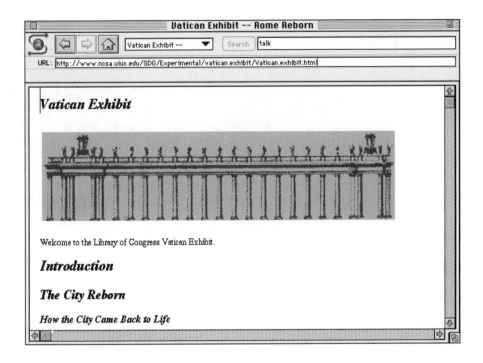

Figure 10.5   *Is the Pope an Internet provider? The Vatican Library on the World Wide Web.*

Service providers and HTML

HTML is the Hypertext markup language used to construct pages for the World Wide Web. It's simple to master, and full details can be found on the Web itself. There are a number of utilities which let users construct pages in Microsoft Word, and other word processors. HTML is proving to be a great way of providing information, via the Web. New servers pop up every day, and many Internet providers will rent out space on their Web servers to almost anyone. This means that the Web has suddenly become the *de facto* standard for electronic mass picture and text publishing, and there are many interesting publications available as a result.

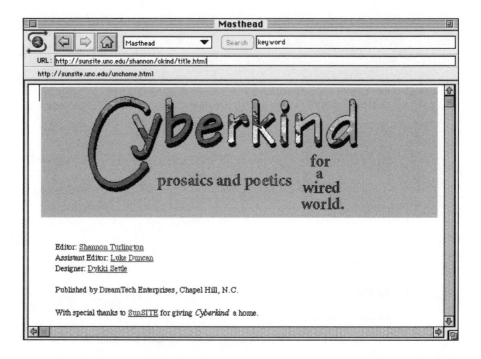

Figure 10.6   *Add 'cyber' as a prefix to anything and you're assured of instant nerdiness. Even poetry is a target.*

Again, the sheer variety of information on the Web defeats the ability of this book to display even a small proportion of it and you're therefore recommended to download a Web client from **ftp.ncsa.uiuc.edu** and fire it up. You'll be delighted with what you see – especially if you have a Mac, Windows or Amiga computer.

Figure 10.7 is from the WWW startup pages and will be out of date by the time we go to publication simply because the WWW is reputed to be expanding at the rate of 350 000 per cent per annum. But the file shows a little of what's available, to whet your appetite. With the real thing accessed via Mosaic or Cello you can click on any of the bulleted items and be taken to another document, which in turn will provide links to other servers and files. If you want a file to be sent to you then WWW will FTP it to you automatically; if you hook into a WAIS server then WWW will provide you with a transparent interface to the WAIS server via telnet. And you can get to all the Gopher services through WWW.

WWW is currently recognized as the 'killer application' that Internet providers have been waiting for. Access to the Web is being

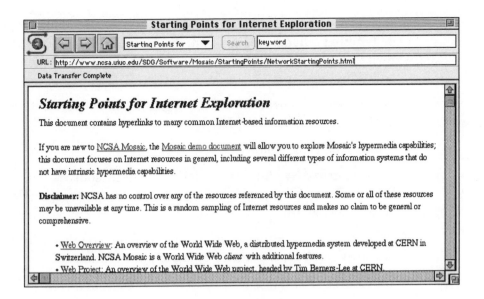

Figure 10.7 *The 'Starting Points' document. Clicking on a site takes you directly there. The document is updated frequently.*

touted as the easiest way to get to most of the Internet services, and providers are distributing Mosaic client software on the basis that it's all you need to start working with the 'Net. In many cases they may be right, although not all Internet services are currently available via WWW. But it may well be the case that WWW provides all the information you need, in one simple-to-use package.

Happy hunting!

Favourite places

The 'Starting Points for WWW Exploration' document contains hyperlinks to many common Internet based information resources.

If you are new to NCSA Mosaic, the original Mosaic demo document will allow you to explore Mosaic's hypermedia capabilities, whilst the 'Starting Points for WWW Exploration' document focuses on Internet resources in general, including several different types of information systems that do not have intrinsic hypermedia capabilities. What follows is a text version of the 'Starting Points' document, which is regularly updated.

- Web Overview: An overview of the World Wide Web, a distributed hypermedia system developed at CERN in Switzerland. NCSA Mosaic is a World Wide Web client with additional features.

- Web Project: An overview of the World Wide Web project, headed by Tim Berners-Lee at CERN.

- Other Web Documents

- Data Sources By Service: A listing of data sources within the World Wide Web, organized by information service (Gopher, WAIS, and so on).

- Information By Subject: A listing of data sources within the World Wide Web, organized by topic and subtopic.

- Web News: The latest World Wide Web news bulletin.

- Web Servers Directory: The central listing of known World Wide Web servers. Servers not yet registered with this list may be noted in the Mosaic 'What's New' list.

- InterNIC InfoGuide : A Web server run by the InterNIC; this is a good place to find general Internet-related information.

- NCSA Mosaic Home Page: The document NCSA Mosaic accesses upon start-up by default; this document tells you what the latest released version of NCSA Mosaic is at any given time.

- NCSA Mosaic Demo Page: A self-guided tour of the hypermedia capabilities of NCSA Mosaic.

- NCSA Mosaic 'What's New' Page: A day-by-day listing of new information resources on the Internet available through NCSA Mosaic.

- NCSA Doc Finder: Quick search-and-jump to any HTML documents on NCSA's web server.

- NCSA Home Page: The home page for the National Center for Supercomputing Applications at the University of Illinois at Urbana-Champaign.

- Other Home Pages: These are some interesting home pages located all around the world. For the complete listing of home pages, see the Web Servers Directory; for new home pages, see the Mosaic 'What's New' page.

- ANU Bioinformatics

- British Columbia

- BSDI Home Page

- Carnegie Mellon

- CERN Home Page

- Cornell Law School

- Cornell Theory Center

- DESY Home Page

- Honolulu Home Page

- Indiana Computer Science Home Page

- National Center for Atmospheric Research

- Northwestern Home Page

- Ohio State Home Page

- Pittsburgh Supercomputing Center Home Page

- SSC Home Page

- WAIS Starting Point: WAIS (Wide Area Information System) is a powerful searching engine in use over the Internet. This document tells you how to access WAIS servers through NCSA Mosaic.

- Gopher: Gopher is a popular menu-based information system in use on the Internet.

- GopherSpace Overview: A comprehensive listing of all the known Gopher servers in the world, organized by continent.

- Veronica: Veronica is a way to search 'Gopherspace' for specific pieces of information.

- NCSA Gopher: The Gopher server for the National Center for Supercomputing Applications.

- CTC Gopher: The Gopher server for the Cornell Theory Center.

- PSC Gopher: The Gopher server for the Pittsburgh Supercomputer Center.

- SDSC Gopher: The Gopher server for the San Diego Supercomputer Center.

- Original (UMN) Gopher: The Gopher server at the University of Minnesota, home of Gopher.

- UIUC Gopher: The central Gopher server at the University of Illinois at Urbana-Champaign.

- UIUC Weather Machine: The Weather Machine contains up-to-the-minute forecasts and weather satellite images.

- USC Math Gopher: The Gopher server for the University of South Carolina Department of Mathematics.

- FTP Sites: This is a comprehensive listing of anonymous FTP sites. This listing is not being actively maintained; it is provided as a proof-of-concept. We encourage others to maintain such a listing and make it available to the network.

- Usenet Newsgroups: This is a comprehensive listing of Usenet newsgroups available at CERN, where the listing is housed. This listing is not entirely appropriate for sites other than CERN; it is referenced here to encourage individual sites to set up such listings themselves.

- Finger Gateway: This is a gateway to Finger, a common utility program used to obtain information about people on the Internet.

- HyTelnet Gateway: This is a gateway to HyTelnet, a comprehensive index of publicly-accessible electronic library catalogs.

- TeXinfo Gateway: This is a gateway to a large collection of TeXinfo documents at Ohio State University.

Other information resources

- Hyper-G Gateway: Hyper-G is another Internet-based hypermedia system; this gateway is located in Austria.

- TechInfo Gateway: Techinfo is another Internet-based information system (somewhat like Gopher).

- X.500 Gateway: X.500 is an Internet-based phone book service.

- Whois Gateway: Whois is another Internet-based phone book service.

Other documents

Here are some additional interesting information resources not listed above that may interest people exploring the Internet.

- ANU Art History Exhibit: An exhibit of art history materials collected and put online by Michael Greenhalgh at Australian National University.

- Bryn Mawr Classical Review: BMCR is a review of classical literature distributed over the Internet.

- CyberNet: the central online 'jumping off' point for alternative information seekers. Their library of topics range from the bizarre, to the downright scary. If you're after information about anarchy, Nirvana, or goofy art, come on over.

- Electronic Visualization Lab: An exhibit of work done at the Electronic Visualization Lab at the University of Illinois at Chicago.

- Internet Services List: A standard list of Internet services collected by Scott Yanoff. (NB – doesn't cost $500 (Author))

- Internet Talk Radio: A collection of radio programs from Internet Talk Radio – because asynchronous times demand asynchronous radio.

- Library of Congress Vatican Exhibit: An exhibit of materials from the Vatican Library.

- Los Alamos Physics Papers (Gopher): The Gopher based interface to a central repository of physics papers at Los Alamos.

- Los Alamos Physics Papers (Web): The Web based interface to a central repository of physics papers at Los Alamos.

- NCSA Access Magazine: A hypermedia version of NCSA Access, a general-interest magazine published by the National Center for Supercomputing Applications.

- Postmodern Culture: Postmodern Culture is an edited journal distributed over the Internet.

- Unified CS Tech Reports: A central index of computer science technical reports from all around the world.

- White House Papers: A WAIS server containing all of the papers from the Clinton Administration from Day 1 to about two days ago.

- Internet RFCs: An archive of Internet Request for Comments documents, the technical documentation of the Internet.

- Zippy The Pinhead: Asynchronous irreverence.

UK information servers by name

Anglia Polytechnic University: ULTRALAB an experimental server of ULTRALAB software and information; general interest stuff; experimental areas. ULTRALAB is a learning technology research centre, so the server will be of particular interest to everyone in the learning/teacher training/educational software fields.

Apollo Advertising: A commercial server holding advertisers' WWW documents.

University of Bath: General information about the University of Bath. (Still under development.)

BBC : This is the BBC Networking Club WWW server.

Bulletin Board for Libraries (BUBL) Information Service: Including BUBL's Academic Information Service, Library and Information Science on BUBL and the GALLERY – a long (unsorted) list of interesting Web links.

The University of Birmingham: The School of Computer Science, degree and course programmes, current research details and information about the School of Computer Science. Also a Birmingham visitors' guide and other local information.

Brunel University: The Computer Centre/Brunel Library and Information Service (BLIS), information about the staff, faculties and library, including local area maps. There is also the Student Server.

University of Cambridge (UoC): University of Cambridge Computer Laboratory maintains links to all known Cambridge information servers:

UoC Institute of Astronomy, Royal Greenwich Observatory and Mullard Radio Astronomy Observatory.

UoC School of Biological Science. This server provides a wide variety of links to useful information resources for biologists. In addition, it supports a BLAST gateway for sequence database similarity searching.

UoC Cambridge Crystallographic Data Centre. Provides information relating to the Cambridge Structural Database System, including documentation in HTML format. Also a slowly growing postcard collection.

UoC Centre for Atmospheric Science (Chemistry). Provides information relating to the Centre (general info, seminars, publications and so on), information on the UK Universities Global Atmospheric Modelling Programme (general, data, software) via links to the anon.ftp server at caesar.atm.ch.cam.ac.uk.

UoC Engineering Department. Contains links to many other information sources relevant to control around the world, including ftp servers and Web servers containing technical reports and papers. It also contains some recent papers and PhD theses by members of the control group here. We have the first coffee machine on the Web so you can see how full it is and hence whether it is worth visiting it.

City University: The City University, London. Contains links to other services and maps of the area and the campus. 'Computer Science' contains information about the department and the School of Informatics.

CityScape Internet Services Ltd: Guides to CityScape products, their headquarters and their newsletter. Also their pub guide for Cambridge.

Cranfield University: University Postgraduate prospectus, Research Directory, and local information on computing services.

Demon Internet Services: Provides information on services and products for sale.

Durham University: Department of Mathematical Sciences. Information and links of general interest to Mathematicians / Theoretical Physicists / Statisticians.

University of Exeter: The Department of Computer Science has research papers, postgraduate study details and personnel information.

University of East Anglia:

> School of Mathematics. This contains information about both the school and Ocean Modelling. The server is officially mandated by the department.

> School of Information Systems. This contains information about the school including its staff.

Edinburgh University (EU): The main Computing Services server provides a hypertext of helpful information for new users of the UNIX operating system.

> EU Chemical Engineering Department. Information about the department, its teaching, research and people.

> EU Tardis Public-Access Service. A free, networked public-access UNIX service hosted by the Department.

Frontline Distribution Ltd: Frontline are one of the UK's largest TRADE distributors of computer hardware, software and services to the UK's computer reseller community.

HEPDATA: The HEPDATA High-Energy Physics database of published numerical results organized by Mike Whalley.

Hillside Systems & Berkeley Software Design International (Europe): The server at Hillside has technical information and a European order form for the BSD/386 UNIX-like operating system for 386, 486 and Pentium PCs. BSD/386 hypertext manual pages and a current patch set for BSD/386 V1.1 are also available. You can use anonymous FTP to get the data too. You will find a full list of titles for Peter Collinson's SunExpert and EXE articles.

Institute of Chartered Accountants of England and Wales, Accounting Information Service: The 'Summa' Project. This is the site of a World Wide Web information server for Accounting Academics, students and professionals. The service is funded by a grant from the Research Committee of the ICAEW. It is at present sited at the University of Exeter, Devon, UK. The Director of the project is Mr Barry J. Spaul.

Imperial College, University of London:

Department of Computing. Has information about the department and the src.doc.ic.ac.uk archive services (includes Archie scanning), the current UK weather and links to all other departmental WWW and other IC information servers.

Centre For Computing Services. Offers information about IC, computing facilities, and other local information.

Department of Chemistry. For details of this department, its staff, facilities and courses. Includes WATOC World Association of Theoretical Organic Chemists.

Theoretical Physics Group. The server contains information on the IC Theoretical Physics Group, as well as links to an FTP server containing recent preprints from members of the group. There are also a number of links to sites of interest to Theoretical Physicists, including all the known UK Theoretical Physics Groups. We also include all the known servers at Imperial College.

Solid State Theory Group.

Space and Atmospheric Physics Group.

Kingston University: This is a new, experimental, service.

Leeds University:

Computer-based learning unit

School of Chemistry

University Computing Service

Central Administration. This is the front page for the Administration web server, and leads to corporate, research and teaching information; this area is growing rapidly.

Loughborough University: High Performance Networks and Distributed Systems archive.

Mac-Supporters: Frequently asked questions (FAQs) and other assorted material related to supporting Apple Macintoshes.

Mailbase: Mailbase is the national electronic mailing list service for the UK academic and research community. It runs over 500 lists on a wide range of subjects with over 40,000 subscribers. The Mailbase WWW allows access to the archives and memberships of the public lists on the system.

University of Manchester: Manchester Computing Centre will shortly be used for the Central NRS (Name Registration Scheme) database.

> Computer Graphics Unit. Computer Graphics services, software, research, images, computer graphics and scientific visualization information. Officially mandated and representative of the CGU.

> Computer Science Department Feb 94. Small setup but growing.

University of Newcastle:

> Theory of Condensed Matter Group, Dept. of Physics.

> Arjuna Project Information. This server provides information about Arjuna, an object-oriented programming system that provides a set of tools for the construction of fault-tolerant distributed applications.

NEXUS: A server for NEXUS, the UK network of student physics societies.

Nexor: Includes full hypertext Archie gateways.

University of Nottingham:

> Communications Research Group : Information on the Department of Computer Science and the Communications Research Group. Also includes an Archie gateway, and UK independent music scene information base.

University of Oxford:

> Department of Earth Sciences. Access to departmental information plus links to other Oxford University information services.

PIPEX Ltd: The Public IP Exchange.

Rutherford Lab: The Rutherford Appleton Lab, UK. Admin: www-master@letterbox.rl.ac.uk.

SuperJANET: An information source of the UK SuperJANET project.

The University of Sheffield:

..is pleased to announce a WWW server based at its Academic Computing Services. Currently there is information from:

Department of Automatic Control & Systems Engineering.

Department of Chemistry. Features include WebElements: a periodic table of the elements database (this is the new permanent home for WebElements), an isotope pattern calculator (an interactive isotope patterns calculator – you supply the chemical formula), and an element percentage calculator (an interactive element percentage calculator – you supply the chemical formula).

The Hartlib Papers Project. News on the publication of the complete text and facsimiles of the Hartlib Papers.

Sheffield Collegiate Cricket Club. Information from Yorkshire's premier amateur cricket club.

University of Southampton:

Southampton High Energy Physics (SHEP). We have some local information and links to other High Energy Physics material.

Astronomy Group.

High Performance Computing Centre. The HPC Centre supports High Performance Computing within the South and South West of England. The Centre runs courses and workshops as well as supporting a number of HPC machines.

University of St Andrews, Scotland: The FIDE Project is part of a multi-site ESPRIT-funded project on database programming languages. This site provides information about project members and access to a number of papers about persistence and the database programming languages PS-algol and Napier88.

University of Strathclyde: This is run by the Computer Centre. Lists courses offered by the Centre, centrally managed clusters and contains links to other WWW servers on campus.

University of Surrey:

The Department of Electronic and Electrical Engineering. Contains information about the department and its reseach. Also EDUPAGE and Science Fiction TV series Guides .

University of Sussex:

School of Cognitive and Computing Sciences. This is a general information server about COGS. There is access to the anonymous FTP site giving access to COGS research papers. Also an index of the School's research papers, a calendar of Seminars and other events at the School. A gallery depicting members of the School.

University of Wales, College of Cardiff:

Department of Computing Mathematics (COMMA)

University of Ulster:

Faculty of Informatics. This server provides information on the staff and research interests of the Informatics Staff of the Faculty of Informatics at Coleraine. This information is officially mandated and is representative of our organization.

Warwick University:

WINFO WWW. Warwick Information WWW Service with lots of info about the University and things relating to it.

NURSE WWW. WWW Service for Nurses.

Law Technology WWW. Experimental service linking to other WWW/Gopher sites

UKOLN – The Office for Library and Information Networking:
Links to various library related services.

University College, London:

Department of Computer Science including info on MICE (Multimedia Integrated Conferencing for European Researchers) and the MBONE (Multicast backBONE).

Part 3

Finale

11 A brief history of crime

'Anti-virus software
is a must for Internet
users...'

You may have gathered from the ten preceding chapters that there is a subculture of sorts permeating the Internet. It's this subculture which adopts self-styled titles like Cyberpunk, uses aliases instead of real names, and attempts to perpetuate the myth that, because the 'Net isn't controlled by a single authority, it therefore represents and provides anarchic freedom.

In fact the 'Net provides less freedom than the average democracy, as the contributors and users of the Internet impose their own conventions and restrictions on each other, much like the kids let loose in *Lord of the Flies*. A pecking order is established and those not deferring to it are penalized, just like in the real world. It's a bit like the joke which asks 'Which colour flag do anarchists use?' The answer is that anarchists have a black flag, but if they were really anarchists, they would all have different coloured flags.

The anarchist/hacker community represents only a small fraction of Internet users, but they shout with the loudest voice, presumably because they have the most to lose by the possibility of controls being placed on the Internet. The recent furore over the proposed Clipper encryption scheme, where US Government bodies proposed the adoption of a data encryption scheme to which they had a back-door key, is a case in point. It's the hackers and 'freedom fighters' on the 'Net who most dispute the point of having a Government sponsored encryption scheme. The average Joe in the street neither uses nor cares about encryption because he has nothing to hide – or more likely, he hasn't yet found the need to protect himself from the CIA or the National Security Agency.

But Joe's computers are under attack, or they soon will be. Hackers and virus writers currently cost US business hundreds of millions of dollars a year in downtime. Phone phreakers and call-whistlers consume a few more million dollars of revenue and keep the cost of calls to genuine users higher than they should be. Hacking, antisocial behaviour and using the Internet as a convenient route into and out of other people's computer systems is considered acceptable to many Internet users on the basis that if you're stupid enough to leave the doors open then you should expect people to walk in.

The reasons for hacking can be found in the various issues of 'Phrack', a hacker-based electronic newsletter scattered around the 'Net. You can get it by Gophering for it. Phrack is a contraction of phreaking and hacking, where phreaking is the gentle art of manipulating telecomms systems. Issues are studded with phrases such as 'vengeance', 'revenge', and 'corporate stupidity', and with opprobrium for those who try to control those involved. Judging from the pages of 'Phrack', the hacker mentality seems based on the male desire for control and power – and the Internet, with its wide-open availability of systems connected to it, provides rich pickings for data-rape.

Of late, hackers have tried to claim some small immunity from being lumped in with the rest of the break and enter community, and now claim that hacking is a legitimate exercise in self-progression and the gaining of technical knowledge. Hackers claim that it's 'cracking' that consists of breaking into computer or other systems with malicious intent, whereas 'hacking' is a mere intellectual pastime. In fact both hacking and cracking are now illegal in the UK courtesy of Emma Nicholson's Computer Misuse Act, a fine example of knee-jerk legislation which mainly serves to keep policemen out of other people's computer systems.

Figure 11.1   *Think hacking is a minority sport? A Gopher search for 'hacker' reveals much...*

How they do it

The transport tools of computer hackers are often the open systems run by educational sites and government computers. The chief means of entry is telnet, which, if you can find a port that takes you out of the public areas into private sections, will then let you telnet from that computer into others scattered all over the world. The most notorious hacks, including those documented in Clifford Stoll's *Cuckoo's Egg*, were carried out by logging into a relatively local site via a modem and humble terminal emulation package, and then using the telnet or 'rlogin' client on the host machine to loop around the Internet sites. The technique is simple – you don't even need TCP/IP software to achieve it, and many of the most infamous UK hacks have been carried out using nothing more exotic than a BBC computer and a 300 baud modem. One favourite tool of the early hackers was the Tandy 100 laptop, which included a built-in terminal emulator and modem and can be seen in pictures from many of the early UK telecomms magazines. In recent years the GNS packet switch network has provided a fine transport mechanism for hackers. Packet switch networks make it possible to dial a local number in most major towns to connect to systems anywhere in the world. And if the hacker gains access to a 'reverse-billing site' his unknowing host will be billed for the privilege. This small irony is not lost on many hackers. Packet switch networks also make it exceedingly difficult for phone numbers to be traced,

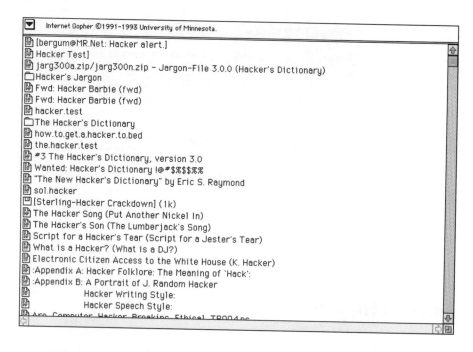

Figure 11.2 *This search revealed over a thousand hacker-related topics.*

as special technical knowledge and equipment is needed to trace packets back to the originating public dial-up node. Consequently many hackers now make exclusive use of the world's packet networks to avoid detection.

There may also be an element of phreaking involved in many hacks – especially in the USA where phone phreaking was a national hobby amongst students during the early to mid 1980s. Steve Jobs and Steve Wozniak founded what was to become Apple Computer on the strength of their expertise in making Blue Boxes – small boxes of electronics which could whistle their way across the world's telephone networks for free. Phreaking is still common in countries like Holland and the USA and to a lesser extent in Germany, but many hackers find it easier to steal credit card numbers and use them either to pay account bills, or to open accounts on commercial dial-up systems. Many systems allow new users to sign up with a credit card whereupon they are given full access, and virtually all of the UK's main systems providers have been caught out by bogus IDs backed up by stolen credit card numbers. Prime times for the activity are weekends and Bank

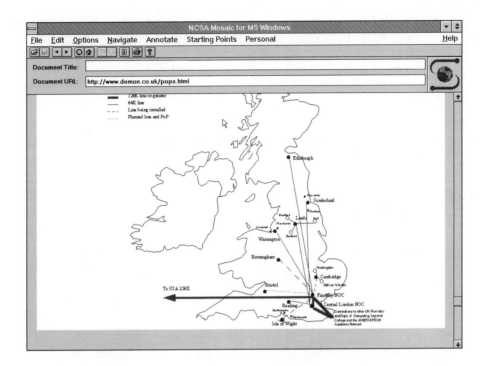

Figure 11.3   *Demon under attack? Telnet and remote login let hackers roam freely around the Internet.*

Holidays, when staff who would normally check card details are absent.

Many telnet sites have now tightened up security, but as soon as one door shuts, several more seem to open. Despite the publicity surrounding the Great Prestel Hack of 1984 in which hackers raided Prince Philip's Prestel Mailbox amongst other sites (two were prosecuted but acquitted – a third is alleged to have gone to ground), Nick Whiteley, a 19-year-old computer operator, managed to hack around many of Britain's top ICL sites, using an alias of 'The Mad Hacker' and a Commodore Amiga computer. Whiteley was able to get into systems and capture System Manager status, which then allowed him almost unlimited control of the computers. The question, of course, is why a 19-year-old, armed only with a decent brain and what's considered to be a toy computer by many contemporary computer writers, was able to cause so much disruption. The answer lies in the hopelessly inadequate precautions taken by software providers and designers to keep computer data from prying eyes.

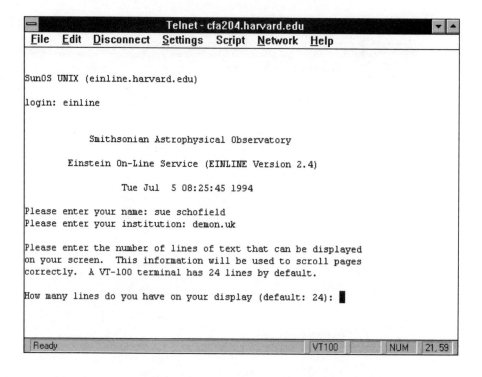

Figure 11.4   *Does telnet let almost anyone in? It can do, if the correct security precautions aren't in place.*

The corporate PC

Take a look at the Windows PC on your desk, for instance. You've read all the magazine articles and installed an anti-virus package, you've enabled the BIOS password protection, and you have password-protected your Word Perfect files and your spreadsheet data. That's about as far as the average corporate user goes. But there's a back door built into the BIOS of your PC which you don't know about. Anyone can get around the BIOS password feature supplied on millions of low price PCs, by holding down the INS key during a cold start.

And those password-protected word processor files? The last time you worked on those files, copies of them or the password used to encrypt them were probably stored in the hidden Windows swapfile on your disk. They are still stored there now as easily readable text unless you've been doing enough work on your PC to overwrite them. And if you've overwritten them, you may have left the imprint of something else – the password you used to access your company file server, or the letter you sent to the boss (or your lover?). It matters not if your data is stored on a distant file server, your local hard disk will carry the imprint of data which has been used in your Windows session. Even if you've taken the data files off your PC, that single large swapfile can contain passwords for your spreadsheets, your word processing files and the dial-up services you use. I found passwords to three dial-up systems, plus the registration passwords for an expensive Windows application, in the swapfile on the PC used for the screen shots, for instance.

Much the same sort of thing applies to the big corporate computers, like the DECs and ICLs. There are back doors built into these systems which even the suppliers themselves don't know about, and it's these areas which are the targets of hackers. Back doors to the VMS and ICL operating systems have been used in major hacks, and as recently as June 1994 Hewlett Packard were releasing software patches to prevent unauthorized access to their larger computers. Most of the Internet providers in the UK have already been hacked to some degree, although you'll find it hard to get acknowledgement of this fact from them. If these experts are open to invasion, what chance does the average corporate stand? The reality is that it is the hacker mentality of much of the Internet which keeps corporates from flocking to it.

So is a connection to the Internet really the best thing for UK business to contemplate? The answer must be that it will suit some, and not others. The UK computer press prints weekly success stories about companies using the Internet to gain on the competition – but rarely features stories about the many companies which have disconnected themselves because of security issues. Like all things, there's give and take, and in many cases an Internet connection can bring huge benefits. But it has to be designed and managed properly from the start.

Staving off the invaders

Keeping hackers and virus writers at bay is a full-time occupation. The prime transport mechanisms for hackers and virus distributors are telnet, FTP, mail and the password utilities of UNIX. Telnet lets unauthorized users gain entry to the port on the host system where throwing the contents of an electronic dictionary at the password prompt will often gain access. Or it's possible to get into many telnet ports with a default maintenance or system manager password. If that doesn't work then it's often possible to find a loophole in the directory structure of the host via FTP, and in some cases download the user log or system files which contain the password information. Going the other way it's possible to upload files to certain systems which give the hacker access to the system files or high-level user privileges, and if you have gaps like this in your system's security then it's only a matter of time before they are found out. Mail programs like 'sendmail' have been used to run commands on remote servers (in much the same way as you might run an Archie search via mail). The sendmail program has long since been updated – but there are some sites which haven't installed the update. And the UNIX password utilities have been hacked in many cases, to present the user with a utility which not only logs them in to the server, but captures the username and password to a file for later collection.

A less technical but more effective technique is simply to steal passwords and IDs from existing users by rummaging through Windows swapfiles as described earlier. It's relatively easy to hook up covert modems or displays to the serial lines used to connect VAX and other terminals to terminal servers, a technique known as sniffing. Sniffing of one sort or another is employed by many IT managers to monitor cabling and other serial line errors. High-level passwords can often be picked up from directors' secretaries who tend to leave them on Post-It notes, or in desktop diaries. But it's reckoned by some that 85 per cent of all computer crime is carried out from within the organization, where passwords can be easily noted, and where tape operators and support personnel often have full supervisor access to networks, including the payroll servers.

Electronic mail is probably the best carrier of passwords and, as mentioned, it's relatively easy to set up a system to monitor TCP/IP packets and decode textual information from them. Before the revolution in GUI based mail clients it was common for the UNIX 'sendmail' utility to be used for mail (it still is in many academic and UNIX sites) and sendmail can be and has been hacked on many occasions. Morris used it to trigger the Internet Worm, which brought most of the Internet to a standstill in November, 1988. The Worm sought out the email address books of the recipient. It used these to mail more copies of itself around the

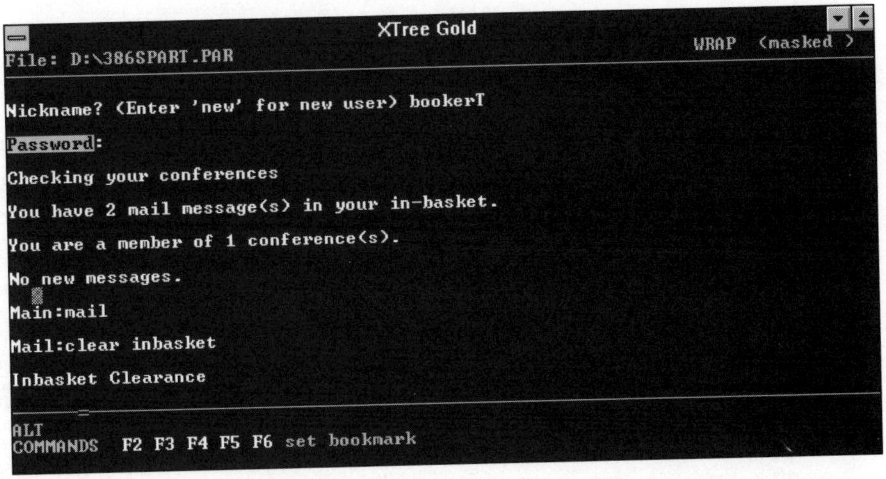

```
                                    XTree Gold                           ▼ ▲
File: D:\386SPART.PAR                                          WRAP   (masked )

Nickname? (Enter 'new' for new user) bookerT
Password:
Checking your conferences
You have 2 mail message(s) in your in-basket.
You are a member of 1 conference(s).
No new messages.
Main:mail
Mail:clear inbasket
Inbasket Clearance
_____
ALT
COMMANDS   F2 F3 F4 F5 F6 set bookmark
```

Figure 11.5 *Windows PCs are completely open to hackers. This particular log of a terminal session doesn't show the password, but if you can see it on the screen it will be saved in the Windows swapfile.*

Internet, growing larger (in the virtual sense) with each mail address it arrived at.

Future crime and the Internet

The level of hacker attacks is set to increase in the approach to the millennium, as more personal computers come into use, and the spread of personal internetworking continues. The techniques outlined in this chapter are public domain and common knowledge on the Internet – but not in many UK company environments where hacking is something we read about in the press but don't take much notice of. We even have the Computer Misuse Act which was intended to keep 'unauthorized' people out of computer systems. Alas, the Act is working too well: police are now effectively being kept out of private 'adult' dial-up systems by a simple login message which claims that they may not enter as they, the police, aren't 'authorized users'.

Viruses are a different matter. Anonymous FTP makes it easy

to inject viruses into a community of 20–30 million users, and I found two major virus releases during the time I researched this book. The first was a Trojan Horse loaded into a program which claimed to make CD-ROMs writable, the second was placed into copies of the well-known McAfee *anti-virus* software. I also used telnet to log into a system containing a virus library – where anyone may log in and grab viruses for either research or more nefarious use, and I was offered a CD-ROM containing the source code for many common viruses.

Uncorrupted anti-virus software is therefore a must for anyone thinking of downloading files from the Internet. As the Internet grows and develops it's going to become more difficult to protect against invasion of your personal and corporate systems. The World Wide Web, with its graphical pages, makes it exceptionally easy for viruses to be distributed, because in many cases your computer is downloading files without you realizing it. And both Archie and Gopher are capable of pointing you towards files which may be infected because they haven't been scanned by the system offering them for access.

Many notable computer evangelists are predicting the overrunning of the Internet by hackers and virus writers, but this may not happen. Governments are slowly transforming the Internet from an open academic institution into a privatized network, and funding for network provision is already being cut. It will take a few years, but the Internet is moving towards a controlled commercial base, where site security might just be taken as a serious topic. But there will always be people around who feel a need to take computer security of other people's systems as a personal challenge.

Moral? You must take precautions against invasion of your computer systems, regardless of size or cost, when you connect to the Internet.

12 Internet past, present and future

'In many cases the
Internet is just a
data dump...'

The Internet was created by the Pentagon's Advanced Research Projects Agency (ARPA) in the Kennedy era. The aim of ARPA was to bring together scientific minds to research and develop technology that would enable America to stay ahead in the Cold War. The guiding light in ARPA was Bob Taylor, a computer visionary who started trying to find better ways of working with computers while he was at NASA. Taylor eventually moved to the Defense Department and was one of the first founders of ARPA.

Taylor launched ARPA by setting up a number of research projects at American universities, and came up with the idea of ARPAnet, the very first transnational computer network. Its purpose was to link the scientists and researchers together. The technology used to transfer data between computers had been developed in the early sixties by Paul Baran, who was working on ways of preventing telephone systems from being destroyed by the electromagnetic pulse (EMP) effect during thermonuclear bomb blasts. Baran developed the first packet switching techniques, which were then incorporated into wide area network (WAN) technology. The firsts tests of NCP – Network Control Protocol – were carried out at Britain's National Physical Laboratory in 1968, and were successful enough to convince the Pentagon's Advanced Research Projects Agency to install the first nodes in 1969, creating ARPAnet. NCP was later superseded by TCP/IP.

ARPAnet operated using DEC PDP-10 computers and the message and data handling was carried out using separate minicomputers known as TIPs (terminal interface processors). The TIPs were linked to other TIPs over leased phone connections and the first nodes connected were the University of California at Los Angeles, Santa Barbara, the Stanford Research Institute, and the University of Utah.

By 1973 the ARPAnet had turned into a national network, but access to the system was limited to universities, research establishments, and defence contractors. The network operated with a great sense of wonder and there was no security anywhere on the system. Virtually any student (or friend of a student) who had access to a terminal connected to a TIP could log into any other computer, and spend hours or days cruising round its insides. Many of the academics who used the system found that electronic mail was much more interesting an application than mailing research papers around, and the beginnings of the social structure of the Internet emerged.

In 1975 the ARPAnet was turned over to the Defense Communications Agency, an organization dedicated mainly to overseeing military and government radio and data traffic. Security on the net was tightened somewhat, but to no great degree. The ARPAnet was at that time limited to 8-bit addressing techniques, which meant that no more than 256 sites could be connected directly at any one time. A new network addressing scheme was introduced in 1982, which meant that thousands of networks could be connected to each other, and the true Internet was born. ARPAnet split from the Internet in 1983 and became Milnet.

The growth of the Internet was rapid, and spread not only to research establishments, but to the corporate sector. In the early days the ARPAnet was used mainly for communications and data generated and sustained by research projects, but by the mid-1980s the Internet was becoming saturated with electronic mail from all corners of the world, including private individuals. This was anathema to those involved at the start, mainly because the costs of connecting to the Internet had dropped to the sort of levels where small corporations could afford connections. By the start of the 1990s it was estimated that the Internet carried over 2 million regular users, much to the chagrin of the universities and government departments who were directly funding the backbone of the service.

Birth of UNIX

In 1969 Ken Thompson, a worker at the Bell Laboratories Science Research Murray Hill labs, decided to invent UNIX. Thompson's idea was to write an operating system for his own use, one that would multitask, and eventually become virtually processor-independent. Thompson's project quickly caught the enthusiasm of co-workers and UNIX blossomed. Various universities also caught the bug, and many of the larger American faculties eventually developed their own implementations of Thompson's work.

UNIX was tailor-made for use on computer networks. Utilities such as ftp, Finger and sendmail became standards for accessing and using the computers connected to the Internet. The early UNIX implementations were often bug-ridden, because anyone and everyone had a hand in its development and there was no central coordination of development amongst the academics who used and 'improved' UNIX. In fact there were so many implementations of UNIX that it was possible to find different versions sitting on adjacent terminals in most of America's universities.

The combination of flaws in UNIX, the curious minds of students, an utter lack of security on the Internet, and the 'hacker mentality' led to huge problems for the Internet on many occasions. The arrival of cheap personal computers in 1982 started the explosion in Internet use. Almost any sort of computer can now be hooked up, as long as the TCP/IP software is available for it. TCP/IP is now truly multi-platform and it's often very difficult to tell just what type of computer is providing the service at the remote end of the link.

Present

The Internet has started to distend with new users in the mid-nineties. The huge sales of personal computers in the West is one reason, the availability of cheap telephone modems is another. It's estimated that there are 50 million personal computers in the USA, and about the same number in Western Europe, although less than a quarter of these are fitted with modems or network access of any kind. That gives a population of about 25 million modem users – about the same as some estimates for the number of Internet users in 1994 – although not all modem users have Internet access.

Hyperbole about the Internet is rife. It's dubbed the Information Superhighway, the InfoBahn, or the Digital Revolution, depending on the thickness of glossy paper your favourite computer magazine is printed on. Some of this might actually be true if you had an Ethernet connection to the Internet, but modems present the Digital Superhighway to the user as an information traffic jam, and few UK journalists seem to be plugged into the Internet over a network cable. Services like Internet Talk Radio demand transfers of files up to 30 megabytes in length, and are not realistically available to users of current modem technology, because of the download costs.

The Internet traffic snarl-up is unlikely to improve even with the arrival of V.34 modems, as there's always more data waiting to be downloaded than there is bandwidth available to get it. At the moment the theoretical bandwidth of modems over European networks is believed to be about 32 kilobits per second. This roughly equates to 2000 words of ASCII text per second, but it's likely that new transport techniques such as ATM will start to erode the supremacy of the analogue telephone modem.

It has to be said that access to the Internet over a phone line is cruddy. It's expensive because it takes a long time to squeeze large files down the limited bandwidth of modems, and it's frustrating because the same bandwidth limitations prevent you from doing something else on the same line while you're transferring data. Unfortunately, alternatives to dial-up access are expensive. A leased line with 64 Kbits per second, enough for a couple of heavyweight users, costs around £8000 per year to install and maintain, and the much-vaunted ISDN is still too expensive for the average punter to contemplate. But enter the Information Superhighway. The phrase itself comes from a visionary speech by Vice President of America Al Gore, and points towards a system of unlimited bandwidth connections direct to businesses and homes in the USA. It's envisaged that the network will be more or less complete in the first decade of the new millennium, bringing unlimited amounts of data and information to businesses, schools and homes. Things are not so clear in the UK and Europe. Over-regulation of telecomms providers is in place in the UK, which specifically forbids telcos (telecomms companies) from 'broadcasting'. This is to give the cable entertainment companies a head start, in return for the investment (and jobs) that the cable companies bring. While it's conceivable that cable will eventually carry Internet connections, the overall policy is shortsighted enough to ensure that Britain will lag behind the USA in information provision, unless policies are changed in the next year or so. Similar policies prevail in much of Europe, and despite Europe being the home of the much-vaunted ITU/U (ex CCITT), European telecomms are a mishmash of systems, technology and policy. The Information Superhighway will be a long time coming as a result.

Neither is the Internet the Information Repository. In many cases the Internet is a sort of data dump, where much useless trivia blocks access to the virtual shelves of pure knowledge. Consequently, you need to wade through an awful lot of garbage to get to real knowledge on the Internet. Alas, some pundits have even said that the Internet now contains all human knowledge, which is, of course, a sad joke.

As this chapter was being written British Telecom announced that it would be providing Internet access in the near future, which is welcome news for subscribers if not for Internet providers. Once the telcos – the telecomms providers – get involved it won't be long before the Internet is available at any phone line – as long as the bill continues to be paid.

The future

Anything written about the techno-future is doomed to be inaccurate. Two years ago I wrote that ISDN was the data transfer medium of the future, and two years later ISDN is still the consumer backwater it was then. High equipment prices and a lack of promotion by the telcos haven't helped, neither has the

Figure 12.1 *Even the BBC is tackling the Internet. It can't be that difficult after all.*

introduction of V.FAST and V.34 modems, which can run a megabyte a minute of text through ordinary phone lines. But there have been advances. Systems which offer video on demand have been demonstrated and there's currently a pan-European test to run ATM. ATM (asynchronous transfer mode) is a technology which allows virtually unlimited bandwidth to be made available over dial-up lines or Ethernet, and looks set to get here in about five years' time. The implications for Internet users are enormous and the promise of unlimited transmission bandwidth means that the only limitation to data transfer will be the speed at which your hard disk can write files. Data will consist of moving images, sound, and all of the stuff we now call multimedia, instead of the plain ASCII text which constitutes the vast majority of Internet traffic today.

The Internet is evolving to meet the future, or perhaps it's the other way around. Services like World Wide Web have become more sophisticated, and multimedia, Internet based voice-mail in real time, and elementary online video conferences are already here. The future, it would seem, holds unlimited promise for Internet users, and the writing is certainly on the wall for providers who continue to lope along with character based terminal interfaces. The days of typing arcane commands into a distant computer are now past, and many Internet providers are beginning to realize this. Some never will, and will slowly fade into the past, just like MS-DOS 2.1 did.

The future of the Internet is bright and multicoloured and doesn't demand that users scrabble with UNIX in order to be able to use it. At least that's how it looks from this end of a GUI.

13 Sex, lies and video-rape

'Using extra hardware, full
motion video data can be
sent over the Internet'

Social issues on the Internet

You've read through this book, you may have used it to open an account with an Internet provider, and glory of glories, you might even be enjoying yourself. On the way you'll have picked up on the various forms of social control and interaction mechanisms on the 'Net and the methods people use to get ideas across via the written word and antiquated 7-bit computer technology. The Internet, as well as offering the most basic of communication methods that computers are capable of providing, has opened up the floodgates of social revolution. This revolution is now so large that Internet users, society and governments cannot afford to ignore the vast electronic subculture which the Internet nurtures. It's a subculture which has more members than three times the population of Belgium.

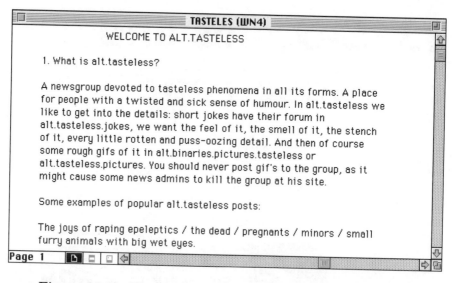

Figure 13.1   *The Alt.Tasteless Usenet Group. Is this really a part of an 'advanced' society?*

This amount of interaction cannot exist without causing disruption to the values and mores of the 'real' culture of everyday society. The edges of the Internet blend into the daily lives of millions of North Americans, and similar effects are now being seen in most Western European countries. The Internet is here, and no amount of head-burying by governments and corporations can make it go away.

Some of the issues discussed in this chapter may not yet have impinged upon you, and it's possible that they never will. But all over America, universities, corporations, individual States and the Government are grappling with the impossibility of coping with the rushing tide of social issues which unregulated mass communication brings. The Internet is causing large waves in the social fabric of the western world, in a similar fashion to the introduction of the railways, or the introduction of gunpowder to feuding Europe. In the UK many of these issues are not yet understood or even discussed, but they will be very soon.

Like the rest of this book, the most difficult choice has not been what to include, but what to leave out, and so this chapter focuses briefly on a few issues which are set to hit the fan in the UK over the next year or so. Some of the issues will be only of passing interest to casual Internet users, but they may become a scourge to schools, universities, corporations, parents, and Internet providers in the future.

Anonymous mail

Many Internet sites now offer anonymous posting of email, and Usenet messages. Anonymous servers take incoming messages, strip out user IDs, replace them with pseudonyms and then pass the 'untraceable' result on to its destination. Anonymous mail was meant to provide Internet users with a mechanism for working with help and support groups without fear of persecution by individuals, or society. But it more often provides a vehicle for transmitting abusive or obscene messages to individuals, who have no real hope of determining who the sender was.

Anonymity closely ties with concepts of identity on the Internet. In reality I'm Sue Schofield, my Internet ID is sue@s-sco.demon.co.uk and both IDs are readily identifiable – as are the 15,000 others at Demon Internet. But many Internet users use aliases to deliberately conceal their names, their social status and their gender. Often they use electronic hacking techniques to falsify their geographical locations.

In general, anonymity is seen as a beneficial side effect of electronic communications because social prejudice is not possible, and an electronic cat may thus talk to an electronic queen. But identity, electronic or otherwise, is the key focus for regulation and law enforcement. If identity is unenforceable on the Internet then it follows that so are any other regulations.

One other disturbing development is the spread of steganography – the ability to hide information in image or other electronic files. Steganography permits covert communication by making senders and recipients undetectable and unidentifiable to anyone who doesn't have the decoder key. It operates by hiding data bits in files, usually graphics files held in or on publicly accessible areas such as Usenet groups, list servers or large on-line services such as CompuServe. Users agree on code/decode keys and use these to send and receive hidden messages to each other. A non-Internet analogy is the hiding of coded messages in television commercials. If you have the correct decoder hardware or software you could pull out the information hidden in the wash of electronic data, just as teletext transmissions carry data in the unused part of TV transmission bandwidth. Steganography isn't thought to be widespread but there are a number of organized electronic experiments being carried out on the Internet at present.

The original concept of anonymous mail was to provide a shield of anonymity for vulnerable groups. However anonymous mail has been largely usurped for nefarious ends, by users feeding corrupt or forged origination domains to anonymous mail servers so that their messages can't be traced. Should UK Internet providers filter out mail from anonymous mail servers as a matter of policy? And if there's no enforceable method of verifying identity on the Internet then how can businesses make commercial transactions over the Internet which stand up in law?

Anarchy

How we laughed at anarchy in the Sixties. We chortled at America's obsession with the Yippies – while we ignored the terrorist

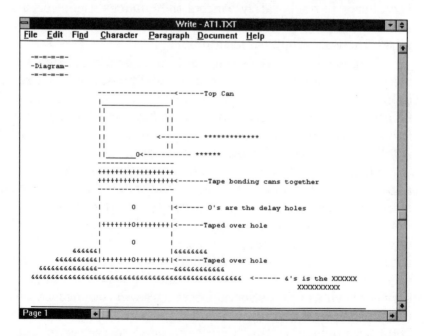

Figure 13.2   *ASCII diagram of a home-brew bomb (details deleted).*

activities of the IRA. The Internet, like most places inhabited by large numbers of students, is a training ground for social anarchists. Here they can find recipes for napalm, land-mines, exploding ball-point pens and much more. In the USA these quirky methods of making a point are superseded by the ready availability of firearms, but they still have over 1000 home-made bomb incidents every year.

Do we just laugh off the availability of 'subversive' and anti-social bomb recipes on the Internet, or do we institute a clamp down on the importation of such material?

Anonymous practical jokes

Extracts from a December 1994 Reuters America release:

> '*SEATTLE (Reuter) – In one of the oddest items yet to come spinning out of Cyberspace, software giant Microsoft Corp. issued a statement Friday denying it was seeking to acquire the Roman Catholic Church. Microsoft, the largest software company in the world, fell victim to an electronic hoax that showed the much-ballyhoo superhighway can just as easily carry nonsense as well as useful data.*
>
> *The hoax forced the company to deny the report circulating on the Internet that it planned to acquire the Roman Catholic Church. A Microsoft spokeswoman said the false report, written in the guise of a news article supposedly issued by a major news organization, was first noticed a little more than a week ago.*
>
> *Since then, it has bounced around on the Internet, generating a flood of angry telephone calls and electronic mail messages to the company. The item was even picked up and mentioned on the air by nationally syndicated radio talk show host Rush Limbaugh, the spokeswoman said . . .*'

This is just one of a number of hoaxes, malicious or otherwise which filtered through Internet nodes in 1994. Other novelties included rumours of viruses circulating in text files (read this book and your computer dies) and various other hoaxes of varying subtlety and realism.

Anonymous hoaxes are rife on the Internet. In the example above Microsoft will have spent rather a lot of time and money sorting out the problem, at their expense. And while it might seem a jolly jape to anyone not connected with either the Catholic Church or Microsoft, most readers will probably agree that the end result of the hoax is embarrassment to one or both parties.

Do hoaxes like this make the Internet a better or worse place, do they make companies think twice about investing money in Internet related business ventures? Or are anonymous hoaxes at the expense of other people and companies just part of human nature, and therefore to be tolerated?

Electronic privacy and security

Most UNIX systems, bulletin boards, corporate networks, digital cellphone systems and commercial dial-up systems carry an internal system of logging user activities. These logs are referred to as accounting systems, and are used to 'audit' or track user access to files and data. Most electronic accounting systems will track which directories were opened, which files were read or downloaded, and the login and logout times of the user concerned. The user's email address becomes the digital signature at the bottom of the list of items accessed.

The information contained in the log file may not be of interest to anyone else, but the electronic signature – the login user identity of the person accessing the system – is. Imagine logging into a World Wide Web site to look at a few video clips of an unusually artistic nature. Unbeknown to you, your electronic ID is sent to the host site automatically by the browser software you have on your computer, and your username, domain and country are logged into the remote system. Imagine your surprise when a few days later your email box contains a message from the operator of the artistic WWW site containing details of your login, and a request for a 'subscription' in exchange for you not receiving any more mail.

Or imagine that the hypothetical **pm@house. commons.gov.uk** logs inadvertently into a server carrying child pornography. Later he receives an electronic blackmail demand from one of the tape ops at the site who thinks he's found a great way to make a few thousand dollars. Or more likely, the tape op makes up the story and sells it to a UK tabloid newspaper. Would it be published?

These are hypothetical cases, but the hooks are already there in many systems and WWW browsers to send the email address of the inquirer to the remote site. Is this a case of Big Brother monitoring you, or would you accept that electronic anonymity on the Internet is a desirable quality?

Privacy and personal security is one of the major problems for commercial enterprises wishing to use the Internet for business. Every login to a remote site operated by an unknown person is a possible trap for email identities and passwords. Every uncoded credit card transaction to a remote site is a possible invitation to credit card fraud. Every email message which passes through a spot gateway (a destination or forwarding gateway) and is spooled to disk for retransmission) can be read by an operator, or the friend of an operator who just happens to be sitting in on a Saturday morning 'watching the traffic'. It happens on nearly every amateur bulletin board, and not a few of the larger UK commercial systems.

From this readers should be able to deduce that unencrypted email on the Internet is not private. Your Internet provider will have employees, possibly unvetted short-term contract employees who will have full access to your mail, and will at some time probably catch a glimpse of it in their normal duties. The number of people who have access to your mail as it routes from site to site will increase drastically, and while the huge amount of traffic on the Internet would make it a time consuming business for anyone to track individual mail from a particular user, it can and has been done. Added to this is the complete anonymity of the nature of the site through which your mail is being routed – how can you tell if a mail server is a university or commercial site, or a PC in someone's back bedroom hooked up to the Internet via a modem or leased line? In the normal course of events you should never imagine that your Internet mail isn't being read by an anonymous and untraceable third party.

The coming millenium will see most of the data records on UK individuals held by the medical profession and the Inland Revenue farmed out to private companies. Should the holding of such intensely personal data records by private companies be governed by law?

Copyright and the Internet

Imagine you are an author who publishes a fairly popular book after lengthy meetings with your publisher to map out distribution and copyright affairs. You sign the contract, write the book, and then sit back and wait for the royalties to roll in. But then you find to your horror that your book has been digitally scanned, and appears in its entirety on an FTP site somewhere in Arizona. It's available free to anyone who drops in to visit.

This happened to Hugo Cornwall's *Hacker's Handbook*, the last edition of which was recalled by the UK publisher in the light of the Computer Misuse Act. Ironically, the text of that banned edition now appears freely on many FTP sites, and on a CD of material taken from the Internet. The entire scripts of all the Monty Python programmes are also available – not from the BBC, but from dozens of American Internet sites. The scripts have been faithfully transcribed word by word from video tapes, and posted onto the 'Net by aficionados of the Pythons. The authors don't receive any payment for work published in this way. And sexually

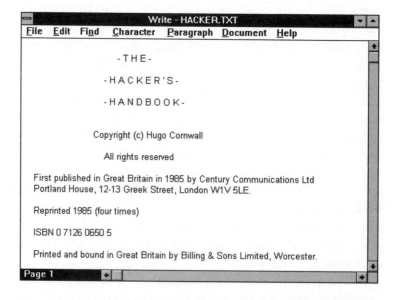

Figure 13.3 *The 'liberated' version of the* Hacker's Handbook, *a British publication itself hacked and placed on the Internet.*

explicit material scanned in by readers of commercial magazines regularly appears in the alt.sex newsgroups – without a hint of a writ from the magazines concerned. Is this freedom of information, or is it freedom of piracy?

Copyright is rigorously affirmed (and enforced in law) in both the UK and the USA, where broadly similar copyright systems exist to prevent pillaging of creative works. Yet the Internet, or its denizens, can openly flout copyright restrictions with little fear of being apprehended – even when they attach their email addresses to stolen copyrighted work (as with some of the Python scripts). By the same token many newspapers provide the reverse function by ripping off interesting or newsworthy stories from Usenet groups, without accrediting authors, or abiding by copyright notices in the material concerned. There was a fine example with the story that Bill Gates was really the Beast, according to the sum of ASCII codes which made up his name. The story appeared in many of the computer magazines and not a few daily newspapers without accreditation – yet it appeared first in an Internet newsgroup, with a readily identifiable author.

Shades of this 'no rights is all right' policy are already affecting UK and US journalists, who are under increasing pressure from magazines and newspapers to sign away all their rights to copyright of articles and features. In the USA, journalists on the *New York Times* went on strike over issues raised when new contracts asked them to sign away 'electronic rights' which had the effect of allowing publishers to republish work without further payment. In the UK, top magazine publisher VNU recently sent out a similar contract to UK journalists who were asked to sign over all rights to their work so that the publishers could republish in any format they pleased.

Electronic rights and the vast amounts of money to be made by selling articles and features to readers over the Internet will be worth far more in the coming years than many writers would ever believe; journalists, artists and writers who today sign away their right to electronic publishing fees will be tomorrow's losers. Or should they give away their work for free distribution over the Internet to the greater benefit of the electronic society?

Culture shlock

According to George Bernard Shaw, America and England are two countries divided by a common language. According to John Updike, 'America is a vast conspiracy to make you happy.'

Whatever your personal view the American influence is undeniably everywhere. Our children watch hours of American cartoons on TV, their main cultural influence comes from American marketing giants such as Disney, McDonald's, and Coca-Cola, their playgrounds are governed by peer group pressure to acquire Power Rangers, video games, baseball caps, trainers and sweat-shirts. Parents succumb to Hollywood box office hits, where artistic talent and interpretation is often replaced by gross violence and ever more implausible special effects.

In the home over 40 per cent of total UK television output comes directly or indirectly from the USA, and intrusive American marketing tools such as British Telecom's 'Caller Line Identification' (banned in many US States) are being inflicted onto a generally unaware British public. It used to be said that what America had now, the British would have in five years' time, but the global communications networks of TV, telecomms, and the Internet are merging global differences into one vast melting-pot, overbearingly based on American value systems. What America has now – shopping malls, drug-related inner-city violence, and the culture of the self – we also have, but we got it second-hand.

This doesn't yet seem to be a problem for many British people. Our children are only too happy to grow up into a world where self, and not family values, comes first, and where parents find it easier to go along with liberalizing change than to maintain brutalizing regimes of the past. Kids and parents now grow up submerged in an overwhelming deluge of Americana, much of which they don't readily understand, but accept nonetheless. And the exciting virtual world of the personal computer is being sold to our children, providing sensations better than the real thing. In many homes it will be the 15-year-old son who pressures his techno-virgin parents into procuring a computer and an Internet connection, egged on by TV ads that infer that the quality of a child's education now depends largely on the power of the CPU in his multimedia PC.

Before the year 2000 the Internet will have become a standard component of the UK entertainment industry. Already BBC

Children's TV promotes the Internet daily, and has its own email address. (Does the BBC sell Internet provision, and promote it at the expense of non-computer owning licence payers?) Youth culture magazines aimed at teenagers carry ads for modems and communications software that five years ago was the sole domain of the comms nerd. 1995 will be the Year of the Modem, with high street shops setting up specialist outlets for comms software and hardware.

But the Internet, and the sub-culture that permeates it, is almost entirely American. Is there a danger that Internet based value systems are already replacing some of the more staid, and level-headed social control systems we used to take for granted in the UK? Pornography is a prime example. Its distribution is controlled in the UK, but not in The Netherlands. Before the Internet, porn mags were smuggled from the Continent into the UK by post, now the Internet supplies porn on demand to any home in the world equipped with a cheap computer and an Internet connection. At the time of writing there are no effective measures in place for controlling the delivery of electronic pornography into the UK. Does this mean that the UK approves (by its lack of legislation) of porn travelling over the Internet; does it mean that only global legislation can stem the tide; or do we simply shrug and say that the Internet represents true freedom, and that pornography on demand is part of that electronic Utopia?

The Internet culture is subversive, complex, based on nothing and everything, controlled by no one, managed by everyone. It's both the anarchist's dream and the culturist's nightmare. At the same time the Internet is one of the world's largest carriers of personal and educational information – if you exclude telephony, the movies, the postal services of the world, newspapers, TV and radio. It provides the world's science labs with the greatest aid to research ever designed. It helps thousands of disabled and lonely people keep in touch. But fewer than one per cent of the world's population have access to the Internet, and whatever the Global Village might to turn out to be, the text based Internet of the late Nineties is not it. According to a recent US Adult Literacy Report, adult literacy has plummeted to just 50 per cent in the US which has a population of around two hundred and fifty million people. Is this an effect of the growing blind acceptance of computer culture values, or is it part of a larger cultural problem afflicting Western society?

Finally, does the Internet bring an invasive, undesirable product and market based culture directly into countries with thousands of years of tradition and craft? Does it displace our personal and cultural values with those of a corrupt and socially dysfunctional country? If it does, is this desirable from the point of view of a UK government?

Video-rape

Just when you thought you'd got the hang of those newfangled fax modems, an uneasy marriage of personal computers and telephony is about to hit the fan. It's called Computer–Telephony Integration (CTI) and according to the marketing spin doctors, CTI will be the Next Big Thing You Can't Do Without.

CTI has been around for a while, as one of those computer based answers in search of a question. It's currently being presented as integrated voice data in the form of AT&T's VoiceSpan, which purports to duplicate the office switchboard on a PC. But CTI is about to surface in the PC marketplace as the voice data modem. While this may not appear to be an earth-shaking device Intel and Microsoft are ploughing ahead with a new communication interface called Tapi. Tapi is a programming tool that allows developers to hang sophisticated voice telephony tricks onto a V.34 modem from within Windows or a Mac. And while it's being developed, a multi-manufacturer video telephony study group is looking at the possibilities of squirting real time video over modem links. The eventual promise is for a combined voice, data, fax, and video modem, bravely dubbed the multimedia modem by enthusiasts. This will make it possible for almost any old PC to send video, voice, fax, and data over a phone or Internet link. The resulting box will turn your PC into a video phone, voice mailer, and video bulletin board system.

While this might seem to be a science fiction nightmare, the voice handling bits are already here and will appear in next year's crop of new modems. V.34 VD modems will control voice and data over the same call and cost little more than existing technology.

If by chance you should accidentally hook all of this into BT's Caller Line Identification you'll have a system that will not only tell you the number of the person calling, but will be able to pull out a customer's name, address and credit rating from a CD-ROM or database, while irritating them with computer derived elevator music. Another interesting possibility is for voice mail fraud, using a PC to sample and re-create digitized voice recordings.

Probably the most exciting CTI application for Internet geeks is in video handling. All that's needed inside the PC is a video input board and a working software standard, which is what Tapi and a video extension will eventually provide. Using Tapi and a little extra software, video data can be encoded into the PC's serial output, although later modems may include their own video handling devices. While frame rates will never reach those of broadcast television, current coding gives very acceptable results on a PC screen.

Quite what the Internet will make of all this is anyone's guess. The voice mail bulletin board already exists in the USA, where instead of sending someone an ASCII based text message, you use your voice modem to post a digital recording. This can be automatically received over a dial-up modem by anyone with a telephone or speaker hooked into a PC sound card and stored on a hard disk. Similar processes can be used with a cheap video camera to produce multimedia electronic mail, which will evolve into the video mail bulletin board as equipment prices fall. Monochrome videocams are already available in the USA for about a hundred dollars, armed with one of these and Tapi you can use your sound card and video-board to create digital home movies for mailing over the Internet.

But questions are already being raised about the obvious issue of electronic porn mail, and the transmitting of unsuitable pictures to unsuspecting people. If anonymous text based email is already a nuisance, just what will be the impact of malicious and anonymous porn mail on your wife, your daughter, or for that matter the Prime Minister? Like most of the other issues raised, there are as yet no clear answers.

Viruses and virus hoaxes

Viruses have been around almost as long as computers. As with most things to do with personal computers Apple users were there first, probably with the mid-1981 Elk Cloner Virus on the Apple II.

Since then viruses have become not only big trouble, but big business to the anti-virus companies. The Internet is alive with virus writers, hackers, and hoaxers. The hoax below is only one of dozens which appear on the Internet each year. Each of these hoaxes costs businesses big money as they take unnecessary anti-virus measures or spend time and money investigating the reality of reported virus attacks. By and large the perpetrators are neither caught nor prosecuted.

If a virus originates inside a British company or institution and the offender is caught he or she can be prosecuted under British law. If your secretary inadvertently downloads a virus from the Internet which destroys valuable corporate data no one will be prosecuted unless the originator of the virus can be brought to book. Is this the correct sort of environment for companies to operate in – or do UK IT managers believe that they have sufficient resources to deal with every outbreak of an Internet virus or virus hoax? And should the non-computer owning public, who indirectly pay for virus attacks and hoaxes through increased prices, have a say in how a public company should manage its anti-virus and anti-hoax systems?

The 'Good Times' hoax

Warning Internet mail virus

The FCC released a warning last Wednesday concerning a matter of major importance to any regular user of the Internet. Apparently, a new computer virus has been engineered by a user of America Online that is unparalleled in its destructive capability.

Other, more well-known viruses such as Stoned, Airwolf, and Michaelangelo pale in comparison to the prospects of this newest creation by a warped mentality.

What makes this virus so terrifying, said the FCC, is the fact that no program needs to be exchanged for a new computer to be infected. It can be spread through the existing e-mail systems of the InterNet. Once a computer is infected, one of several things can happen. If the computer contains a hard drive, that will most likely be mostly destroyed. If the program is not stopped, the computer's processor will be placed in an nth-complexity infinite binary loop – which can severely damage the processor if left running that way too long. Unfortunately, most novice computer users will not realize what is happening until it is far too late.

Luckily, there is one sure means of detecting what is now known as the 'Good Times' virus. It always travels to new computers the same way – in a text e-mail message with the subject line reading simply 'Good Times'. Avoiding infection is easy once the file has been received – not reading it. The act of loading the file into the mail server's ASCII buffer causes the 'Good Times' mainline program to initialize and execute. The program is highly intelligent – it will send copies of itself to everyone whose e-mail address is contained in a received-mail file or a sent-mail file, if it can find one. It will then proceed to trash the computer it is running on.

The bottom line here is – if you receive a file with the subject line 'GOOD TIMES', DELETE IT IMMEDIATELY! DO NOT READ IT! Rest assured that whoever's name was on the 'From:' line was surely struck by the virus. Warn your friends and local system users of this newest threat to the Internet! It could save them a lot of time and money.

And the response:

There is a rumor running rampant on the Internet and on several commercial BBS systems about a virus called the 'Good Times' virus. Allegedly, this virus wipes out everything on the hard disk of your PC/Mac/Unix system when downloaded (or read or...).

This rumor has been investigated by several of the FIRST teams and found to be false. We know for certain that this was started as a hoax by a student at a small college in the Northeast US. There are no verified reports of any virus of this nature, and much of the activity reported to be caused by this 'virus' is dubious or impossible. The rumor has since taken on a life of its own, and it is being spread widely by well-meaning people who are failing to check its accuracy.

Furthermore, the story is being changed slightly as each person has passed it on. PLEASE do NOT pass this rumor on to anyone! It is false and only serves to help cause anxiety and possibly panic. Feel free to pass this notice along to your users and colleagues at Purdue.

If you encounter something that you believe is a virus or attack on your machines, please report it to pcert@cs. purdue.edu and we will analyze it for you. Please be considerate and do not get caught up in posting false or misleading warnings.

Gene Spafford, COAST Project Director
Software Engineering Research Center & Dept. of Computer Sciences
Purdue University, W. Lafayette IN 47907-1398
Internet: spaf@cs.purdue.edu phone: (317) 494-7825

End notes

Many of these issues, and a thousand others, will govern the future of the Internet as we UK users will see it. Issues such as the Clipper chip, and other cryptography technology will become more important, especially when the US Government stop grading them as 'munitions' and let the world share in their development. The social impact of the Internet is already huge in the USA, where a much

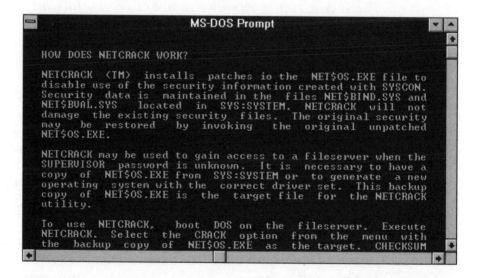

Figure 13.4   *The Netcrack files – used to hack commercial Novell 2.11 systems.*

larger proportion of the population has access. These issues will grow in the UK – does your 11-year-old's school have a policy on computer use? Does the BBC Network Club accept that they may be inadvertently distributing illicit material, some of it ripped off from their own BBC copyright sources? (Their response to date has been to limit access to some newsgroups.)   And how will UK Internet providers keep the short sight of the law at bay when it comes to charges of distributing pornography?

For further reading plug yourself into Gopher and search on privacy, Clipper, computer use policy and any other topic mentioned here. And then ask yourself how relevant these issues are to you, and what you will do with them, now that you are part of the Internet Culture.

See you on the 'Net.

More reading

Cryptography

NIST (US National Institute for Standards and Technology) publishes an introductory paper on cryptography, special publication 800-2 'Public-Key Cryptography' by James Nechvatal (April 1991). Available via anonymous FTP from csrc.ncsl.nist.gov (129.6.54.11), file pub/nistpubs/800-2.txt. Also available via anonymous FTP from wimsey.bc.ca as crypt.txt.Z in the crypto directory.

Phil Zimmerman's PGP (Pretty Good Privacy) package for public key encryption is available at numerous sites. See the newsgroup *alt.security.pgp*. Mailing list requests to *info-pgp-request@lucpul.it.luc.edu*.

Privacy related newsgroups

alt.comp.acad-freedom.news
alt.comp.acad-freedom.talk

Moderated and unmoderated issues related to academic freedom and privacy at universities. Documented examples of violated privacy in email. Documented examples of 'censorship' as in limiting Usenet groups local availability.

alt.privacy – General privacy issues involving taxpaying, licensing, social security numbers, etc.

alt.privacy.anon-server – Debate regarding anonymous servers.

alt.privacy.clipper – Group dedicated to discussing technical and political aspects of the Clipper chip.

alt.security & comp.security.misc – Computer related security issues.

comp.society.privacy – Privacy issues associated with computer technologies. Examples: caller identification, social security numbers, credit applications, mailing lists, etc. Moderated.

comp.org.eff.news & comp.org.eff.talk – Moderated and unmoderated groups associated with the Electronic Frontier Foundation started by Mitch Kapor for protecting civil and constitutional rights in the electronic realm.

Part 4

Appendices

Appendix 1

How Al Gore invented the Information Superhighway

Author's note: Part of Al Gore's Address, concerning the Information Superhighway. The text and grammar are unchanged from the Public Domain original.

... Invest in an information infrastructure

Objectives

Today's "Information Age" demands skill, agility and speed in moving information. Where once our economic strength was determined solely by the depth of our ports or the condition of our roads, today it is determined as well by our ability to move large quantities of information quickly and accurately and by our ability to use and understand this information. Just as the interstate highway system marked a historical turning point in our commerce, today "information superhighways" – able to move ideas, data, and images around the country and around the world – are critical to American competitiveness and economic strength.

This information infrastructure – computers, computer data banks, fax machines, telephones, and video displays – has as its lifeline a high-speed fiber-optic network capable of transmitting billions of bits of information in a second. Imagine being able to transmit the entire Encyclopedia Britannica in one second.

The computing and networking technology that makes this possible is improving at an unprecedented rate, expanding both our imaginations for its use and its effectiveness. Through these technologies, a doctor who needs a second opinion could transmit a patient's entire medical record – X-rays and ultrasound scans included – to a colleague thousands of miles away, in less time than it takes to send a fax today. A school child in a small town could come home and through a personal computer, reach into an electronic Library of Congress – thousands of books, records, videos and photographs, all stored electronically. At home, viewers could choose whenever they wanted from thousands of different television programs or movies.

Efficient access to information is becoming increasingly more important for all parts of our economy. Banks, insurance companies, manufacturing concerns, and many other businesses now depend on high-speed communication networks. These networks have become a critical tool around which many new business opportunities are developing.

And, by harnessing the power of supercomputers able to transform enormous amounts of information to images or solve incredible complex problems in record time, and share this power with an ever-expanding audience of scientists, businesses, researchers, students, doctors and others, the potential for innovation and progress multiplies rapidly. Supercomputers help us develop new drugs, design new products, predict dangerous storms and model climate changes. They help us design better cars, better airplanes, more efficient manufacturing processes. Accelerating the introduction of an efficient, high-speed communication network and associated computer systems would have a dramatic impact on every aspect of our lives. But this is possible only if we adopt forward-looking policies that promote the development of new technologies and if we invest in the information infrastructure needed for the 21st Century.

Actions

A.   Implementation of the High-performance Computing and Communications Program established by the High-Performance Computing Act of 1991 introduced by Vice President Gore when he served in the Senate. Research and development funded by this program is creating (1) more powerful supercomputers, (2) faster computer networks and the first national high-speed network, and (3) more sophisticated software. This network will be constructed by the private sector but encouraged by federal policy and technology developments. In addition, it is providing scientists and engineers with the tools and training they need to solve "Grand Challenges", research problems – like modeling global warming – that cannot be solved without the most powerful computers.

B.   Create a Task Force on Information Infrastructure. Government telecommunication and information policy has not kept pace with new developments in telecommunications and computer technology. As a result, government regulations have tended to inhibit competition and delay deployment of new technology. For instance, without a consistent, stable regulatory environment, the private sector will hesitate to make the investments necessary to build the high-speed national telecommunications network that this country needs to compete successfully in the 21st Century. To address this problem and others, we will create a high-level interagency task force within the National Economic Council which will work with Congress and the private sector to find consensus on and implement policy changes needed to accelerate deployment of a national information infrastructure.

C.   Create an Information Infrastructure Technology Program to assist industry in the development of the hardware and software needed to fully apply advanced computing and networking technology in manufacturing, in health care, in life-long learning, and in libraries.

D.   Provide funding for networking pilot projects through the National Telecommunications and Information Administration (NTIA) of the Department of Commerce. NTIA will provide matching grants to states, school districts, libraries, and other non-profit entities so that they can purchase the computers and networking connections needed for distance learning and for hooking into computer networks like the Internet. These pilot projects will demonstrate the benefits of networking to the educational and library communities.

E.   Promote dissemination of Federal information. Every year, the Federal government spends billions of dollars collecting and processing information (e.g. economic data, environmental data, and technical information). Unfortunately, while much of this information is very valuable, many potential users either do not know that it exists or do not know how to access it. We are committed to using new computer and networking technology to make this information more available to the taxpayers who paid for it. In addition, it will require consistent Federal information policies designed to ensure that Federal information is made available at a fair price to as many users as possible while encouraging growth of the information industry.

Appendix 2

All about modems

Parts of this appendix are copyright © Demon Internet Services 1994 and reproduced with their kind permission.

Modems for Internet users

You'll need to use a modem to connect to the services of your Internet provider, unless you have a direct connection to the Internet via a leased line or other means. In the UK the vast majority of Internet users will be modem users, and interfacing the TCP/IP software to the Internet via a modem is considered to be a black art by many people.

Get a grip on modems

You'll need to master the CCITT numbers which are used to describe modem performance before you do much else. The CCITT (now the ITU) is part of the UN, and ratifies recommendations from modem manufacturers. These recommendations are then given reference numbers which correlate to the technical ability of the modem. The current fastest ITU standard for transmission speeds is V34.

ITU-ratified modem speeds – Items marked * are suitable for use with a TCP/IP Internet connection

V21: 300 bps transmit/receive. Almost unused these days but still present in new modems for backwards compatibility with older systems. Not suitable for TCP/IP use.

V22: 1200 bps transmit/receive. Seen mainly on older portable modems. Superseded by V22 bis and hardly used. Not generally suitable for TCP/IP use.

* V22 bis: 2400 bps transmit/receive. The minimum realistic specification for a modem to be used with an Internet connection.

V23: 1200 receive/75 bps transmit. Archaic split rate standard. Not generally suitable for TCP/IP use.

* *V32*: 9600 bps transmit/receive. Superseded by V32 bis although still common. OK for medium duty Internet use, but not really fast enough for World Wide Web use. OK for email and Archie searches.

* *V32 bis*: 14,400 transmit/receive. Today's standard for fast data transfer. Most providers now have V32 bis connections available. OK for medium to heavy Internet use and will cope with graphic applications such as World Wide Web.

V32 Terbo: 19,200 bps transmit/receive. Proprietary non-ITU ratified mode, not used by Internet providers. Don't buy V32 Terbo modems unless they have V32 bis modes as well. Most do.

V.FAST/CLASS: 28,800 bps transmit/receive. Proprietary non-ITU-ratified mode, not used by Internet providers. Don't buy V.FAST/CLASS modems unless they have V32 bis modes as well. Most do.

* *V34*: The ITU-ratified mode (broadly speaking) of V.FAST. Should give 28,800 bps on most dial-up lines – once Internet providers have started to install them. You can buy V34 now, as almost all V34 modems will run at V32 bis speeds for compatibility with older systems.

Modem types

Modems that provide V21, V22, V23 and V22 bis are often called quad (four-speed) modems. A quad modem with V32 is sometimes quoted as having quin-standard capability. Most V32 bis modems have all or most of the quad modes built-in, while V34 modems will retain 32 bis, V32 and V22 bis. Desktop modems are recommended over card or internal modems, all other constraints being equal. Desktop modems can be easily transported between machines, and are fitted with indicators which can help troubleshoot installation problems.

Hayes compatibility

Modems from other manufacturers are often touted as being 'Hayes Compatible' but the truly Hayes compatible modem is rare. The term is used to show that the modem in question uses part of the 'Hayes AT Command' set – but you should be aware that all manufacturers tend to use different subsets. This causes confusion when trying to set a modem up from scratch, as a command that works with one modem is not guaranteed to work with another.

Error correction and data compression

All modern modems are now fitted with V42 error correction. This monitors data throughput and, as line conditions deteriorate, packets of data are retransmitted if found to be faulty. This results in clean data transfer, at the price of lower throughput if errors are found.

A V32 bis modem has a maximum transmission speed of 14,400 bits per second but the actual throughput of the modem is increased by the use of data compression. V42 bis compression automatically compresses the data within the modem at the transmit end, and decompresses it at the receive end. This increases the actual data throughput by a factor of four in ideal circumstances, and a V32 bis modem using V42 bis can manage throughputs of up to 57,600 bits per second in perfect conditions. Actual throughput depends on the quality of the phone line, the ability of the computer at each end of the link to control data flow and, in PCs, the ability of the chip driving the serial port to handle high throughputs without loss.

Older modems use MNP5 compression, which manages compression by a factor of around two times, but MNP5 does not work well with already compressed data. These figures represent theoretical maxima – in practice V42 bis compression results in an increase of around two to three times, depending on line noise, the compressibility of the data, and the ability of the transmitting computer and modem to keep up. Most text and graphics files are highly compressible, but archived data tends to be already compressed and cannot be further compressed by the modem. This is why you'll see lower transfer rates with compressed files; typically they travel at around 1600 cps through V32 bis modems.

Computer to modem speeds

This increase in throughput means that the speed of the connection between the computer and the modem has to be higher than the transmission speed of the modem by a factor of two to three times. Most V32 bis users set a speed of 38,400 to 57,600 bps to gain the benefit of data compression, but in practice there is little to be gained by going above 38,400 bps. In fact there can be significant data loss on slower computers at 57,600 bps, especially those running Windows, or occupied with driving networks at the same time.

Modem benchmark freaks should also realize that throughput will depend entirely on what is happening at the far end of the link. A heavily loaded remote server will not be able to keep up at maximum rates, but despite this buying a V32 bis modem makes sense – it removes one more data bottleneck from your end of the system. If you are buying a new modem you should consider V32 bis to be the minimum standard, with V34 providing a degree of future-proofing for when Internet providers start installing similar equipment. Approved V34 modems are already starting to appear in the computer magazines.

Flow control and handshaking

Fast modems interface with the computer via a process called hard handshaking, and the modem-to-computer cable needs to have the handshake wires connected so the computer can sense flow control signals to and from the modem. You can't therefore use any old cable with a fast modem, nor can you generally use cables designed for use with earlier modems unless they have those extra handshake lines. You need to set your modem and computer to use 'hard handshaking' – a technique where the modem raises and lowers voltages on two or more of its connections, to provide start/stop signals to the computer. This prevents data 'over-run' where the computer or modem sends data faster than the other can receive it. Flow control schemes used on slower modems often embedded codes into the data stream from the modem (called XON/XOFF or 'soft' handshaking) but soft handshake codes will interfere with the transmission of packets over a TCP/IP serial link, and cannot therefore be used. You need to make sure that whatever modem and cable you use with a TCP/IP link has hard handshaking enabled. Your modem handbook will advise; generally the code to set a Hayes modem for hard handshaking is AT&K3.

BABT approval

In the UK you cannot legally attach unapproved telephony equipment to services run by BT, Mercury, the Kingston Upon Hull telephone system, or the cellular mobile networks. Approved modems carry an approvals notice, usually on the underside, and will normally work without problems with other approved modems, as used by Internet providers. The author specifically recommends that you buy or use only approved modems.

Setting up a modem for SLIP or PPP use

You'll need to make sure your modem is properly configured before you leap into setting up SLIP or PPP utilities. Normally this entails checking your modem's ability to work with hard handshaking, and at the correct speed. One way to do this is to dial up your favourite Bulletin Board and attempt to download a file with the Zmodem protocol. You should get a continuous download with no errors, overruns or time-outs. A compressed file such as a ZIP or SEA archive should travel at around 1600 characters per second on a correctly set-up V32 bis link. A plain ASCII text file should travel at about 3000 characters per second or more through V32 bis modems. Actual throughput will vary, and any repeatable indication of errors or time-outs should be investigated. The Hayes BBS on 0252 775 599 carries ASCII test files, and is driven by fast modems. You should get at least 3000 cps from this site under optimum conditions.

If you are a PC user running Windows you may have problems driving modems at speeds much over 19,200 bps, especially when multitasking. This can be corrected by fitting a serial port fitted with a 16550A chip to your computer. You can check which chip you have by using the MSD.EXE utility supplied with Windows, but run it in DOS, not Windows. If you have an 8250 chip, you may need to upgrade. If you have problems with faster modems then most PC dealers or Internet providers can advise. Macintosh computers, from the Mac Plus upwards, can drive V32 bis modems at 38,400 bps, although older 68000 based Macs may slow down if other interrupt driven processes are running, such as AppleTalk or Quick-Keys. Most Amiga users of 600 and 1200 computers will find that their serial ports will run at speeds of up to 38,400 bps, the speed needed to get the best from V32 bis modems, although some tuning may be needed to go higher than this when V34 becomes popular. The newer V34 modems will not run at full speed on many computers, including Macs and Amigas, at the time of writing, and they should be used with a speed of 38,400 bps at the computer.

You will need a comms or 'terminal emulation' package such as Telix, Procomm, Windows' Terminal, or Zterm for Macs, or Term for Amigas and so on, to set up a modem.

(1) Set the speed of the comms package to 2400 bps.

(2) Set the parity to none.

(3) Set 8 bits, and hard handshaking. Some comms packages refer to it as RTS/CTS handshaking.

(4) Go to communications mode if the package has it (it's sometimes called 'direct online mode').

(5) Type AT followed by the <return> key.

(6) You should see 'OK'. If you don't, and the modem's lights flash, type AT&F (<return>), ATZ (<return>) and try again. This resets the modem to factory defaults. If you still don't see OK when you type AT, you'll need to refer to your modem's instructions, and the instructions for the comms package in use.

(7) Set hard handshaking on the modem. On a Hayes modem you type AT&K3 followed by <return>. You should see OK. (Many newer modems have hard handshaking set as a default.)

(8) Save the setting in your modem's non-volatile RAM. You do this by typing AT&W or AT&W0, but check your manual first, as modems vary.

IBM PC compatibles running DOS

Some modems send back 'OK' when sent ATZ (the reset command) even though they are not ready. This means that the dialer program will try to ring out even though the modem is not ready. The effect is that you will see ATZ on the screen followed by OK and then the program will not dial. Eventually it will time out. To avoid this, send AT instead of ATZ in the modem initialization string.

Extended memory drivers can interfere with the correct operation of your serial communications. If you suspect this, rename your CONFIG.SYS and AUTOEXEC.BAT files and then reboot your computer to see if the connection improves.

Troubleshooting

If you are getting garbled characters on the screen then something is wrong. Garbled characters are often a sign of mismatched speeds, lack of hand-shaking, or incorrect parity settings. You need to have your modem working properly before you attempt to set up SLIP or PPP so make sure that you get an OK from the modem before continuing.

Some common modem user setups

* PSION PDM 60F modem, from: mark@yrsk.demon.co.uk

MODEM INIT STRING : at e1 f0 m1 q0 v1 x4 &c1 &k3 &r0 &s1 %c3 s0=1
ROM REVISION : PDM60F V5.04
O/S : VAX (VMS V5.2)
Protocol : CMUIP (which is a version of SLIP)
DTE/DCE Speed : 19200 (LAP-M , V42 BIS)

* USR Sportster 14400 Internal Fax/Modem, from: john@jhall.demon.co.uk

Rom revision : Supervisor rev 044-4.1 – DSP rev 10
SLIP, PPP ?: PPP
Modem Init string : ATZ
DTE-DCE speed : 14400
PC/Mac/Amiga/Archimedes/other : PC
Dip switch settings are (left to right):

Switch	Position	Effect
1	Off	&D2
2	On	V0
3	On	Q0
4	Off	E1
5	On	Auto answer suppressed
6	Off	&C1
7	On	Load factory (ROM) defaults
8	On	AT command set recognition enabled

* US Robotics Sportster 14.4 + Fax (Internal), from: al@loonat.demon.co.uk

Rom version : 1444
SLIP Windows 3.1 Trumpet WinSock 1.0 Rev A
Modem Init String : AT&F&A3&B1&H1&R2X4S0=0S7=90
DTE-DCE Speed : 14400

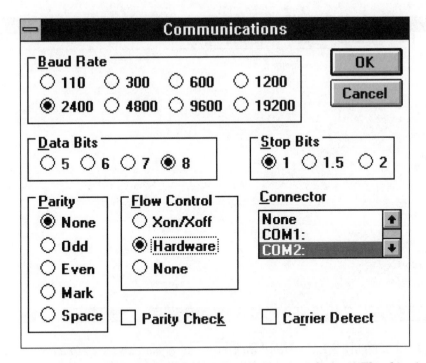

Figure A2.1   *Setting up a modem for Internet dial-up. The objective is to make sure that settings for hard handshaking are stored in the modem's memory. Start with 2400/8/N/1 settings for most modems...*

* Global Village modems for Mac PowerBooks

These use a non-standard set-up, but try:

AT \J0 %C1 \N4 \G0 \Q3 W1

for SLIP or PPP.

* Hayes Optima modems, from: sue@s-sco.demon.co.uk

Hayes modems tend to work out of the box with a simple AT&F&C1&D2 set-up. You can fine-tune Hayes modems to only negotiate an error-corrected connection by setting S36=4. This prevents hiccups in negotiating error-corrected connections from some Internet providers.

* Intertex IX22,33,34, from: sue@s-sco.demon.co.uk

The Swedish Intertex IP33 modems work out of the box, with AT&K3W1&C1. These modems come with speed buffering between the computer and modem disabled, so they should be easy to set up. They also conform fairly closely to

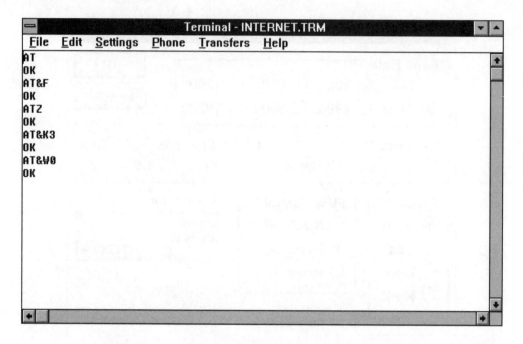

Figure A2.2   ... *and then make sure you can see the modem returning OK for each command you type in. This simplifies setting up procedures later on.*

the Hayes Command Set, so S36=4 can be used to ensure an error-corrected connection. The modems are recently BABT-approved.

* US Robotics/Miracom modems from Demon

To set up your modem, use a standard communications package.
Type ATZ <RETURN> and see the response OK. Then continue to make the settings. You can type ATI4 <RETURN> and ATI5 to see what your current settings are.

B0	V.32bis modulation rather than HST
C1	Transmitter enabled
E1	Local echo ON
F1	Duplex OFF receiving system sends duplicate data
Q0	Result codes displayed
V1	Display result codes in verbal (not numerical) mode
&A3	Enable additional error control indicator
&B1	Serial port remains at fixed setting
&C1	Modem send CD (Carrier Detect) on connection
&D2	Terminal sends DTR (Data Terminal Ready)
&H1	Hardware CTS (Clear to Send) transmit data flow control

&I0   Received Data software flow control disabled

&K3   MNP5 data compression disabled

&N0   Variable link speed negotiation

&R2   Received Data h/ware (RTS) flow controlled by computer

&S1   Data Set Ready (DSR) controlled by the computer

For example, type AT&K3 <RETURN>. When done, type AT&W <RETURN> to save the settings to non-volatile RAM (NVRAM) so that they are remembered when the modem is reset.

* Supra modems

Supra 14.4k fax modems need ROM revision 1.70B (or later).
ACTIVE PROFILE:
B0 E1 L0 M1 N1 Q0 T V1 W0 X4 Y0 %C1 %E0 %G0 \N3 &C1 &D2 &K3 &Q5 &R0 &S0 &X0 &Y0
S00:000 S01:000 S02:043 S03:013 S04:010 S05:008 S06:002 S07:050 S08:002 S09:006
S10:014 S11:095 S12:050 S18:000 S23:055 S25:005 S26:001 S36:007 S37:000 S38:020
S40:087 S46:138 S48:007 S95:000 S109:062 S110:001

* Yoriko modems

Yorikos work OK with a simple AT&F&C1&D2 set-up.

* Zoom modems

To force a Zoom modem to talk at only one speed use AT&Q6S37= 11M0X3&K4

Part of the Hayes command set

AT command summary

Comands need to prefixed by AT, and followed by a carriage return.

Command	Description
A	Enter answer mode; go off hook, attempt to answer incoming call, and go online with another modem
A/	Re-execute previous command line; not preceded by AT nor followed by CR
D	Enter originate mode; go off hook and attempt to go online with another modem

Modifier	*Description*
T	Dials using Tone method
P	Dials using Pulse method
'	Pauses before continuing
W	Waits for second dial tone

Command	*Description*
E0	Do not echo characters from the keyboard to the screen in command state
E1	Echo characters from the keyboard to the screen in command state
H0	Hang up and place modem in command state
I0	Display product code (3-digit number)
I1	Calculate ROM checksum (3-digit number)
I2	Verify ROM checksum of modem (OK or ERROR)
L0-L1	Set low speaker volume
L2	Set medium speaker volume
L3	Set high speaker volume
M0	Turn speaker off
M1	Turn speaker on until carrier detected
M2	Turn speaker on
M3	Turn speaker on until carrier detected, except during dialling
Q0	Return result codes
Q1	Do not return result codes
Q2	Return result codes in originate mode, do not return result codes in answer mode
Sr?	Read and respond with current value of register r (r=number of register; ? requests value)
Sr=n	Set the value of register r to n (n=value within range of register r)
V0	Display result codes as numbers
V1	Display result codes as words

W0	Do not return negotiation progress messages
W1	Return negotiation progress messages
W2	Do not return negotiation progress messages; return CONNECT messages using modem-to-modem (DCE) speeds instead of modem-to-DTE speeds
X0	Provide basic call progress features to enable connection, no carrier, and ring detection
X1	Provide basic call progress features and connection speed with appropriate result codes
X2	Provide basic call progress features, connection speed, and dial tone detection
X3	Provide basic call progress features, connection speed, and busy signal detection
X4	Provide basic call progress features, connection speed, busy signal and dial tone detection
&C1	Track the status of carrier detect signal
&C2	Presume presence of carrier detect signal until online, then track status of signal
&D0	Ignore the status of DTR signal
&D1	Monitor DTR signal. When an on-to-off transition of DTR signal occurs, the modem enters command state. Return to the online state (if the connection has not been broken) when the 00 command is issued.
&D2	Monitor DTR signal. When an on-to-off transition of DTR signal occurs, hang up and enter the command state
&D3	Monitor DTR signal. When an on-to-off transition of DTR signal occurs, hang up and perform a reset&F Recall factory configuration as active configuration
&K0	Disable local flow control
&K1	Enable RTS/CTS local flow control
&K3	Enable RTS/CTS local flow control
&Q0	Communicate in asynchronous mode
&Q5	Communicate in error-control mode
&Q6	Communicate in asynchronous mode with automatic speed buffering – for interfaces requiring constant speed between the DTE (computer/terminal) and the DCE (modem)

&R0	Track CTS according to RTS
&R1	Ignore RTS; assume presence of CTS
&V	View active configuration, user profiles, and stored telephone numbers
&W0	Write storable parameters of current configuration in memory as profile 0
&W1	Write storable parameters of current configuration in memory as profile 1
&Y0	Specify stored user profile 0 as power-up configuration
&Y1	Specify stored user profile 1 as power-up configuration

RS232 connections

Pin	EIA	V.24	Signal direction	Description
1	AA	101	N/A	Protective Ground
2	BA	103	To modem	Transmit Data
3	BB	104	From modem	Receive Data
4	CA	105	To modem	Request To Send
5	CB	106	From modem	Clear To Send
6	CC	107	From modem	Data Set Ready
7	AB	102	N/A	Signal Ground
8	CF	109	From modem	Data Carrier Detect
12	CI	112	From modem	Data Signal Rate
15	DB	114	From modem	Transmitter Clock
17	DD	115	From modem	Receiver Clock
20	CD	108.2	To modem	Data Terminal Ready
22	CE	125	From modem	Ring Indicator
23	CI	112	From modem	Data Signal Rate
24	DA	113	To modem	Transmitter Clock

Appendix 3

Getting started with an Internet provider

Author's note: The UK Internet Book is pleased to be associated with Demon Internet Services who have provided much of the text in the following Appendices. Demon were chosen because they have a large number of regional access points (PoPs), they are an established company, and they offer a range of low-priced start-up options for newcomers.

The following instructions will allow you to open a full TCP/IP Internet account with Demon Internet Services and install Demon software on your hard disk, and will point you to the remaining documentation.

All the necessary software is available from Demon Internet Services on disk, or it may be downloaded from their system using a standard comms program and a modem.

Read the rest of this appendix before you make the call, so you're familiar with the information you'll be asked to provide. You'll also need a modem of at least V22 bis capability, and a standard comms program to get going. (V32 bis modems are recommended for use with TCP/IP based software.)

If you are using the voucher enclosed with the book, you need to send this to Demon first. They will process your account within a day of receipt and send you a joining letter. If you contact Demon by phone they will need some time to set up the account, although this can often be done the same day.

Open an account

You will need to open an account with Demon before you proceed, and the following administrative data will be required:

- Your name

- Your address (must be same as that on the credit card)

- Your credit card number and expiry date

- Your choice of monthly or annual billing

- Your telephone number
- Your first and second choice of nodename. See the example below.

Nodename example: your nodename can be either

(1) your name:

xxxx@bloggs.demon.co.uk, or

(2) your company:

xxxx@bloggs-co.demon.co.uk.

You only need to inform Demon about the text after the @ sign, as anything before it is the 'username', as in:

username@nodename.demon.co.uk

or

fred@bloggs.demon.co.uk

The nodename needs to be between 4 and 8 characters and Demon do not need to know the username@ part as you can have unlimited mail addresses per nodename.

You are recommended to keep your nodename simple and recognizable as it will be attached to all your mail messages. It's not recommended that you use aliases such as *infobahn-surfer@hades.demon.co.uk* if you want to be taken seriously by other Internet users.

The suffix *demon.co.uk* is added to all nodenames. You should also choose your nodename on the basis that you will be using it for a long time, as it will cost you money to have it changed at a later date. Also be prepared to sign up with a second choice of nodename, especially if you decide to use your surname as a nodename. (The nodename *doesn't* have to be your surname.)

It will be helpful if you have all the above information to hand before you sign up.

Getting an IP address

When you contact Demon with the above information, you will be allocated your nodename, such as *bloggs.demon.co.uk*.

NB: You cannot proceed further until you have been allocated your nodename by Demon.

You need to set up a password for your account and also get your unique IP address (for example 158.151.23.102). To do this, configure a standard terminal (communications) package for 8 bits, no parity and one stop bit. Dial the Point of Presence (PoP) of your choice (for example, London 0181 338 4848). Demon have lots of these, and more are being added all the time, so ask for the one nearest to you.

At the login prompt, type your nodename (for example, bloggs), not your username (for example, fred):

Login: bloggs

(Don't add the .demon.co.uk)

- If the system prompts you for a password, your account has not yet been set up. Try again later.

- If the system takes you into a password selection program, your account has been set up. Set up a password, taking care with upper and lower case.

- You will then be given your IP address. Note both your IP address and password down carefully.

UK phone numbers

These are the current UK phone numbers for Demon servers. Use the one nearest to you for access. Lines are busiest during the cheap rate periods for BT and Mercury, so try to call during UK office hours, if possible.

Current PoPs	*Number*
London	0181 338 4848
Birmingham	0121 275 4848
Manchester	0161 385 4848
Bristol	0117 981 4848
Cardiff	01222 274848
Coventry	01203 284848
Gloucester	01452 354848
Leeds	0113 298 4848
Leicester	0116 290 4848
Liverpool	0151 210 4848
Luton	01582 644848
Newcastle	0191 247 4848
Nottingham	0115 954 4848
Preston	01772 484848
Reading	01734 284848
Sheffield	0114 238 4848
Wolverhampton	01902 464848

That's it. You should now have:

- an IP address, such as 158.151.22.105 (example only), and
- your own password for TCP/IP access.

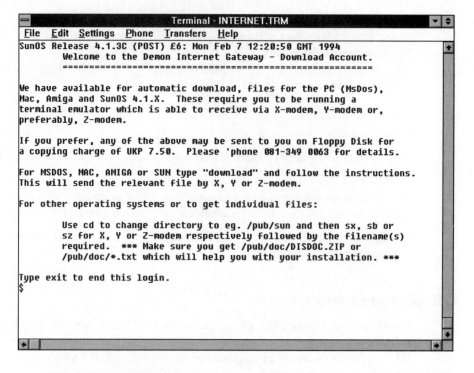

```
─                    Terminal - INTERNET.TRM                ▼ ‡
 File  Edit  Settings  Phone  Transfers  Help
SunOS Release 4.1.3C (POST) £6: Mon Feb 7 12:20:50 GMT 1994    ▲
       Welcome to the Demon Internet Gateway - Download Account.
       ===========================================================

We have available for automatic download, files for the PC (MsDos),
Mac, Amiga and SunOS 4.1.X.  These require you to be running a
terminal emulator which is able to receive via X-modem, Y-modem or,
preferably, Z-modem.

If you prefer, any of the above may be sent to you on Floppy Disk for
a copying charge of UKP 7.50.  Please 'phone 081-349 0063 for details.

For MSDOS, MAC, AMIGA or SUN type "download" and follow the instructions.
This will send the relevant file by X, Y or Z-modem.

For other operating systems or to get individual files:

       Use cd to change directory to eg. /pub/sun and then sx, sb or
       sz for X, Y or Z-modem respectively followed by the filename(s)
       required.  *** Make sure you get /pub/doc/DISDOC.ZIP or
       /pub/doc/*.txt which will help you with your installation. ***

Type exit to end this login.
$                                                               ▼
◆                                                               ◆
```

Figure A3.1 *The Demon screen you'll see when you log in to download software. You'll need to use a standard comms package such as Windows 'Terminal' to log in.*

You can now use these to set up your computer for TCP/IP working.

Getting TCP/IP software for your computer

You'll need TCP/IP access software for your new Internet network account, such as SLIP, PPP or a Windows variant, and TCP/IP based 'client' software for mail, news, ftp, gopher and so on.

You can either use commercial software, or download all the Shareware software you need, ready packaged, from Demon.

To download TCP/IP software from the server, you can use the 'guest' download account. First you'll need the password of the day from Demon, which can be obtained by dialling Demon's office number. (This is not the same as the password you just set up for your account.) You use this access password to download Demon's latest start-up software and documentation for DOS, Windows, Mac, Sun, and Amiga computers. The password is changed daily, so if you don't go into the server immediately you should contact Demon by phone for a new password on the day you intend to set up your software.

To do this dial any PoP using standard communications software and a modem, type 'guest' at the login prompt (without the quotes) and then type in the daily password given to you by Demon. On-screen prompts will then guide you through the download process.

Getting software for an existing account

If you want to download software once your account is opened, you'll need the password of the day from Demon. Using an ordinary comms program and modem login as 'guest', with the daily password (not your TCP/IP password), and follow the on-screen prompts.

Appendix 4

Getting started with Demon and DOS

Author's note: Parts of this Appendix are copyright © Demon Internet Services 1994 and reproduced with their kind permission. Readers are advised that this information is liable to change as new software becomes available, and that this appendix is provided for general guidance only.

PC users are recommended to try the Demon DOS software, even if they are running Windows. It offers a fast set up and ease of configuration, and is a quick way of getting on to the 'Net. Once there, you can use the DOS software to FTP all the Windows software you need.

The following instructions will allow you to install the Demon DOS software on your hard disk and point you to the remaining documentation. The software is available from Demon Internet Services on 0181 349 0063 as a high-density floppy PC disk, or it may be downloaded from their system.

Introduction

DIS.EXE is an easy to use installation program for the DOS based NOS/NET programs, and for SNEWS/ PCELM, the offline news and mail readers. Once installed, it allows configuration and maintenance of these packages. The idea is to obviate the need to go to the DOS prompt and to provide a common interface for the maintenance of the packages. Having successfully installed the software, you should refer to DISPC.TXT for full information.

Quick start

You are strongly recommended to read through this document before proceeding.

(1)   Before running the installation program you should get your Internet address and set up your password as described in Appendix 3. You should have got one self-extracting zip file from Demon called DISnnn.EXE, where nnn is the version number, e.g. 212. You will probably have got this by downloading from our guest account or alternatively on a disk. A copy of UNZIP.EXE is included in DISnnn.EXE. All the zip files should be in the same directory. IT SHOULD NOT BE NECESSARY AT ANY POINT DURING THE INSTALLATION FOR YOU TO USE UNZIP OR PKUNZIP YOURSELF ON THE COMMAND LINE – THE PROGRAM WILL DO EVERYTHING FOR YOU. In case you don't have a suitable editor (and the EDIT in DOS 5 takes up a *lot* of memory and is best avoided), we have also included TED.COM. If you wish to use *any* editor, please copy it to a directory in your DOS PATH. To see what your path is set to, type PATH at the DOS prompt. If you don't want to do this by hand (or forget to do it) the installation program will warn you. If you want to use the TED.COM supplied it will offer to move this program for you.

(2)   Run DIS.EXE and follow the questions on the screen. If anything goes wrong during installation, please refer to this document first.

General guide to using DIS

The process you are in is titled at the top of the screen on one or two lines depending on the contents of the rest of the screen. The bottom line of the screen is the prompt line. This tells you what is going on and gives a guide to what data should be entered. When it asks you to 'Press' you simply have to press any of the valid keys. When it asks you to 'Enter' there will be a flashing cursor at which your data should be typed in, followed by pressing Enter or Return. Additionally you may move the cursor up or down and use the function keys F1 to F10 where appropriate. When in an input field with a flashing cursor, you may press CTRL and HOME together for a help screen on editing features. The F1 Key is for Help information and is available virtually everywhere in DIS.EXE. ESC (or F2) is used to abandon the screen you are on and take you back one level. The F3 Key is used when you are happy with the data on a screen and wish to move forward. Additional functions, where available, will appear on Function keys F4 to F12. A description of their use will appear one line above the prompt line.

Creating a brand new installation with DIS

You will need at least 4 Mb of free disk space on your hard disk to install the software and at least 540 kb of conventional memory free in order to run the tools. If in doubt, consult your DOS manual regarding Memory Managers.

(1)   Insert the disk into your 3.5 inch drive high density. I will assume this drive is A:, substitute B: if necessary.

(2)   From DOS type:

```
C:
MKDIR C:\DEMON
CD C:\DEMON
A:\DIS215B.EXE
```

(3)   You now have the base software installed on your hard disk. You should then review the document C:\DEMON\README.1ST. This can be read as a text file in (for example) the Windows Notepad, or EDIT on more recent versions of DOS; if all else fails there is an editor provided, in which case type:

```
C:\DEMON\TED C:\DEMON\README.1ST
```

This will explain to you how to complete the installation. You may want to print this file out to refer to during the remaining steps.

(4)   Having completed the installation, documentation on the software packages installed is available in the following files in the c:\demon directory:

DIS.DOC	Tutorial on the front end package (essential reading)
DISPC.TXT	Tutorial on main packages (essential reading)
MODEM.TXT	How to configure modems for correct working (essential reading)
PROBLEM.TXT	Problem report form
WELCOME.TXT	General Internet introduction

Should you have any problems, feel free to contact technical support on 0181 343 3881. Support hours are Monday to Friday 9:00 a.m. till 9:00 p.m. and Saturday 10:00 a.m. till 5:00 p.m.
    Type

```
DIS <return>
```

The first question asks you if you wish to maintain the colours straight away. If you are running on an LCD or similar display, the default colours may be unusable. In fact you may not even be able to read the first question! In that case simply press Y for Yes and you will be able to maintain your colours before proceeding. The colour maintenance program allows the flashing parameters to be set – that is, if you want to set or turn off flashing colours you can do so. You will now be given the opportunity to specify the directory you wish NET to be installed in, and the program can make the directory for you if it does not already exist. Please note that it can only make one new subdirectory at a time – thus on an otherwise blank drive C: it can make C:\NOS but not C:\DEMON\NOS. If you wish to create the latter you must create C:\DEMON first and then C:\DEMON\NOS.

The program will look in the current directory for the zip files. If it cannot find them there you will be prompted for the directory in which they are located. You will then be asked to enter the configuration information – this configures two files called AUTOEXEC.NET and DIALER which are used by NET.EXE, the communications package. You will then be able to set up some general options such as your DOS editor. As there is a built-in editor you can use that for all of the standard files. Enter the details on each screen, pressing F3 to Update when you are ready. You will then be led through the installation of SNEWS and PCELM in a similar way. Keep pressing F3 when ready to update each screen. Finally, the program will create a batch file called DEMON.BAT which should be used to call DIS.EXE. From now on you should type DEMON to access the program and not DIS. The files DIS.EXE and COLOURS.CTX need to be in the same directory as the NET.EXE programs and they will be copied there automatically by the program (DIS.EXE). See the section on DEMON.BAT further down for more details. You are now ready to connect for the first time. From the Main Menu Press A. More detailed info is available in DISPC.TXT and a variety of other documentation.

DIS.EXE will create a batch file called DEMON.BAT. In this program a few environment variables will be set. If you are short on environment space you could see the DOS error message 'out of environment space' flash up to the screen. To fix this, on DOS have a look in your CONFIG.SYS file for a SHELL= line. This will call COMMAND.COM and, if there is not one there already, you can add a /E:1024 so that the resultant line may look like: SHELL=C:\DOS\COMMAND.COM C:\DOS /P /E:1024. If running in a Microsoft Windows DOS box, change the pif info to have a similar setting – make sure you are using command.com to load the program. You can do this in another way by adding the following line to windows\system.ini, in the [NonWindowsApp] section:

CommandEnvSize=1024

This means that .bat files would also get this amount of environment space, so DEMON.BAT could be run directly or via a pif rather than from a DOS box.

Installing DIS on an existing, working installation

Copy DIS.EXE and COLOURS.CTX to the directory containing NET.EXE. Run the program by typing DIS <return>. The program will take you in to the general configuration screen. If it was able to find any of the relevant directories for SNEWS and PCELM, it will put defaults on the screen

Complete the details and then Press F3 to update. If you do NOT get the configuration screen but get a screen asking you where to install NOS then you have started from the wrong directory – copy DIS.EXE and COLOURS.CTX to the correct directory and start again.

Upgrading an existing installation

If you just want to upgrade DIS.EXE then simply unzip DIS.ZIP in the NET.EXE directory optionally using the -o switch to overwrite any existing files.

DIS configuration file – DIS.CFG

DIS creates a file called DIS.CFG so that it knows where to find News and Mail etc. Should you wish to re-install DIS on an existing working set-up, then simply delete this file. If you wish to start again from zip files then delete AUTOEXEC.NET as well. For a completely clean start, delete all files and clear any environment variables (for example, set SNEWS= and set HOME=)

The built-in editor

DIS.EXE has its own built-in editor. It's fairly primitive but it is wonderful if you don't have one of your own :) Also it is quicker to use if editing small files. One redeeming factor is that it enables online help – this is fully implemented when editing AUTOEXEC.NET which will save some laborious searching in the documentation. Please note that it does not handle tabs and leaves them as a graphics symbol so they are not destroyed.

When using it to edit other standard files, F1 for Help will tell you what that file is used for and sometimes it will give examples of what could be included.

Common problems

(1)   You go into the mail but when you press return on a message the screen flashes and you don't see any message. Or you go into News and when you post an article it doesn't take you into an editor to type any text. This is because you have specified an editor or viewer that is not in your DOS path. Please reread 'Creating a brand new installation with DIS' above.

(2)   There is a program called Health Check which checks some of the more common problems. Please use it after your installation to make sure everything is OK.

(3)   4DOS users sometimes have trouble when they get to create the newsgroups for the first time. If you get a problem here then change to

the SNEWS sub-directory and type: addgroup demon.announce. One of our users also had this info to add which I cannot verify:

> In article 743184915snx@lazy.demon.co.uk Andrewb@lazy.demon. co.uk writes: I *think* it would have worked in 4DOS, too, had I put a line in the 4dos.ini file that said "EnvFree=1024", which expands the environment space for secondary shells. I also reset UMBEnvironment to NO in the same file. But I have bottled out from testing it yet again. The odd thing is that I have successfully installed DIS under 4DOS before. So I suspect that the UMBenvironment thing, which I only have on this machine, may be at fault.

Improvements

Any bug reports and/or suggestions should be mailed to internet@demon.net or posted to the demon.ip.support.pc newsgroup.

Demon Internet Limited   0181 349 0063

Appendix 5a

Setting up Windows Shareware for the Internet

By Grahame Davies, Demon Internet Services.
(Copyright Demon Internet Services 1994 and reproduced with kind permission)

Author's note: An automated set-up routine for Windows Shareware was under development as we went to press. The following is included to assist with earlier installations, and with troubleshooting Windows set-ups.

The latest version of this document is available electronically from:

ftp.demon.co.uk:/pub/doc/os/windows.txt

Overview

This is the first in a series of documents:

windows.txt: How to set up Windows software for the Internet.

wintcp.txt: Advanced configuration for Windows software TCP/IP and dialling.

winmos.txt: Configuration of Mosaic for windows.

One of the main reasons for setting up Microsoft Windows software for connection to the Internet is so that you can run a W3 (World Wide Web) browser such as Cello or Mosaic.

The rest of this document assumes that you wish to install Public Domain and/or Shareware software and will help you set up TCP/IP software so that you can dial and have TCP/IP running. Having done that just once, you can simply download other applications and with the minimum of configuration they should work. Some examples are included.

Having read this document and followed its instructions you should be able to use all Windows programs to:

- Dial out and connect

- Use W3 (World Wide Web) with a graphical browser

- Use ftp, Finger, Archie and telnet software.

Other applications such as Gopher and IRC are not covered yet but these are normally easy to install.

What you *won't* be able to do (in the first instance) is:

Receive/send mail or receive/send news

You need to set up a piece of software called Winsock. This software can dial and pass information between the Internet and your Windows applications. The other things you run are your applications. To date there are few news and mail applications available so for now you can use your existing DIS PC software.

The extra software detailed in this allows you to receive and send mail/news from within Windows. Mail and news readers available are still in the early stages of development and so you may wish to continue using DOS based NEWS and PCElm.

Do you have a powerful enough computer?

You need a 386 or 486 computer running Microsoft Windows 3.1 (or later); 4 Mb RAM is OK but more helps. Ensure you have a good-sized swap space of at least 8 Mb. Check the available memory by clicking on Program Manager – Help and then selecting – About Program Manager... . Alter your swap space by choosing Control Panel and 386 Enhanced. You need about 5 Mb of disk space (not swap space) to ensure you have enough room to download and install the files. Use dir at a DOS prompt to see the available space.

Software needed and where to get it

All other files are available from ftp.demon.co.uk.

Note: The filenames referred to here were correct at the time(s) of writing. The Internet world is developing quickly and so new versions of programs are being made available all the time. Thus you may find that there is a choice of filenames or that the name suggested here no longer exists. Simply choose the filename with the later version number or the most recent date.

You need something called a Winsock stack. The most popular is Peter Tattam's, which is Shareware. It's in:

/pub/ibmpc/winsock/stacks/trumpwsk/twsk10a.zip (about 110K)

This contains a program to do the dialling and logging on sequence (called a dialer).

You can actually use a different dialer with this Winsock software but for now keep it simple. The reason for wanting to use a different dialer is that the one included in Tattam's Winsock is primitive and will not auto-redial or allow you to select a different PoP (Point of Presence).

On top of this you need to run some applications. There are a large number available which you can get going in your own time. For now it's suggested you start with FTP and then Mosaic (W3 Browser). Just get FTP first, as Mosaic is a large program.

/pub/ibmpc/winsock/apps/ws_ftp/ws_ftp.zip (about 73K)

Installation and configuring

You should by now have (at least):

twsk10a.zip
ws_ftp.zip

It is a matter of personal taste as to where you put these programs. One suggestion is a set of subdirectories below your Windows directory. For example, from DOS:

```
cd \windows    (change to your Windows directory)
md wapps       (make a directory for your Windows applications)
cd wapps       (change to the wapps directory)
md twsk        (make a directory for Trumpet Winsock )
md ws_ftp      (make a directory for the ftp client ws_ftp)
```

Or from Windows, use File Manager, File, Create Directory to create these.

You will then have:

\windows \windows\wapps
\windows\wapps\twsk
\windows\wapps\ws_ftp \windows\wapps\etc

and so on. Change to the twsk directory:

cd \windows\wapps\twsk

and unzip the Trumpet Winsock zip file using the unzip or pkunzip program. The command for this might be:

pkunzip \tmp\twsk10a.zip or unzip \tmp\twsk10a.zip

depending on where you have put your zip files. Change to the ws_ftp directory and unzip the ws_ftp zip file. You can continue for any other applications you may have downloaded.

Alternatively you may have a Windows unzipper and you may of course use that instead.

Let's configure the Winsock program. Change to its directory:

cd \windows\wapps\twsk

There is a fair amount of documentation included which you can read later (after it's all working).

There are some files that need configuring:

hosts	(tells Winsock how to talk to the Demon gateway)
login.cmd	(the login dialer script)
bye.cmd	(the hang up the modem script for when your session has ended)
trumpwsk.ini	(the defaults for the trumpet winsock program)

You need to do some editing so that your host's file looks similar to the following:

localhost 158.152.1.65
gate.demon.co.uk 158.152.11.1
walm.demon.co.uk

except the last line should be *your* IP address and *your* nodename, for example 158.152.n.n yourmc.demon.co.uk.

The sample login.cmd file is quite complicated. The following is all you really need:

```
# initialize modem
#
set DTR on
wait 30 DCD
# if this script doesn't work it might be the above lines causing the
# problem so you can remove them both. However this may indicate that
# you either do not have a full spec modem cable or that your modem
# is not configured for hardware handshaking. See /pub/doc/Modem.txt
# for some advice.
output atz\r
```

```
input 10 OK\n
#
# send phone number
# This example has the London PoP number
#
output atdt01813434848\r
# simply replace 01813434848 with your favourite PoP number. If it's not
# London input 60 CONNECT
#
# wait till it's safe to send because some modems hang up
# if you transmit during the connection phase
#
# yes the first characters *are* meant to be missing
input 60 ogin:
# change yourmc to be your nodename (without .demon.co.uk)
output yourmc\r
input 60 assword:
# change xxxxx to be your password
output xxxxx\r
input 60 otocol:
output SLIP\r
input 60 HELLO
```

You may have noticed that we are only checking for ogin:, assword: and
otocol: This is so that should Demon change operating systems, the login
sequence will still work regardless of the case of the letter(s) of the words
(Login: or login:, Password: or password:). Also, at the Protocol: prompt, we
are sending SLIP. This is because the Winsock driver we are installing runs
SLIP. Other software, such as NET.EXE/KA9Q, runs PPP. Your account with
Demon does either and so you can use SLIP or PPP software as suits you.

The file bye.cmd should be simple:

```
output +++
input 10 OK\n
output ath0\r
input 10 OK\n
```

The trumpwsk.ini file can be configured from within the application.
However, the following is included for your reference:

```
[Trumpet Winsock] ; change the IP address on the following line to be
*your* IP address
ip = 158.152.n.n
netmask = 255.255.0.0
gateway = 158.152.1.65
dns = 158.152.1.65
```

```
time = 158.152.1.65
domain = demon.co.uk
vector = 00
mtu = 576
rwin = 2048
mss = 536
slip-enabled = 1
; The slip-port should be 1 for com1, 2 for com2, etc.
; note that if you have a com port on a non-standard IRQ then simply
; enter the com port here and use Windows Control Panels to set up the
; IRQ so that the whole of Windows knows rather than just this program.
slip-port = 1
; the following is the speed at which your modem talks to your computer.
slip-baudrate = 19200
; of course you may wish to make this speed higher (38,400) or slower
; depending on the speed of your modem and the type of serial chip you
; have. See /pub/doc/Modem.txt for some help.
slip-handshake = 1
slip-compressed = 0
dial-option = 0
online-check = 0
inactivity-timeout = 5
slip-timeout = 2
registration-name = ""
registration-password = "h[G?"Rgl"
```

Now add the TCPMAN.EXE to Windows as a program icon. This is the program that runs Winsock and can do the dialling. Double-click on it and check your configuration. The following is mainly taken from /pub/ibmpc/winsock/DIS_docs/ws_bg_v5.txt and my thanks go to the authors of this excellent document.

Click the menu bar FILE and then SETUP on the drop down menu.

```
Enter:
your address in IP address      158.152.n.n
netmask                         255.255.0.0
default gateway,                158.152.1.65
name server                     158.152.1.65
time server                     158.152.1.65
Domain suffix                   demon.co.uk
```

'Check' (make sure it is selected) the Internal SLIP box (this 'greys out' the net mask and default gateway options but ungreys (!) some of the later options).

Set SLIP Port, Baud rate and Hardware handshake to the same values as you used in configuring the Demon software. There are some other buttons and options in the set-up. These can usually be left alone. The SLIP port is your serial port (com1, com2, and so on). Note that if you have a serial port on a non-standard IRQ then you tell Windows about this using the configuration program in the Windows Control Panel group.

Also set:

> TCP mss 536
> mtu 576
> TCP rwin 2048

Click OK
Click OK on message "You will need to restart......"
Close TCPMAN with FILE, EXIT

Done!

You can now test that it works by starting up TCPMAN and then selecting Dialer and login. Watch the screen. You should see the program initialize the modem and then dial out and connect and go through the login sequence. If it does then you are on! Do not select Manual Login unless you wish to use a different dialer and then tell TCPMAN to start SLIP.

If you unzipped the ws_ftp package, then add an icon for it and double-click on that icon. There are some defaults that you may wish to set but you can do that later – it should just work! Try connecting to ftp.demon.co.uk and retrieve a file from, say, /pub/doc.

When finished, go back to the TCPMAN program, select Dialer again and then select bye which will run the log off script.

Occasionally you might find that selecting bye does nothing. Or that you cannot exit the TCPMAN program. This often indicates that there is either a bug in your login.cmd script or something went wrong with the connection. If this happens, press ESC to abort the script. You can then select a new script (login, bye) or File, Exit to close TCPMAN.

Troubleshooting: if the above doesn't work first time then it could be due to modem problems, configuration problems or a scripting problem.

Modem problems: Check out Modem.txt and make sure your modem is configured correctly, you have a proper cable, it's turned on, and so on. If you haven't got a copy of this file or want the latest version, get /pub/doc/Modem.txt.

Configuration: Check the COM (serial) port you are using. Try altering the speed at which your computer is talking to your modem.

Scripting: Check login.cmd to make sure there are no spelling mistakes and no spaces at the end of any lines.

Assuming you are successfully working then what should you do next? Configure more packages. Most are as easy as the ws_ftp package in that you simply unzip them, add a program icon and they run. Mosaic or Cello (W3 browsers) will also work like this. However they have far more features that can be configured and most of these are not configurable from within the program so you have to edit the .ini file by hand. This is certainly true of Mosaic.

Clients versus servers

You are probably familiar with the term 'application', that is, a program that runs on your computer and allows you to put information in and get information out. Over the past few years there has been quite a bit of talk and action on the client/server front. Without getting into too much detail, most of the things you do on the Internet you are acting as a client and talking to a server. Examples:

Sending mail, using FTP, accessing Archie, using W3 browsers

The most common exception, where you are running as a server, is when you are *receiving* mail. Other occasions include running an FTP server to allow others to log in to your computer and retrieve files.

I have only drawn attention to this here so that if I mention the term client or server later in this document, you may have an idea of what is meant.

Mosaic – a W3 (World Wide Web) browser

You should have successfully got your Winsock connection to work by following the above section before attempting to get Mosaic running.

Mosaic is available from ftp.demon.co.uk in the following directory:

/pub/ibmpc/winsock/apps/wmosaic

In that directory there are various versions of Mosaic and some extra picture viewers. The latest version of Mosaic at the time of writing is 2.0 alpha 5 and the file is called wmos20a5.zip. Get that file and create a directory to put it in, for example:

cd \windows\wapps md mosaic cd mosaic

and now copy the Mosaic zip file to that directory and unzip it.

pkunzip wmos20a5.zip

Alternatively do not copy it and just put the path in the pkunzip command, for example:

pkunzip c:\tmp\wmos20a5.zip

Once again you can use Windows features and utilities to do the above if you prefer.

There are various files you can read now or later (readme.txt, faq.txt, install.txt, and so on). Copy mosaic.ini to your Windows directory, for example:

copy mosaic.ini \windows

You need to edit mosaic.ini to get maximum use out of the package but we can leave this to later as you are probably getting eager to give this program a try soon!

The later versions of Mosaic require WIN32S which is 32-bit Windows system software and there is a large file win32s.zip which is in the wmosaic directory. If you have already got this then you don't need to download this file. Check by seeing if you have a \windows\system\win32s subdirectory as this is where it normally goes.

If you do download this file (/pub/ibmpc/winsock/apps/wmosaic/win32s.zip) then change to the \windows\system directory:

cd \windows\system

and then type

pkunzip -d win32s

The -d is important as it creates the necessary subdirectories. The above works if your win32s.zip file is in \windows\system. If it isn't then simply type in the full pathname to find it, for example:

pkunzip -d c:\tmp\win32s

This will have created two subdirectories DISK1 and DISK2. You should start Windows, select File and Run and then run the SETUP.EXE program that you will find in the \windows\system\disk1 directory. Follow the instructions on the screen (they are quite straightforward).

The other files in the wmosaic directory of ftp.demon.co.uk include picture viewers, video players and sound players. These are not essential to the running of Mosaic so let's come back to them later.

That's about it! To test, start TCPMAN and select login and, when you are on, double-click on Mosaic and away you go. Our W3 server is http://www.demon.co.uk/ and you can check out my home page which is:

http://www.demon.co.uk/subscribers/w/walm/

Other applications

Finger

A Finger client is very useful. From ftp.demon.co.uk get:

/pub/ibmpc/winsock/apps/wsfinger/fingv11.zip (6,724 bytes)

Make a directory for it, for example:

```
cd \windows\wapps    (change to your Windows applications directory)
md finger            (make a directory for your finger client)
cd finger            (change to that directory)
```

Now unzip the fingv11.zip file into this directory in the normal way. Add an icon for it by running File Manager and dragging fing.exe to a Windows Application Group and dropping it. This default icon is not very pretty so select close or minimize File Manager and select Fing (as it's so delightfully called!) by clicking on it just once. Press Alt-Return to edit the program item properties and then select Change Icon… to select an alternative icon. At the same time you may wish to alter the name to Finger!

To test Finger, bring up TCPMAN in the normal way. Double-click on Finger and then select Finger and then Finger Client. You will be presented with a box asking for host name. To see your mail queue enter post.demon.co.uk.

The next box asks you for a username in which you then enter your nodename. So I would enter walm. This is the same as doing finger walm@post.demon.co.uk (see /pub/doc/Welcome.txt for details of this).

There is a lot of information available via Finger and it is popular as it requires no login procedure so it is a simple way of getting information. Other examples:

```
motd@gate.demon.co.uk    See the message of the day
hel.demon.co.uk          See who is logged on to our Warrington PoP 'hel'
```

As you are part of the demon domain, you can use a short cut and miss off the .demon.co.uk. For example, for post.demon.co.uk just enter post.

Archie

Archie is an archive searching system enabling you to locate filenames and ftp sites easily. A worked example follows. You can in fact access Archie using a telnet command. Far neater is to use an Archie Client, so from ftp.demon.co.uk get:

/pub/ibmpc/winsock/apps/wsarchie/wsarch05.zip (170,113 bytes)

As for all the other applications, create a directory for it; for example, c:\windows\wapps\archie and unzip the program. Run File Manager and drag and drop wsarchie.exe into your desired program group so that an icon is automatically created.

There is only one thing to set up (and that is optional): double-click on Archie to start the application. Select Options and FTP setup. You will see that it already defaults to ws_ftp which we installed earlier. It needs to know where this program is on your hard disk and so you should alter this accordingly: for example, c:\windows\wapps\ws_ftp\ws_ftp.exe and leave the other parameters showing (%h:%d/%f) as they are essential.

The setup will default to src.doc.ic.ac.uk as that is your nearest server – we have a 64K line directly to it (it being the Department of Computing, Imperial College, London).

There are various preferences you can alter by using the Option, Preferences menu.

To test, type in a word such as 'spade' and press Return or click on search. You will see the heading change as the Archie Client interrogates the Server. I suggest spade as for me it found a handful of files in a short amount of time. When it is finished it will fill in the three columns headed Hosts, Directories and Files. A line in each will be highlighted to show the current selection.

The Hosts column gives a list of FTP sites that contain files that matched your search. The Directories column lists the directory paths in which the file(s) are located. The Files column gives the actual file names. You may find that a host has several matches, some of which are in the same directory, and the display will sort this out for you. Select different combinations to look at the matches. You will note that there is a set of lines at the bottom of the screen giving you a bit more information about the selected file, including two most important bits of information: the date and the size.

If you wish to retrieve one of these files simply double-click on the highlighted filename and your FTP client (ws_ftp) will be fired up and will automatically retrieve the file. It will put it into your Archie directory, for example:

c:\windows\wapps\archie

A number of things could go wrong with this:

(1)   You have not got an FTP Client such as ws_ftp set up and so it can't retrieve the file – go and set ws_ftp up.

(2)   It fails to find your FTP Client – you have incorrectly configured the Options, FTP setup option and it can't find the program. Edit that entry as recommended above.

(3)   The FTP Client fires up but after a while stops without retrieving the file – perhaps the FTP Server selected was not available (down for maintenance, too many users, and so on). Or perhaps the file wasn't where Archie thought it was. Try using FTP by hand to see the error message or discover if the file really is there. Archie Servers work by logging on to FTP servers around the world, making a note of their directory structures and filenames and then building an index of them. When your Archie Client asks questions, it has a look in its indexes and sends you the results. The frequency with which Archie Servers log on to FTP servers around the world to check on the latest state of play depends on the Archie Server Administrator. That person has to balance bandwidth, CPU power and other resources against the desire to have up-to-date information. Typically they will be configured to be updated no less than once per month. This is more than adequate for most requirements.

Of course, you don't have to use the local server – a list of others is included and their servers will quite possibly give different results as their set of FTP Servers probably differ from src.doc.ic.ac.uk's ones.

Telnet

Trumpet's own version of telnet is fairly good, although a little lacking in features. It is also quite small. It is available from:

ftp.demon.co.uk:/pub/ibmpc/winsock/stacks/trumpwsk/trmptel.exe
(65,792 bytes)

and that file is the executable itself and not a self-extracting archive. No documentation is supplied. Download it to the directory of your choice, for example c:\windows\wapps\telnet, and then use File Manager in the normal way to add it as an icon and then use it!

To try it out you could telnet to a Gopher client, for example:

telnet gopher.sunet.se

More help

The Windows software is best supported in the demon.ip.winsock* newsgroups. You will get the fastest and most accurate responses by asking there. The support mailbox internet@demon.net and the support help line can only offer assistance with the login and not with any applications, so please try to use the newsgroups.

What next

Install more packages. Do some more configuring on TCPMAN. Read wintcp.txt which contains more advanced information on configuring and using TCPMAN. Read winmos.txt which contains more advanced information on configuring and using Mosaic.

This document was written by Grahame Davies and I would ask you to please give feedback where possible in the newsgroups. I can be mailed at:

grahame@walm.demon.co.uk

which is the mail address for the wee hours of the morning. My work mail address is:

grahame@demon.net.

Stop press

Demon Internet have their own complete comprehensive Windows installer on their ftp server ftp.demon.co.uk in /pub/ibmpc/DIS called diswin.exe. Beta test versions of this are available from /pub/ibmpc/DIS/beta.

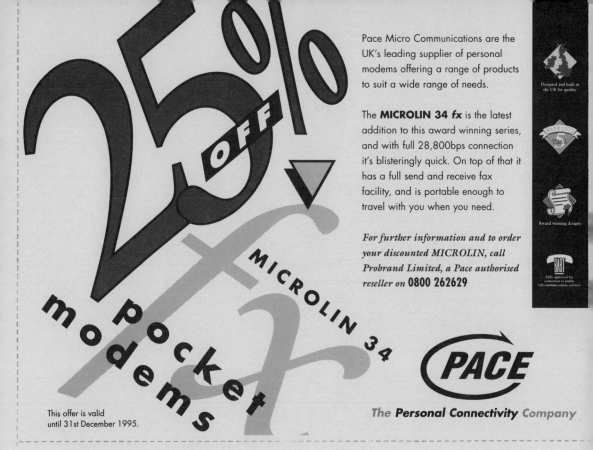

25% OFF

OFF

MICROLIN 34

fx

pocket modems

Pace Micro Communications are the UK's leading supplier of personal modems offering a range of products to suit a wide range of needs.

The **MICROLIN 34 fx** is the latest addition to this award winning series, and with full 28,800bps connection it's blisteringly quick. On top of that it has a full send and receive fax facility, and is portable enough to travel with you when you need.

For further information and to order your discounted MICROLIN, call Probrand Limited, a Pace authorised reseller on **0800 262629**

Designed and built in the UK for quality

Award winning designs

Fully approved for connection to public telecommunications services

This offer is valid until 31st December 1995.

PACE

The Personal Connectivity Company

Ethix Distribution Ltd are pleased to offer:

1 copy of

Net*Manage* Internet Chameleon

at a special price of £99 *plus VAT, shipping*

Normally £139 *plus VAT, shipping*

Internet Chameleon includes:

- WebSurfer, Archie, Gopher, Email, NewsReader, FTP client & server, Telnet and more!
- Windows user interface
- 5 minute installation
- Easy dial-up; supports SLIP, CSLIP, PPP and ISDN
- 256+ colour support

This offer is valid until 31st December 1995.

NAME (AND COMPANY NAME IF APPLICABLE) _____

ADDRESS _____

_____

_____

POST CODE _____   TEL NO: _____

PLEASE SUPPLY _____ MICROLIN 34FX(S) AT £ _____ : _____ (RRP EACH)

LESS 25% PACE DISCOUNT £ _____ : _____

DELIVERY £ _____ : _____

VAT £ _____ : _____

SIGNED _____   **TOTAL £ _____ : _____**

TO OBTAIN THIS SPECIAL DISCOUNT PRICE YOU MUST PRESENT THIS CARD
(PHOTOCOPIES ARE NOT ACCEPTABLE) TO:

PROBRAND LIMITED,
49 CAMDEN STREET
BIRMINGHAM, B1 3BP
TEL: 0800 262629
FAX: 021 626 0268

E & O E

PACE

The **Personal Connectivity** Company

Internet Chameleon Order Form:

Please send me a copy of the Internet Chameleon!

Quantity	Product	Price
1	Internet Chameleon	£99 special price plus VAT
	VAT	£17.32
	Shipping	£8.00
Total		**£124.32**

Credit Card Information:

☐ VISA   ☐ Access/Master Card

Card Number .... Expires ....

Full Name on Card (Please Print) ....

Please Ship to:

Name: ....

Address: ....

....

Postcode: ....   Telephone Number ....

All orders and enquiries to be sent to:

Ethix Distribution Ltd, Ethix House, Meadow Court, South Normanton, Derbyshire DE55 2BN
Tel: +44 (0)1773 863666   Fax: +44 (0)1773 863919   E-mail: sales@calibra.demon.co.uk

Appendix 5b

Setting up NetManage Chameleon for Windows

(Parts of this revised chapter are copyright 1994 Demon Internet Services)

Author's note: This appendix has been revised from Jim Evans's original to include instructions for setting up NetManage Chameleon version 4.1, launched in December 1994. If you have an older copy of NetManage Chameleon you are recommended to download the text file ***chamel.txt*** from ***ftp.demon.co.uk/pub/doc/general***. Readers may like to keep an eye on the ***alt.chameleon*** Usenet group for ongoing news and support for the product.

What is Chameleon?

Chameleon from NetManage is a combined suite of Internet utilities for Windows 3.1 computers, connected to the Internet via a modem. It provides everything you need to navigate the Internet, and provides mail, news, and file search and retrieve facilities including Archie, Gopher, and – in version 4.1 – a World Wide Web browser. You'll need a TCP/IP based Internet account from an Internet provider before you can use the program. You can't use Chameleon with terminal accounts such as those provided by CIX, CompuServe, or Delphi.

What's new in version 4.1?

Version 4.1 includes an Archie client (see Chapter 7), a World Wide Web browser (see Chapter 10) and enhanced news features. It's also being sold at a lower price than the previous versions (see discount coupon).

Installing Chameleon

What you need:

You'll need a 286 or better PC with Windows 3.1 installed, or OS/2 Warp

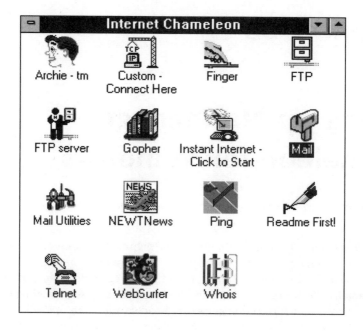

Figure A5b.1

installed over the top of Windows 3.1. The installation takes up about seven megabytes of disk space, but you'll need more than this to accommodate files and data you download with the program. A minimum of 15 megabytes free disk space is therefore recommended.

8 megabytes of RAM is recommended for all Windows PCs, although Chameleon will run on machines equipped with a minimum of 4 Mb.

You'll also need a modem and cable (see Appendix 2).

You can install Chameleon to operate with any Internet provider who provides full TCP/IP access. You cannot use Chameleon with a terminal type Internet account. These are sometimes called 'shell' accounts. You must therefore already have an IP address such as 158.152.24.106 and a password from the Information provider you are using.

The program comes on three separate 3.5" disks. The disks are protected by a serial number. If you don't have the serial number you won't be able to configure Chameleon to work correctly.

If you have previously installed any versions of Chameleon you are recommended to delete the old files, and the directory they live in, before you install the new version.

Installing

(1)   Backup your Windows INI files by copying them to another directory:

From DOS type:

C:\
MD inibup

copy c:\windows*.ini c:\inibup

You can use these backups to restore Windows if the installation fails midway for any reason.

(2)   Return to Windows and put Chameleon Disk 1 into Drive A:

- Choose Run from the File menu
- Type A:\Setup and select OK

Fill in the Serial Number and Key Code dialogues with the numbers supplied with the package and choose the DOS directory where you want to put the files. The default is C:\NETMANAG.

When the installation is complete you'll find a new program group in Windows called Internet Chameleon. From here you'll need to configure your dialling and Internet set-up from information given to you by your provider.

Important note:
If you decide to use anything other than the default C:\NETMANAG directory you must check the [TCP/IP] section of the WIN.INI file to ensure that Chameleon has installed the correct path. You should also check your AUTOEXEC.BAT file to make sure that the correct path is included.

Setting up for Demon users

These instructions are mainly for subscribers to Demon Internet Services, although they provide a model for users of other services. In the example the account is set up for SMTP mail, although Chameleon also operates with POP3 mail servers.

(1)   Ignore the 'Instant Internet – Click to Start' icon unless your Internet provider has sent you a custom start-up file for Chameleon.
Click on the 'Custom-Connect Here' icon instead.

(2) Configure interface:

- Click Interface.
- Click Add.

An entry box appears and defaults to Ethernet0 – unless you have upgraded from a previous version.

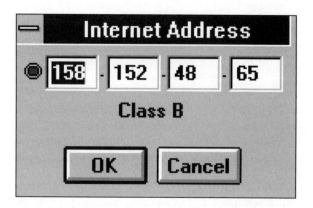

Figure A5b.2   *IP address settings.*

- Click on the down arrow to drop the alternative interface types.

- Click PPP or use the down arrow key to highlight PPP – accept the name of PPP0.

The Name should show PPP0 and the type should be PPP. Press Enter or click OK to set up the interface.

PPP0 should now be highlighted as the interface that you will continue to configure. Additionally, under the Name section you should see an asterisk. This means that this is the default interface.

(3)   Configure setup:

Select the Setup menu and work down the available options as follows:

- IP address - enter your IP address.

This is the IP address of your node as in 158.152.24.106. (Don't use these numbers, or you'll get a bill from the Author for using her account.)

The type of IP address will automatically change to Class B. This is correct. See Figure A5b.2.

- Subnet Mask – don't change anything here. The Subnet Mask should be 255.255.0.0.

- Host Name – add the 4–8 character name you agreed with Demon as 's-sco' as in s-sco.demon.co.uk Do not enter the '.demon.co.uk'.

- Domain Name – enter demon.co.uk.

- Port – select the modem configuration you use – see Figure A5b.3.

Baud 38400 (for V32 bis modems or 9600 for V22 bis modems)

```
┌─────────────────────────────────────────────────────┐
│ ━             Port Settings                         │
├─────────────────────────────────────────────────────┤
│ ┌─Baud Rate──────────────────────────────────────┐  │
│ │   ○ 2400        ○ 9600         ○ 19200         │  │
│ │   ◉ 38400       ○ 57600        ○ 115200        │  │
│ └────────────────────────────────────────────────┘  │
│ ┌─Data Bits────────────────┐ ┌─Stop Bits─────────┐  │
│ │  ○ 5  ○ 6  ○ 7  ◉ 8     │ │ ◉ 1  ○ 1.5  ○ 2 │  │
│ └──────────────────────────┘ └───────────────────┘  │
│ ┌─Parity───┐┌─Flow Control─────┐┌─Connector───────┐ │
│ │ ◉ None   ││  ◉ Hardware     ││  ○ None        │ │
│ │ ○ Odd    ││  ○ None         ││  ○ COM1        │ │
│ │ ○ Even   │└──────────────────┘│  ◉ COM2        │ │
│ │ ○ Mark   │ □ Parity Check    │  ○ COM3        │ │
│ │ ○ Space  │ ☒ Carrier Detect  │  ○ COM4        │ │
│ └──────────┘└──────────────────┘└─────────────────┘ │
│              ┌──────────┐  ┌──────────┐             │
│              │   OK     │  │ Cancel   │             │
│              └──────────┘  └──────────┘             │
└─────────────────────────────────────────────────────┘
```

Figure A5b.3   *Com port settings for Windows3.1.*

Bits 8
Parity n
Stops 1
Flow control – Click 'Hardware'
Port COM1 (Or COM2 if you have a mouse on COM1)
Parity Check – No. (The check box should be empty)
Carrier Detect – Yes. (The check box should have an X) BUT.....

Your modem MUST be configured to sense Carrier Detect. On a Hayes modem the command is AT &C1. You must add this command to your Initialize string to use Carrier Detect (CD) sensing. If you don't, or if you don't have the correct set-up, Chameleon will not run the login script (defined in SLIP.INI) as it cannot see the carrier detect signal from the modem. If your login script refuses to run on login then check this modem setting first.

- Modem – Hayes modems will work the defaults of Dial = ATDT and Initialize = ATQ0V1E0M1&C1 (see Figure A5b.4). Hayes 'compatible' modems will demand that you read the modem manual to set hard handshaking and Carrier Detect to on (See Appendix 2).

If you have to use Pulse (rotary) dialling (sometimes called Loop Disconnect or LD) set the Dial entry under Setup Modem to ATDP.

If you have Network Services Redirect installed (bleeping dial tone) your modem will not recognize the dial tone. Put X1 (for Hayes modems) at the end of the Initialize string. For non-Hayes modems check the manual for a

Figure A5b.4 *Modem settings – make sure you set hard handshake on with a Hayes command.*

command which tells the modem to ignore dial tone and place it in the Initialize string.

● Dial – increase the time-out to at least 60 seconds and click on Start Log so that there is an X in the box. While you are setting up Demon you may find it useful to set the time-out to 120 seconds.

Put in the phone number of the nearest PoP for your provider (see Appendix 8). If you are going via a PABX put a 9, (nine comma) before the number to make the PABX give the modem an outside line.

● Check the Redial after Timing out and Signal when connected boxes, (an X will be seen).

If you are using a Hayes Optima or other advanced modem you can tell the modem to drop carrier if an error-corrected connection isn't made (see Appendix 2). If you do this then check the 'Redial After Carrier is lost' box.

Login – enter the following three fields:

● User Name, enter your Demon nodename. This is the same as Host Name as entered above, i.e. your 4–8 character name as in *s-sco*. This is not your mail user name, as in *sue*.

● Password – enter your password.

● Startup Command – enter PPP.

● Interface Name – accept PPP0.

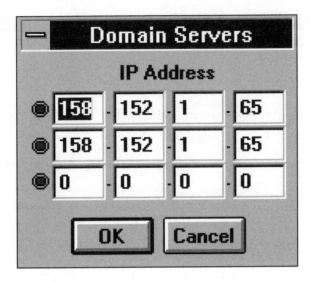

Figure A5b.5   *Setting domain servers for Demon.*

- Route Entries – all should be 0.0.0.0.
- BOOTP – leave as 0.0.0.0.

Configure 'Services'

Click on Services.

- Default Gateway – enter 158.152.1.65 (this is gate.demon.co.uk or another Demon default gateway).
- Frequent Destinations – ignore it for dial-up use.
- Domain Servers – enter 158.152.1.65 in the first entry and 158.152.1.193 in the second. (see Figure A5b.5)
- SNMP – ignore this field.
- Host Table – this should be empty.

Close the Custom application and save the changes when asked.

Setting up the SLIP.INI file

There's a copy of the SLIP.INI file in the Demon directory on the disk that accompanies this revision of the *UK Internet Book*. If it's missing or corrupt then use NotePad or a similar text editor to edit a SLIP.INI file in your NETMANAG directory to look like Figure A5b.6.

```
─                    Notepad - SLIP.INI                    ▼ ▲
 File   Edit   Search   Help
[DEFAULT]                                                      ↑
SCRIPT=login: $u$r word: $p$r Protocol: $c$r HELLO $r
TYPE=SLIP

[SLIP0]
SCRIPT=login: $u$r word: $p$r Protocol: $c$r HELLO $r
TYPE=SLIP

[PPP0]
SCRIPT=login: $u$r word: $p$r Protocol: $c$r HELLO $r
TYPE=PPP

|
                                                              ↓
←                                                             →
```

Figure A5b.6   *The SLIP.INI file for Chameleon and Demon.*

Note that SLIP0 and PPP0 contain zeros, not the letter O. There's a space after HELLO, a CR/LF before the 'TYPE=' statement and between each line. Miss them out, and you'll have problems. See p. 36 of the Chameleon manual for scripting examples.

Making a modem connection

- Connect your modem to the correct port and power it on.
- Click Custom – there will be a short delay.
- Click Connect – you should get a dialling box.

If you wish to see a log of what is happening then click on Setup and choose Log. This will allow you to see the progress of the Login including any messages. You should see the AT command sequences beginning with AT and with a response of OK which sets up your modem. Then you will see the dial string ATDT or ATDP (for Tone or Pulse dial), the modem will dial, get the connect message and then the user ID and password handshake with the Demon machine.

The Login is finished when the Word HELLO appears, and a second or two later the word Connect on the menu bar changes to Disconnect.

If the program connects successfully the connection dialog box disappears and, if you have the audio box checked, you will hear a beep. You are now connected to the Internet.

Other Chameleon applications

Before you can use any of the applications other than Mail you must have a connection open to Demon – start Custom and do Connect.

You can prepare Mail, and read previously recovered mail offline without starting custom.

For Demon users, the most useful applications with Chameleon are Mail, FTP and telnet. Mail and News require further configuration, described below.

Configuring Mail

- Start the Mail application – the icon with the mailbox. If there is no connection open, there may be a delay while Mail tries to communicate and gives up.

- Select the one predefined user, Postmaster, and click OK.

- Under Services, Mailboxes, User, type the name without spaces that you wish to use for your mail, for example *sue*. Click Add.

In the box that results, you may type a password. This prevents anyone else reading mail from your PC – it is not passed to your Internet service.

- Put the full name that you want to be known by in the 'In real life' box.

- Accept the default mail directory that is offered unless you have a good reason not to.

- Click OK.

If other members of the family have separate mail IDs on a Demon account, you can add them as well with different names. Demon allows multiple names at one machine. Chameleon provides that support. However you cannot have multiple names if you are using Demon's POP3 mail service.

- When you have finished adding names, click Save, to save the name configuration.

- Click File, Exit and Save the changes.

Now you have to configure each user you have added.

For each user,

- Re-start the Mail application. Login to Mail, with the user ID and password that you just gave them.

- Under Settings, Network, Mail Gateway, enter the Demon Mail Machine you use, as in *post.demon.co.uk*. (This is for SMTP mail use.)

- Under Settings, Network, Mail Server, enter nothing unless you have taken out POP3 mail service which is an extra charge. If you have, then type the following:

Host: the full name of the PC you are using – e.g. ***yourpc.demon.co.uk***.
User: the user name that you just logged into mail with.
Password: the password that you just used to login to mail with.
Directory: the full directory where that user's mail is stored, e.g. ***c:\netmanag\email\sue*** (your username). See Figure A5b.7.

- Click on the Delete Mail from Server to remove the X (cross). You can put this back later when you have proved that Mail is working correctly.

Demon users:

Each time you log in to Demon you should start mail, log in with the user ID you want to collect mail for and click the minimize box. This will leave the mail application running in the background, ready to be probed by Demon if there is mail waiting. When mail arrives the PC will bleep, the mailbox icon will change to open with a letter sticking out of it.

POP3 users:

You will keep getting duplicate copies of your mail every few minutes until you change the Settings, Network, Mail Server, Delete Mail from Server to Yes, that is put a X in that box and save the configuration file (File Save). Do that when you know that Mail is working OK and you don't want to use another package to receive copies of the mail as well.

Read the manual about setting up folders, composing mail, setting up the address book etc.

Configuring NewtNews

Before you use NewtNews you should have configured all users you need as users of mail.

- Double-click the News Icon.

- Click OK on the NewtNews – what happens next depends on whether Mail is running. If you are already logged into Mail, you will not be asked to log in to News. Otherwise log in as your mail user ID which will be available when you drop the login box.

- Click Connect on the NewtNews Menu, enter news.demon.co.uk in the Host Box and click OK.

Accept the offer to create a list of groups.

If you use ALT-TAB to go to another application in Windows, you risk the communications timing out. If you have a fast machine you may be able to do other work – if you have a slower machine then the communications will take most of the capacity and you will find other applications sluggish.

Figure A5b.7   *Setting up Chameleon up for POP3 mail.*

Use Windows Techniques to select the Groups you want to 'subscribe' to. To select groups scroll through the list and hold the control key down while you click the groups that are of interest – they will be highlighted. Don't choose more than six to start with! You can add to them later. Click the + symbol and an S appears beside the groups you subscribe to.

● Double-click the Close box and Chameleon will update the groups. This will take some time.

● Save to save the configuration.

● Double-click on the Group you want to read.

Scroll through the list of messages, double-clicking on ones that interest you, or start at the top, read the first message and use the right and left arrows on the tool bar to read next or previous. Messages are read in date and time order. When you see something you want to comment on, click on the 'Reply to article' button. Compose your reply. In the From: box enter your nickname and formal mail address (if it is not already there).

Do File, Save to save the configuration - to keep the modified mail address which will now be used for News and Mail postings.

When you have read all the articles in a group that interest you, click Groups, Catch-up or Control-U. Then, immediately, do File, Save. Otherwise if your machine hangs before you exit News, you will get all the news you have already read next time.

Thanks to Jim Evans for parts of this appendix.

Appendix 6

Getting started with Macs

The key to Mac Internet working is a single control panel called MacTCP. It's not included with System 7.1 but it is included in System 7.5. (System 7.1 users can get a free update, courtesy of Apple UK and Demon. Details are on the Demon coupon enclosed with the book.) You install it by dropping into your System folder, rebooting, and then assigning your SLIP or PPP driver to it (see below). You'll need MacTCP before you can get going, so mail the coupon off straight away.

You will need a second utility to allow you to use your Internet connection over a phone line. There are two methods: Point-to-Point Protocol (PPP) or Serial Line Interface Protocol (SLIP). Demon will supply you with a Mac installer disk if you want to use Shareware programs. However, the process of getting going is much easier with VersaTerm Link, which is available as part of the VersaTerm set, available from Mac dealers.

You'll need a modem and Mac cable configured to use hard-handshaking (RTS-CTS) because use of XON/XOFF codes will interfere with your TCP connection. We used Intertext IX33, Hayes Optima 144 and Pace Microlin modems with the Macs used in the production of this book.

Electronic mail presents a problem for Mac users. There are two main mail 'standards' in use on the Internet; Post Office Protocol 3 (POP3) and Simple Mail Transfer Protocol (SMTP). Many of the Shareware and commercial programs use POP3 but until recently this service hasn't been available from Demon. The trick is to use an SMTP mail program called LeeMail to get your mail, and a second program (Eudora) to send it. Demon also offer POP3 mail, which you'll need to get the best from VersaTerm if you use it. At the moment there is a hefty charge for Demon's POP3 service but this may be reduced as more POP3 users sign up.

NB: If you opt for POP3 mail you will lose the ability to have multiple user names at your node.

Other POP3 mail programs which will now work over dial-up include TechMail-S, which has its own built-in SLIP software.

At the moment there are no Mac Shareware programs which will read news onto disk for later perusal. This means you are paying fees to read news live over a phone line. However, VersaTerm Link has a fine offline newsreader built-in which can save the costs of the program within a short time. Again, more Shareware news utilities are in beta-test and Demon will be able to advise you on their availability.

For file transfers most recreational Mac users will be happy with Fetch, an FTP application, and there are dozens of programs for telnetting around the Internet. Demon also keep many Mac TCP/IP utilities on their server at ftp.demon.co.uk, and there is no shortage of good Gopher, WAIS, FTP and other utilities for the Mac. Support for Mac users is widespread in Usenet newsgroups.

If you can afford it, the author recommends VersaTerm Link and a Demon POP3 mail account for unrivalled ease of use. VersaTerm Link is a one-shot mail/offline news/ftp/ and telnet utility. It is bundled with VersaTerm 5, together with MacTCP – everything you need for £149.00 net. Details from the distributors: Principal on 01706 832000.

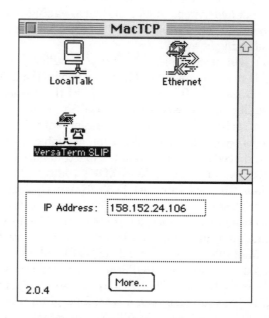

Figure A6.1 *First you'll need a working credit card and a machine name. Make your name something recognizable: like fred@smith. demon.co.uk. Then phone Demon and open an account. If you want to use Shareware ask for the Mac Starter Kit disk. Demon will supply MacTCP on receipt of the coupon from this book.*

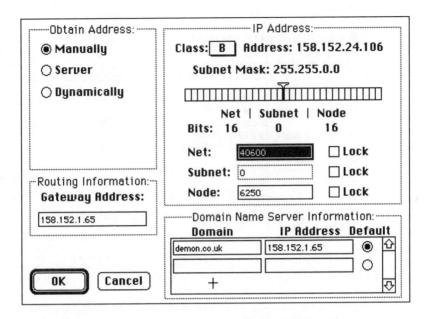

Figure A6.2   *You'll need to set up MacTCP with your machine name. Here's what it looks like set up for my account (158.152.24.106). Put your machine number there. You'll need to copy the gateway address and domain details if your screen doesn't look like this.*

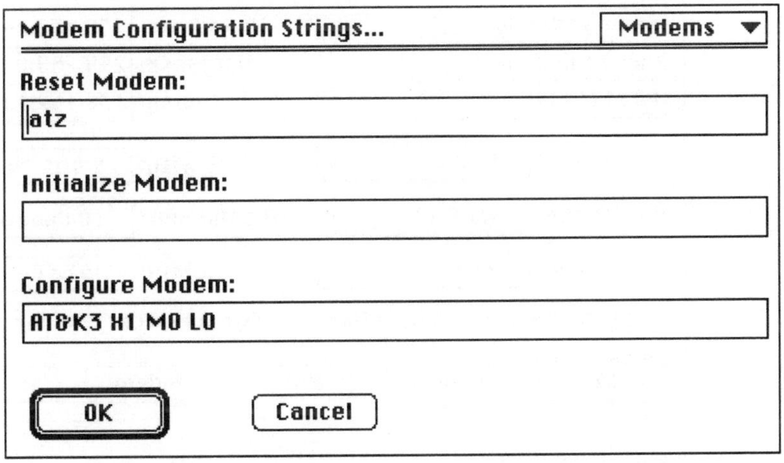

Modem Configuration Strings...   Modems ▼

Reset Modem:

atz

Initialize Modem:

Configure Modem:

AT&K3 H1 M0 L0

OK   Cancel

Figure A6.3   *You'll need to tell SLIP or PPP how to set your modem. These are the commands to make PPP work with a Hayes Optima. The most important is AT&K3 which sets hard handshaking.*

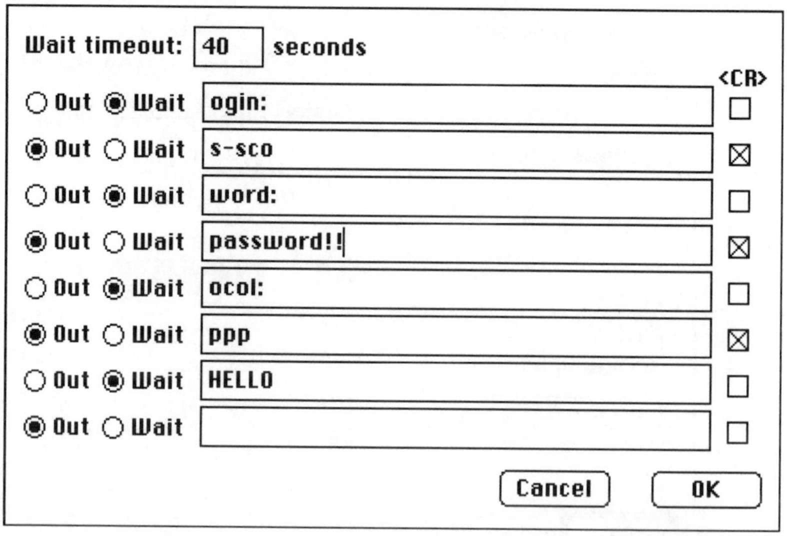

Wait timeout: [40] seconds

<CR>

○ Out ◉ Wait [ogin:] ☐

◉ Out ○ Wait [s-sco] ☒

○ Out ◉ Wait [word:] ☐

◉ Out ○ Wait [password!!|] ☒

○ Out ◉ Wait [ocol:] ☐

◉ Out ○ Wait [ppp] ☒

○ Out ◉ Wait [HELLO] ☐

◉ Out ○ Wait [ ] ☐

[Cancel] [OK]

Figure A6.4   *Config PPP and SLIP utilities offer scripting to log you into the host server. Your login script will look broadly similar – don't forget to click the box to add a carriage return to the end of each string you send.*

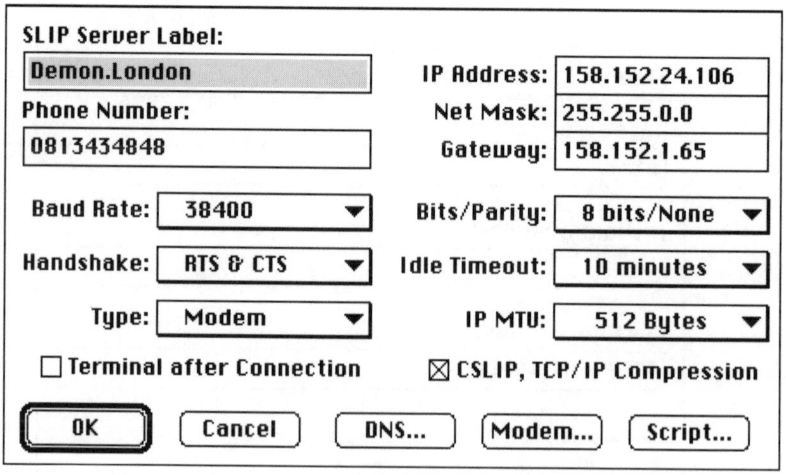

SLIP Server Label:

[Demon.London]   IP Address: [158.152.24.106]

Phone Number: Net Mask: [255.255.0.0]

[0813434848]   Gateway: [158.152.1.65]

Baud Rate: [38400 ▼]   Bits/Parity: [8 bits/None ▼]

Handshake: [RTS & CTS ▼]   Idle Timeout: [10 minutes ▼]

Type: [Modem ▼]   IP MTU: [512 Bytes ▼]

☐ Terminal after Connection   ☒ CSLIP, TCP/IP Compression

[OK] [Cancel] [DNS...] [Modem...] [Script...]

Figure A6.5   *Make sure that SLIP or PPP uses the correct addresses. This is a SLIP configuration screen...*

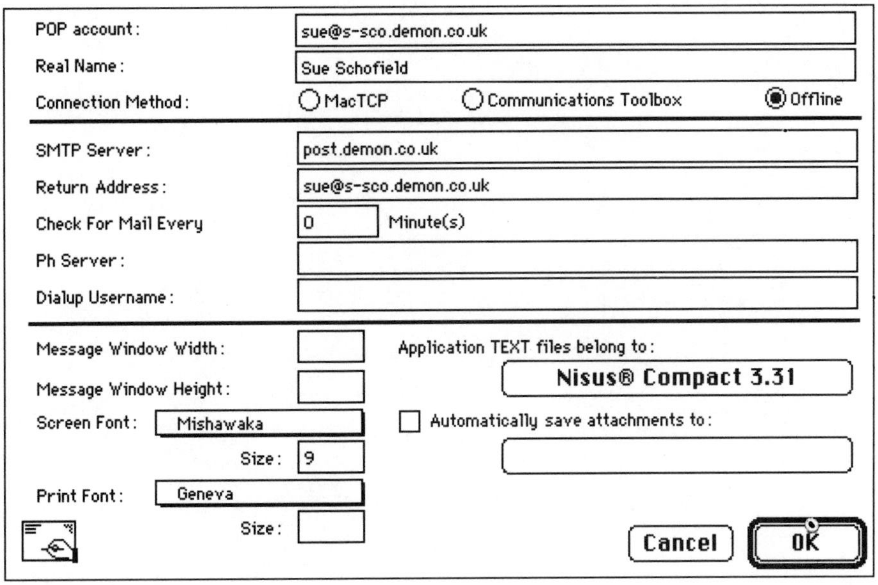

POP account :	sue@s-sco.demon.co.uk

Real Name :	Sue Schofield

Connection Method : ○ MacTCP   ○ Communications Toolbox   ● Offline

SMTP Server :	post.demon.co.uk

Return Address :	sue@s-sco.demon.co.uk

Check For Mail Every	0	Minute(s)

Ph Server :	

Dialup Username :	

Message Window Width : [ ]

Application TEXT files belong to :

Message Window Height : [ ]

Nisus® Compact 3.31

Screen Font : [Mishawaka]   ☐ Automatically save attachments to :

Size : 9   [ ]

Print Font : [Geneva]

Size : [ ]   (Cancel) (OK)

Figure A6.6   *... and the setup for Eudora. Eudora will handle all of your mail for you if you get the new mail-in add-on.*

Appendix 7

Getting started with Amiga computers

(Copyright Demon Internet Services 1994 and reproduced with kind permission)

Author's note: As for all the other computer platforms, Internet software for the Amiga computer is burgeoning, and readers are advised to contact Demon for information about the latest software. My thanks to Oliver at Demon Internet Services for his assistance with this section of the book. The complete electronic version of this file contains instructions for setting up and using utilities such as ping, Gopher, telnet, and so on. It may be worth noting that the initial download now provided by Demon for Amiga users is AmigaDIS rather than the AmiTCP software described in this appendix. Feedback from Amiga-nauts indicates that they seem to prefer AmiTCP, so the instructions are included here.

Introduction

If you are already using AmiTCP and you don't see why you should read lots of 'waffle', then rather than ignore this text completely, please at least read the section 'Using AmiTCP' as a minimum.

If you are new to comms completely, read through this introduction and the following section on installation carefully before beginning the installation.

The AmiTCP FAQ (answers to Frequently Asked Questions) is 'AmiTCP:Doc/AmiTCP-FAQ.Txt'. Please read this file carefully before phoning technical support with lots of questions. You may also find it interesting to skim through before using AmiTCP as it contains lots of interesting tidbits.

About AmiTCP

AmiTCP is an Amiga Shared Library that implements a Berkley Sockets API within the AmigaDOS environment. Or, in English, AmiTCP is a standard Amiga 'library' of routines that allows your Amiga to become a part of the

Internet; it does this by providing an interface through which programs on your computer can talk other programs without having to worry too much about where the other programs are located or what kind of machine they are running on. This interface is known as a 'Socket API' (API stands for Application Program Interface, of course :). AmiTCP also implements the TCP/IP protocol which is required for your machine to talk to the Internet.

AmiTCP is unlike other Amiga networking packages in that:

- Unlike DNet it actually brings the net to your machine; you can run existing 'sockets' based applications on your machine which talk directly to the Internet.

- Unlike AmigaNOS it is not a 'closed' package; you can add new external programs such as Mosaic, Gopher, and so on. Also, it does not provide any 'built-in' programs for news, mail, and so on. It simply provides TCP/IP on your machine and an interface for applications.

- It is 'SANA II' compliant (a standard developed by Commodore) which means you can use it with any SANA II compliant device driver, such as Ethernet cards, parallel port network drivers, and so on, or modem drivers such as CSlip or PPP. You can get some weird and wonderful SANA II drivers, such as those that allow you to network Amigas via the floppy disk drive interface!

About the installer

This installer is free, but designed for use by Demon Internet subscribers. Whilst there is no rule saying non-Demon users can't use it, there isn't much point in trying. Certain assumptions are made which are only valid if you intend connecting through a Demon Internet account.

The installer is intended for use with a Standard Dialup account. If you wish to use it on a local Ethernet, for example, it is recommended that you use the initial installation and then modify as required.

Installation

Basic requirements

- Amiga compatible computer running 2.0 or above.

- Hard drive or at least 2 x 1.4 Mb floppy drives. (Running on floppies is probably possible, but will restrict you so much as to make it pointless.)

- 640 K of free RAM (at least.)

- An account with Demon Internet.

Note: This installation is designed for a Standard Dialup (£10 per month) account.

Additional requirements

If you wish to use some of the flashier applications, such as Mosaic, 2 Mb of RAM is required as a bare minimum, and 4 Mb to be realistic. You may require other libraries, and so on, for other packages; for instance, Mosaic requires MUI. MagicWB is recommended – it makes the Amiga look so much nicer.

Installing AmiTCP

Log on to Demon using ordinary comms software. Log in using the nodename you asked for without the demon part; thus if you asked for 'kfs-uk', you would see:

    login: kfs-uk

(where you enter the 'kfs-uk').

You will then be asked to choose a password. Make a note of this. You will also be told your IP address (158.152.x.y), which you also need to make a note of. My IP address is 158.152.16.231.

Having done this, you should now be able to complete the installation by double-clicking on the 'Install_AmiTCP' icon in the AmiTCP directory. Answer the questions asked, they should all be pretty simple. And then you're away!

The installer provides you with the following:

Service	Program(s)
Archie	Archie
AmiTCP Chat	Chat (only works between AmiTCP systems)
DNS Checking	AskHost
Finger	Finger
FTP	NCFTP or old BSD-style FTP
Gopher	Gopher
Hop Check	TraceRoute
Mail	GW-Mail (and henchmen)
Messages	XMsg and AmiMsgD
News	GW-News (and stooges)
Ping	Ping
Telnet	Napsaterm or 'telnet' script
Unix Talk	Talk

Installing other packages

This installer is only intended to 'get you going'. It installs AmiTCP and configures the various files required, and it installs some 'essentials' such as mail, news, telnet, ftp and a few other niceties. It doesn't, however, install any of the more fancy AmiTCP applications. You will, no doubt, want to install Mosaic. You will generally find a good collection of AmiTCP utilities on

ftp.demon.co.uk:/pub/Amiga/amitcp/utils or
ftp.demon.co.uk:/pub/amiga/amitcp/extras

Which means 'On the machine "ftp.demon.co.uk" in the directory /pub/amiga/amitcp/...'

You should install and correctly set up your basic installation before trying to add any of the other bonus features.

For example, to download the current version of Mosaic (at the time of writing), you will need to connect to Demon and, once connected, do something like:

1.> ncftp ftp.demon.co.uk

<login waffle>

ncftp> bin
ftp.demon.co.uk:/
ncftp> cd /pub/amiga/amitcp/extras
ftp.demon.co.uk:/pub/amiga/amitcp/extras
ncftp> dir Mos*
-rw-r--r-- 1 oliver group 390519 Jun 25 23:14 Mosaic_1.2_AmiTCP.lha
-rw-r--r-- 1 oliver group 320 Jun 25 23:14 Mosaic_1.2_AmiTCP.readme
ncftp> get Mosaic_1.2.AmiTCP.lha...
ncftp> quit

You should then extract the archive, consult the documentation and follow the installation procedure specific to the individual package.

Installing Mosaic

Firstly, you need to follow the instructions above; maybe not to the letter, as a new version of Mosaic may be available. Please use a little bit of noddle. If you see 'Mosaic_1.3_AmiTCP.lha' then download that instead of 1.2 (unless it contains the word 'update', in which case use a bit more intelligence and download the previous version as well).

You will also need MUI (The Magic User Interface). It is worth checking ftp.demon.co.uk:/pub/amiga/amitcp/util/wb for the latest version; please note, you only require the mui??usr.lha, not the mui??dev.lha, which is the extra bits and pieces for people wishing to write programs that use MUI. Install this first (it's fairly straightforward, and has become even simpler with version 2.1, which now uses a single directory rather than splatting stuff all over the place).

Once this is installed, extract Mosaic into the AmiTCP: directory (this will create a subdirectory in AmiTCP: called Mosaic). You should then be able to run Mosaic simply by double-clicking on the Mosaic icon.

Using AmiTCP – starting AmiTCP and connecting

The DIS AmiTCP installation is designed for users who are not permanently connected to their providers, and who are generally using a dial-up device. The original AmiTCP installer assumed that it should configure all 'interfaces' as though you were permanently connected. The DIS installation assumes that you may want to have AmiTCP running without being connected to Demon. This installer allows for that.

Starting up

To load AmiTCP, issue the 'StartNet' command (amitcp:bin/startnet). This loads the shared library and all the relevant modules, and leaves you ready to go, all bar one minor detail – it doesn't connect you to Demon. You are an Internet island :). Some programs, such as guess what, Mosaic, won't load unless AmiTCP is active, although they aren't generally fussy about whether the link is up or not. In order to be able to experiment with such programs, or if, like myself, you simply wish to have AmiTCP loaded all the time, this StartNet script does not cause AmiTCP to try to dial out. You can quite safely place 'execute amitcp:bin/startnet' in your user start-up script without fear of incurring any additional phone bills.

[DIS]Connecting

The ARexx script 'amitcp:bin/link' is used to control the connection. Entering the command:

    1.> link up

should cause your machine to dial in to your chosen PoP and establish a SLIP connection, bringing your machine online to the Internet. It tells the system about a 'route' to the Internet via your serial port and tells the system that this is the default route for any destinations your machine doesn't already know about; so this set-up will quite happily coexist with a local Ethernet or AX25 set-up, and so on.

    1.> link down

will delete the above route and tell the SLIP driver (gwcslip.device) to disconnect from Demon by hanging up.

I personally use the 'fkey' commodity so that Alt-F6 executes 'link up' and Alt-F7 executes 'link down', thus giving me key-press access to the Internet.

When you're connected

Once you've connected, there are no flashy graphics, no prompts, no requesters. You may have a window appear reporting 'GWCSlip.device is on-line (again)'. But that's it. AmiTCP provides you with a connection. What happens over that connection depends on what software you choose to run.

The first time you connect, or any time you are unsure whether your connection is working, you should try to verify that you can 'reach' onto the Net. Start by using the following command:

    1.> ping gate or 1.> ping 158.152.1.65

If only one line of response comes back within 30 seconds or so, or if you get a message saying 'Network down' or 'Destination unreachable' then something is awry and you should check your installation or possibly re-install AmiTCP.

To get out of 'ping' press CTRL-C.

Assuming that you get messages saying '64 bytes received from...' or similar, then the first stage of your connection is working. Next you should try:

    1.> ping ftp.wustl.edu

which is a huge archive on the other side of the pond. If you experience messages saying unreachable or network down, again check your configuration or re-install. If, however, you get responses back, then your system is ready to go.

Note: having asked him nicely, Graham Walter (author of GWCSlip) is looking into the possibility of 'dial on demand', whereby GWCSlip will tell AmiTCP there is a connection available and, whenever AmiTCP tries to send a packet out, if the link has been dropped GWCSlip will re-establish it.

Utilities

The Internet is a vast place. Different computers on the Internet provide different services of all kinds. In order to use any of those services, all you need is your standard dial-up, the address of the remote machine, and appropriate software to make use of the services. Many of the services are purely text based, and simply using telnet will be sufficient to use them. Others, such as FTP or the World Wide Web, require extra software. There is a large and growing range of applications available for AmiTCP. You can get them from Demon Internet Services.

Oliver@demon.co.uk

Appendix 8

List of Internet access providers in the UK as of 30 June 1994

Prices and services offered may change without notice. Readers are advised to ensure that services and pricing offered meet their need before signing service contracts.

Author's note (1): This compilation is copyright 1994 Paola Kathuria and reprinted here with kind permission. (Additions for this reprint only are by the author.) All other rights reserved. There's an updated list on the sampler disk.

Please send any additions and corrections to

paola@arcglade.demon.co.uk.

This modified list contains information on providers who offer commercial and private users a connection to the Internet. Providers offering access to any of e-mail, Usenet, telnet or ftp are included and entries are prepared by the providers themselves. Facilities offered have not been verified by the author in every case.

The original long and summary lists can be obtained in two ways:

Usenet:
Posted monthly to alt.internet.access.wanted, uk.net, uk.telecom, uk.misc.
(The summary list is additionally posted to alt.answers and news.answers)
FTP:

ftp.demon.co.uk:/pub/archives/uk-internet-list/inetuk.lng
ftp.demon.co.uk:/pub/archives/uk-internet-list/inetuk.sum

Author's note (2): Additions to the list by me include the following tags:

- *full TCP/IP connections*
- *You'll need TCP/IP software for your computer, and TCP/IP based client software to access systems flagged with 'full TCP/IP connections'. These providers will set up your own domain on the Internet. You can use either character based software or the latest graphic based client software such as GUI based World Wide Web and Gopher clients.*
- *terminal Internet access*
- *You'll need ordinary modem based communications software to access systems flagged with 'terminal Internet access'. These suppliers cannot provide your own domain, but they can give you an Internet-savvy email account, and access to telnet or other character based services. You can't use GUI based World Wide Web or Gopher clients with these services, but you can use their character based equivalents.*
- *You'll need specialized front-end software to get the best from CompuServe, CIX, and PSILink as supplied by those companies.*
- *In all cases a V32 bis or faster modem is recommended – if the supplier supports it. Newer V34 modems will slowly appear at providers' sites towards the end of 1994.*

Provider	Email for more details	This list updated
CityScape	sales@cityscape.co.uk	02 Jun 94
CIX	cixadmin@cix.clink.co.uk	19 Jun 94 -ss
CompuServe	70006.101@compuserve.com	03 Jun 94
Demon	internet@demon.net	19 Jun 94 -ss
Direct Connection	helpdesk@dircon.co.uk	07 Jun 94
Direct Line	sysop@ps.com	06 Jun 94
EUnet GB	sales@Britain.Eu.net	08 Jun 94
ExNet	sysadmin@exnet.co.uk	14 Feb 94
GreenNet	support@gn.apc.org	09 Jun 94
infocom interactive	info@infocom.co.uk	07 Jun 94
On-line	sysop@mail.on-line.co.uk	08 Jun 94
PC User Group	info@ibmpcug.co.uk	24 May 94
PC User Group – WinNET	help@win-uk.net	24 May 94
Pipex	sales@pipex.net	02 Jun 94
PSILink	psilink-info@psi.com	12 Apr 94
Sound & Vision	Rob@sound.demon.co.uk	02 Jun 94
Specialix	keith@specialix.co.uk	23 May 94
Spud's Xanadu	jamie@spuddy.uucp	24 May 94

CityScape – full TCP/IP connections

CityScape Internet Services Ltd
59 Wycliffe Rd
Cambridge
CB1 3JE

Email: sales@cityscape.co.uk
Phone: 01223 566950
Fax : 01223 566951
WWW : http://www.cityscape.co.uk/

Introduction

CityScape Internet Services was started eighteen months ago to provide Internet connectivity to small companies, individuals, clubs and societies. We are attempting to make the power of the Internet available to all levels of user, especially those to whom computing is a second language.

Our products are not intended to be the cheapest possible, but excellent quality and value for money. Our emphasis is on both commercial quality and ease of use.

Product summary

CityScape IP-GOLD

CityScape, in collaboration with PIPEX and Unipalm, are proud to announce IP-GOLD, a professional, low cost, simple-to-use Internet IP service. The service will be available from 11th May 1994.

Cost: £50 Initial Charge + £180 per annum.

The CityScape Global On-Line Disk gives MS/Windows and Macintosh users Internet access in one simple to use, quick to install package. The GOLD service includes:

- A World Wide Web browser giving simple, graphical access to most Internet services.

- Access, via W3, to CityScape's Global On-Line services.

- E-mail package (Unipalm's Mail-it, worth over £100).

- CityScape SLIP Connection.

- CityScape POP Connection.

- Windows/Macintosh Usenet News software.

- Windows/Macintosh SLIP software.

- A 'Guide to the Internet' Book, title to be announced.

CityScape email

Cost: £400 per annum.

A simple-to-use Internet Electronic Email package for Windows 3.1.

CityScape Email is a new concept in Internet connectivity – it presumes no prior knowledge of inter-networking or communications – a simple installation from a single floppy disk is all that is required to start sending and receiving electronic mail. CityScape charge a fixed yearly subscription rate with no hidden extras, bandwidth or online charges.

Includes:

• User-friendly Installation Software

• Customized copy of Unipalm's Mail-It Remote

• CityScape UUCP Connection (single user)

CityScape MHS

Cost: The gateway software and one year's subscription costs only £999.00, £599.00 for each subsequent year.

MHS Email to Internet Gateway Service.

The software installs onto the MHS hub, connecting networks of MHS-enabled mail products to the Internet. The fixed, yearly charge includes an unlimited user licence, unlimited world-wide Email traffic to anywhere on the Internet and access to CityScape's FTP, Archie and Usenet News gateways. Note that there are no additional charges for connection time or data carried.

Includes:

• Full support for MHS attachments

• Guaranteed minimum user to modem ratio

• Optional Internet site-name registration

• MHS 1.5 and GMHS 2.0 compatible

Service details

CityScape Slip connections

CityScape will provide 6 UK PoPs from which to access the Internet, with a total of 210 lines:

London (60), Edinburgh (30), Manchester (30), Bristol (30), Birmingham (30) and Cambridge(30).

Each PoP is connected by at least a 64K connection to PIPEX's backbone (2M from London PoP, 128K from Edinburgh, direct to backbone at

Cambridge). From there, PIPEX provide a 768K (+compression) link to Alternet and 2M to JIPs – full details can be obtained from the maps held at ftp.pipex.net. IP addresses are randomly allocated from a central pool – this allows users to use any of the PoPs and move between them without informing CityScape.

All connections support V32 bis, and have 24-hour support. User to modem ratios are guaranteed not to drop below 30:1.

CityScape UUCP connections

CityScape offer high quality UUCP connections, with all the service guarantees of their other Internet connections. CityScape UUCP connections come with full 24-hour support and unlimited send and receive for Email, with a guaranteed modem ratio of 7:1.

CityScape UUCP connections can be purchased individually – please phone for a quote.

CityScape POP connections

If users wish to receive Email, they will require a POP (Post Office Protocol) connection. CityScape POP connections can be purchased individually for £50 per year. Email addresses will be of the form:

user@your_host.cityscape.co.uk

Registered domains and bulk discounting available on request.

CityScape GOLD disks

Users who wish to upgrade from other CityScape connections, or who wish to continue using another vendor's connection, can purchase these disks for £150.

CIX – terminal Internet access

Compulink Information eXchange
  Suite 2/5
  The Sanctuary
  Oakhill Grove
  Surbiton, Surrey
  KT6 6DU

CIX Admin: 01492 641 961
CIX Tech Suppt: 0181 390 8446
CIX Data Lines: 0181 390 1255
                          or 1244
Fax: 0181 390 6561
E-mail: cixadmin@cix.compulink.co.uk

Information

CIX, the UK's largest computer conferencing system, offers a broad range of services to both private and corporate users. These services include E-Mail / Usenet privileges, FULL Internet access, online conferencing, a database full of files for download, and much more!

CIX's direct connection to the Internet allows for the use of such facilities as telnet, ftp, Gopher, Archie, and the World Wide Web. (Files that are retrieved by ftp are held in the user's IP directory from which they can be downloaded to the user's computer in the normal way; via Zmodem, and so on.)

CIX users with accounts on other systems on the Internet can telnet into CIX to access it, thus saving their telecom charge. Inversely, users with accounts on other, telnet-able services, can telnet to them via CIX! CIX is also accessible via PSS.

Pricing (ex. VAT)

Connection rates:
£0.04/minute off-peak.
£0.06/minute peak.

There is a monthly minimum of £6.25 which is billed only if usage falls under £6.25. The one-time registration fee is £25.00 and this includes a user manual.

Mail charges: Email to all addresses, both national and international, is covered in the 4/6p a minute charge.

Fax machine billing: A facility to send outgoing faxes by emailing a daemon account which parses the messages for control lines, and so on, and then sends the text is available, and is the only service available on CIX for which you pay more than 4/6p a minute. Prices for the CIX fax gateway run as follows:

UK: 30p first page + 20p per additional page.
European: 70p first page + 45p per additional page.
World: 175p first page + 125p per additional page.

AMEOL

CIX now provides full support for an offline reader software package called AMEOL. The purpose of an offline reader is to maximize your online time by compressing waiting messages (be it conference messages, email, or Usenet) and downloading them to your machine, to be read offline. Your replies are similarly composed offline. AMEOL is a Windows software package, and it is

Shareware. Registration of AMEOL (which is only mandatory if you choose to continue using the product after the 30-day trial period) costs as follows:
AMEOL REGISTRATION (price includes AMEOL manual): £45.00

Notes

Peak time is Mon–Fri 08:00 to 17:00. It is the logon time that determines whether a caller is billed at peak or cheap rate.

While AMEOL is the officially supported CIX OLR software, one can connect to CIX with just about any comms software that works with their set-up. CIX staff will try to answer any technical questions about any software or hardware product used in connection with CIX.

You can register to join CIX either by filling in and returning the forms included in a CIX information pack, or online with your credit card details.

To receive your CIX information packet, including an evaulation copy of the Shareware offline reader, AMEOL, or if you have any queries please email 'cixadmin' or telephone us on either 0181 390 8446 or 01492 641 961!

CompuServe – terminal Internet access

CompuServe Information Service

Customer Service UK Freephone: 0800 289458

1 Redcliff Street
PO Box 676
Bristol BS99 1YN

E-mail: 70006.101@compuserve.com

Information

Established in 1979, the CompuServe Information Service provides its worldwide membership of over 2 million with online access to more than 2000 databases and services to meet both business and personal interests. CompuServe can be accessed by any modem-equipped personal computer utilizing the CompuServe Information Manager graphical interface or any general communications software.

CompuServe expects to launch outbound access to newsgroups by Summer 1994 and full outbound access to the Internet by the end of 1994.

CompuServe also have local support offices in Germany and France, providing freephone support for Germany and Switzerland and 0345-equivalent support in France. All other European countries are supported by either the UK, German or French offices.

Costs (in US$)

Charge = Membership Fee + Connect + Communications Surcharge.

Membership fee:
Free for the first month, thereafter $8.95/month.

Connect charge:
Free for basic services (70+ products)
Extended services
300/1200/2400 baud = $4.80/hour
9600/14400 baud = $9.60/hour

Communications surcharge
As CompuServe calls are quite likely to be to a local number, this charge covers the use of the comms network to the central CompuServe location, rather than you having to pay long distance telephone charges.

Peak time is 0800–1900 and off-peak is 1900–0800.
All CompuServe nodes in UK & Europe: off-peak free, peak $7.70 per hour.

Rest of UK
GNS Dialplus: $4.20/hour $7.70/hour
Mercury 5000: $2.50/hour $7.70/hour
Other European networks: Charges vary.

Demon – full TCP/IP Internet access

Cliff Stanford   Email: internet@demon.net
Demon Internet Ltd
42 Hendon Lane   Phone: 0181 349 0063 (Office)
London N3 1TT   0181 343 3881 (Help Line)

Information

The facilities offered are:

- SLIP or PPP Dial-up access to the Internet
- 14.4K and 64K leased line access to the Internet
- No online charges or charges for mail and so on
- Full read/write Usenet news
- ftp directly to your desktop computer

Do you want to explore the Internet?

For a limited time only, Demon Internet Ltd offers you the opportunity to connect to the Internet for up to **ONE MONTH FREE** with no cost.

Take the chance while you have it,

THIS OFFER IS ONLY VALID UP TO AND INCLUDING 31st DECEMBER 1995.

Macintosh Users:

MacTCP will be provided by Demon free of charge for the duration of this offer when taking a Demon Internet Account.

(See Reverse side for details)

Terms of special voucher offer
(The "small print")

Demon Internet Ltd offer a trial connection to the Internet making use of our full services and support lines for up to one calendar month via a Standard Dial Up account.

We work in calendar months so to make the best use of this offer, you should apply at the start of the month. By accepting this offer you are subscribing to the service on an on-going basis until you cancel. Cancellation should be made to us in writing and if you cancel during the first month you will have paid nothing. If you carry on, as we hope you will, you will then pay the joining fee and start paying the monthly fee which is due in advance of using the service.

Joining fee £12.50 plus VAT   Monthly fee £10.00 plus VAT

There are no usage or online time charges. When joining you must send payment details in the form of one of the following:

1) Credit Card details (Visa or Mastercard)
2) Post-dated cheque for £132.50 + VAT = £155.68 for the 1st of the following calendar month
3) 12 post-dated cheques. The first is for £12.50 + £10.00 + VAT and is to be made for the 1st of the following month. The 11 others should be for £10.00 + VAT = £11.75 and dated the 1st of each of the subsequent months.

In any event you will not be paying for the first month.

We regret that no other forms of payment are acceptable. Accounts are deemed to be annual but you may pay monthly as described above. We do not issue VAT receipts for monthly accounts and businesses are therefore advised to join annually.

We regret that we cannot accept vouchers that do not enclose payment and these may be returned or destroyed.

Please Read Carefully

In order to get connected to the Internet for **ONE MONTH FREE, starting on the first day of any calendar month,** fill out this order card indicating how you would like to pay for continued Demon Internet Service. If you decide to stay connected to the Internet after your month's free access you will be charged a joining fee (see details of charges below). If you decide NOT to remain connected to the Internet, you **MUST** inform Demon Internet Ltd, **in writing,** before the end of the month. This will prevent you from being charged the joining fee. Please note that without receipt of either a cheque or credit card information you will NOT be connected for this trial offer.

Charges if you stay connected:

By credit card (Mastercard, VISA...)   £12.50 + VAT joining fee, plus £10 + VAT monthly charge

By cheque (cheques should be postdated, for the first day of a calendar month and **MUST** be submitted with this offer)
    £155.68 (includes 12 months' connection, £12.50 joining fee and VAT)

If you have submitted a cheque and you decide not to continue your Demon account it will be returned to you if you have included an SAE otherwise it will be destroyed. VAT receipts can only be issued for people paying annually.

Your Name (Full name please)... Company Name (if applicable)...

Address:...

.... Business Tel No:..................................... Home Tel No:.....................................

Credit Card No:.. Expiry Date...................... Monthly or Annual account?...........
(if paying by Mastercard or Visa).
Credit Card address: (if different from above) ....

Machine name 1st choice _____ .demon.co.uk 4 to 8 characters
Machine name 2nd choice _____ .demon.co.uk 4 to 8 characters

I am a Macintosh user but don't have MacTCP. Please send me my **free** copy of MacTCP.   Please Tick Box ☐

Signed .... Date..

Please complete this original voucher only (photocopies are not acceptable) and post to
Demon Internet Ltd, Gateway House, 322 Regents Park Road, Finchley, London N3 2QQ.
Cheques should be made payable to Demon Internet Ltd.   Tel 0181-371 1234. Please dial carefully.

- multiple mail addresses

- local IRC server with telnettable clients

Current PoPs:	Number	Lines
Edinburgh	0131 552 8883	8
London	0181 343 4848	112
Reading	01734 328989	8
Warrington	01925 411383	8
(Local to Manchester & Liverpool)		
Sunderland	0191 522 5005	8
(Local to Newcastle and Durham)		
Leeds	0113 241 5890	16
Sheffield	0114 270 5565	
Hull	01482 495580	
Bradford	01274 755066	

Getting started

To get started, you will need to mail the following details to internet@demon.net or phone/fax them.

(1) Credit Card Number ⎱ or Company purchase order

(2) Expiry Date ⎰

(3) Address

(4) Phone Number

(5) Machine Name: something.demon.co.uk (4–8 chars)

Free/Shareware software for most computers is available for download using standard comms programs.

The support number (voice) is 0181 343 3881. Please do not hesitate to ring us if you need any further assistance.

Pricing

(Prices exclude VAT)

£12.50 joining fee and then £10.00 per month (both plus VAT).

These are collected monthly in advance from your credit card. Companies are requested to pay annually in advance.

Please see ftp.demon.co.uk:/pub/doc/Services.txt for details about network connections, dedicated and leased lines or telephone 0181 349 0063 and ask for an information pack.

The Direct Connection – optional full TCP/IP access

The Direct Connection
helpdesk@dircon.co.uk
Tel: (0181) 317 0100 (voice)

Information

TDC is directly connected to the Internet via permanent high-speed data circuits. This provides for almost instantaneous news and mail, as well as enabling subscribers to access all the standard Internet facilities (telnet, FTP, Gopher, Archie, and so on).

Our most popular connection methods are:

LOGIN ACCOUNTS – Dial into one of our host machines using any terminal emulation package. The host then provides a 'menu-driven' front end to enable you to connect to all the Internet facilities.

TCP/IP ACCOUNTS – Require TCP/IP software on your computer. TDC acts as a gateway into the Internet enabling you to access all the Internet facilities using your own interface.

For further information on our services and pricing you should access the online demonstration facility. Users with credit cards can also sign up online for faster access.

Modem call (0181) 317 2222: 8-N-1, any speed, login as demo
Telnet to dircon.co.uk: login as demo

All enquiries should be directed to the TDC Helpdesk:

Telephone: (0181) 317 0100
Email: helpdesk@dircon.co.uk

Login accounts

Dial into one of our hosts using a terminal emulation package. The host machine then provides you with access to the features listed below through a simple menu-driven interface.

Every TDC subscriber has access to his/her own personal file area. Uses for this facility include: storing electronic mail, batching Usenet News articles for reading offline, and compressing and archiving files so that they can download in the shortest possible time. A choice of shells are provided for accessing the User File Area: either Unix shells or the simple-to-use TDC Easy-Shell.

Batch FTP

Allows you to queue requests for files to be retrieved from other sites. The files are retrieved as part of a batch and placed in the user's file area. The user simply downloads the file to his/her computer at leisure.

Archie

Specify part of a filename and Archie will search some of the world's largest databases, in real time, to find all matching files. You can then download the files using FTP or batch FTP.

Gopher

An amalgam of the most powerful facilities from telnet and FTP. Full menu-driven access to text and data files with powerful searching facilities.

World Wide Web

A single facility bringing together FTP, telnet, Gopher, Archie, and News under one simple-to-use menu-driven interface.

Hytelnet

A 'hypertext' style database offering comprehensive information and easy-to-use access to major Internet catalogues, libraries and other interactive sites worldwide.

IRC Chat

Join Internet users from all over the world in a multi-user, multi-themed conferencing (chat) network.

Electronic mail

Send and receive mail. We offer mail connectivity to many well-known hosts including: MCI, Fido, AT&T, Bitnet, NSFNET, JANET, CompuServe. With a choice of mail-readers including Pine and Elm.

Outgoing FAX messages

Electronic mail can also be directed to our FAX gateway where it is converted into FAX format and transmitted to the specified recipient.

Usenet News (Usenet Conferencing)

Full reading and posting capability. A choice of newsreaders including tin, trn, rn and nn.

Offline News and Mail

Batches of compressed electronic mail and Usenet News can be downloaded. These can be read by a range of offline readers, saving you the cost of a call to read them online. You can also produce replies offline and send them when you next connect.

Computer Newswire

24-hours a day/7-days a week news updates on the latest stories in the computer and technology industries. Includes the popular Newsbytes articles and stories from the UPI newswires.

TCP/IP accounts

Running TCP/IP software on your computer you can use SLIP or PPP protocols to connect through us into the Internet.

We provide access to all the usual Internet services. You can access all those supported in your software.

Internet services provided include:

NNTP: access to reading and posting Usenet News
POP3 and SMTP: For receiving/sending electronic mail
TELNET: 'Log in' to other systems on the Internet
FTP: For receiving/sending files direct from your computer
GOPHER: A hierarchical worldwide database
WWW: Use the latest multimedia/hypertext Internet facility
IRC: A multi-user chat system
ARCHIE: Find files on some of the largest file repositories
WAIS: Search vast databases

Plus other services: PING, FINGER, DNS, and so on.

We can provide suggestions and copies of suitable TCP/IP packages for most popular platforms.

Other services

We offer a range of additional services including:

UUCP connections

For sites just requiring Usenet News and electronic mail UUCP is an efficient protocol to use. We offer everything from small individual feeds through to large site feeds.

Your own domain

With all of our accounts we can register you with a unique domain name ending in either '.co.uk', '.com' or 'org'. Useful where you want a greater 'presence' or want to ensure that you never have to change your mail address.

Mailing lists and publishing services

We can set up and help you to administer mailing lists or private FTP, WWW or Gopher areas. Useful where you want to distribute text or data to a group of customers.

Pricing

We offer various levels of account on The Direct Connection, starting from just £10 per month (excluding VAT).

Direct Line – terminal Internet access

Direct Line
10 lines, 24hrs, All Speeds to 14400 v32bis, 16800 HST
Contact : sysop@ps.com

Information

Direct Line is a large London based system offering access to Internet email and news. Each member has their own email address as first.last@ps.com.

Services

- 10 Lines, 24 hrs, 365 days, operational now for 6 years
- Gigabytes of software online, including the latest files
- Software support for DOS, WINDOWS, OS/2, MAC, Z88, and PSION
- Message echoes from several Networks, including MSI Support, TheNet, WildNet and so on
- Internet email and newsgroups. The newsgroups viewed online or received via QWK mail can be set by the user, with approximately 800 major ones currently available for immediate download, and with others added by simple request from the thousands listed on the system
- Automatic UUencoding of files for transmission by email
- News services such as Newsbytes, Satnews, Satellite Journal and so on
- RIP graphics, ANSI graphics, Mono, all available

- Fax/Answerphone member support on 0181 845 8952

- Large, friendly Sysop team, and powerful easy to use system

- Direct-Line allows:
  - Downloading of News/Mail in a QWK packet
  - Uploading of reply News/Mail in a QWK packet
  - Ability to Add/Remove/Request newsgroups on the fly

- Mail/News can then be read and replied to offline using any QWK compatible software. Online reading/reply with full screen editing also available

Lines

Numbers	Lines	Speeds by Line
0181 845 8228	3	300/1200/1200-75/2400/9600/14.4k(v32bis) HST 9600/14400/16800
0181 841 4114	3	3/12/1275/24/96/14.4k(v32bis)
0181 841 1847	1	3/12/24/96(v32) + HST 96/14.4
0181 842 2030	1	3/12/24/96(v32) + HST 96/14.4
0181 842 4176	1	3/12/24/96(v32) + HST 96/14.4
0181 845 5811	1	3/12/24/96(v32) + HST 96/14.4

Cost (annual subs)

£25 + VAT for Full System and Internet Access

EUnet GB – full TCP/IP Internet Access

=== Connecting Europe since 1982 ===

EUnet GB
Wilson House
John Wilson Busines Park
Whitstable
Kent CT5 3QY

Tel 01227 266466
Fax 01227 266477

E-mail: sales@Britain.EU.net

Introduction

As the only commercial pan-European Internet provider, EUnet is well placed to serve the business and organizational Internet user. Active in 28 countries of Europe, North Africa and the former Soviet Union, serving 8000 corporate and multinational organizations across the region, with over 540 users in the UK building their business applications with EUnet.

EUnet has been providing Internet services for over 10 years, and is a full member of the Commercial Internet Exchange.

EUnet is unique in running its own in-house network across Europe, without dependency on academic backbones like Ebone. The infrastructure is doubling every 9 months, and includes 1024K routes to the USA (due for upgrade to 1512K in November 1994), considerable intra-Europe links, and extensive backup routes and so on.

A range of services are offered, ranging upwards from dial-up services such as the worldwide email UUCP access 'EmailLink', to full leased-line access, with the provision of customer site hardware and so on available as a complete package to suit any site's particular needs.

Prices start as low as £95 per quarter for the bottom-end services. Organizations can start off at the low end, and move up as their demands dictate, staying with one supplier for a smooth upgrade route.

Email gateways to Lotus CC:mail, X400 and MHSmail are available.

Full on-site support, consultancy and configuration support services available.

Up-time guarantees and 24-hour support services are provided.

Points of Presence are currently operational in Birmingham, Bracknell, Cambridge, Canterbury, Glasgow, Manchester and London.

Price matrix overview

Prices are in pounds sterling, exclude VAT, and are billed quarterly in advance.

Service	Basic Service		Equipment lease	
	Set-up	/ Qtr	Set-up	/ Qtr
EmailLink	–	95 *	–	–
EmailLink + News	–	145 *	–	–
IP-Dial – shared	300	450	300	300
IP-Dial – dedicated	1000	600	300	300
IP-Dial – Dial-back	1200	650 +	300	300
ISDN – shared	300	750	1000	450
ISDN – dedicated	1000	900	1000	450
ISDN – Dial-back	1300	950 +	1000	450
IP-Line	1000	1250	nil	250

Services marked * incur International Traffic charges. UKP0.075 per 1 Kbyte sent overseas only, free to receive from anywhere, free to send to UK sites.

Services marked + incur additional PTT usage charges, incurred when EUnet dials out to customer site with incoming packets. The regular PTT charges are passed on at cost.

Shared service means access to a pool of shared modems. Dedicated means one modem and line dedicated to a single customer. Dial-back means the EUnet modem dials *out* to customer site as needed. Equipment lease is for customer-site equipment supply.

IP-Line services exclude cost of PTT line from nearest EUnet Point of Presence.

Please ask for written quotation to include these costs. Current PoPs include Birmingham, Bracknell, Cambridge, Canterbury, Glasgow, Manchester and London.

On-site equipment lease includes:

IP-Dial	V32bis modem and IP-Router
ISDN	single port Terminal Adaptor and IP-Router
IP-Line	serial port/ ethernet port IP-Router
V32bis modem	normally US Robotics Courier
IP-Router	normally Netblazer PN2
ISDN Terminal Adaptor	normally Controlware Citam
IP-Router for IP-Line	normally Span NAT290B

If alternative hardware is required, please ask for a written quotation.

Customers upgrading from one service to another incur only the differential in initial fees, rather than the full initial fees for the new service.

NB – Domain Name Registration Price change

Since 1 March 1994, EUnet GB has been jointly responsible for the commercial name space in the UK (that is, .co.uk names) and thus there are now no charges for registering such domain names. .ac.uk and .org.uk names will still incur a registration charge of £175.

EUnet GB (GBnet Ltd), Kent R&D Business Centre, Giles Lane, Canterbury, CT2 7PB
Tel 01227 475497 Fax 01227 475478 Email sales@Britain.EU.net

ExNet – terminal based mail and news service

Damon Hart-Davis
London
Tel/Fax: 0181 244 0077

Introduction

Prices exclude VAT (currently 17.5% for UK users) and are in UK Sterling.

There are three levels of service. Discounts are available for early payment. Payment for the subscription is a minimum of three months in advance.

Services

Basic service

This lets you connect to our system and use our computer to read and send worldwide email and news.

You will need a terminal (or a computer with a communications package like CrossTalk) and a modem. A suitable modem can be bought for about £90 (we can sell you one), and a minimal communications package called 'Kermit' is free.

UUCP service

With UUCP your machine can automatically collect and send news and mail for you. You do offline email and news reading/composing, drastically cutting down on charges. This Service allows use of a fast modem (at least 9600 bps, V.32).

For added speed, our machine can call yours when mail arrives, for which we only charge the cost of the Mercury connection plus 10%.

This service also includes a normal Basic Service account for free, which you will typically use for small amounts of administration of your own news and mail connections (such as choosing which types of news items you want sent to your machine automatically).

We also create and maintain an entry in the worldwide UUCP maps for you, plugging your machine into the world's electronic mail and news systems in its own right.

Although we are running UNIX on our machines, you can run any software on your machine that can use the UUCP protocols. For example, for MS-DOS there are programs such as Waffle and UUCP to do this for you. We can provide a pre-configured version of Waffle for you, if you wish, for a small charge. Waffle and UUCP are free.

Full-feed service

This essentially gives you all of the UUCP Service but with unlimited volumes of mail and news in your feed and unlimited time to collect that feed. We will also help you set up your own unique worldwide mail address at which you can add or remove extra users and email boxes at will. This is ideal for a company-wide connection to electronic mail and news.

Restrictions

The 'reasonable usage' limits are not detailed here. The main one is a limit of an hour per day connected to our system on the Basic Service login account.

Costs

Prices exclude VAT (currently 17.5% for UK users) and are in UK Sterling.

BASIC :	£60 per year
UUCP :	£100 per year
FULL-FEED:	£300 per year

GreenNet – terminal based Internet access

GreenNet
Global computer communications network for
Environment, Peace, Human Rights & Development

4th Floor
393-395 City Road
London EC1V INE

Tel: +44/(0)171 608 3040
Fax: +44/(0)171 253 0801
e-mail: support@gn.apc.org

Information

GLOBAL CO-OPERATION THROUGH COMMUNICATION

What is GreenNet

GreenNet is part of the only global computer network designed specifically for environment, peace and human rights groups. GreenNet users have access to all users and facilities of the other members: NordNet (Sweden), Ecuanex (Ecuador), ComLink (Germany), Chasque (Uruguay), GlasNet (Russia), GLUK (Ukraine), Histria (Slovenia) LaNeta (Mexico) PeaceNet, EcoNet, HomoeoNet, ConflictNet (USA), Web (Canada), Alternex (Brazil), Pegasus (Australia), and Nicarao (Nicaragua), Wamani (Argentina). There are also close working relationships with other networks in Africa, Asia, the Pacific, and Eastern Europe.

Who is running GreenNet?

GreenNet is run by an independent non-profit organization. Staff have extensive experience and contacts in the international peace, development, human rights and environment movements, coupled with expertise in information technology and its applications.

How is GreenNet funded?

Fees from users make up the main proportion of income. Grants and gifts are used to fund development of new features and expansion. Past funders include the Joseph Rowntree Charitable Trust, the MacArthur Foundation, New-Land Foundation and the Wayward Trust.

Access methods

- Direct dial modems (London numbers), speeds 1200–14,400 plus PEP
- X25 (NUA: 234212301371)
- Dialplus (use our account, 3 pence per minute added to your bill, gives local call access at speeds up to 2400 baud in most of UK)
- Internet (telnet gn.apc.org)

Services

- Electronic mail (Internet + wider connectivity)
- Computer conferences – Usenet plus around 800 of our own
- Internet access (telnet)
- Fax service (email to any direct dialable fax number)
- User support and Training (lots of handholding if you need it...)

Pricing

	Registration	Monthly charge	Connect charge
Non-commercial	£15	£5	4 or 6 p/min
Commercial use	£30	£10	10 p/min

- (£5 registration discount for low income)
- Connect charge does not include phone company charges.
- There are no extra charges for sending mail within GreenNet; mail to other networks goes at cost.
- All EU users pay an additional 17.5% VAT; non-UK EU users do not need to pay this if they supply a VAT number with their subscription.

● Full price list (with high and low use options) on request.

Notes

GreenNet has 1500 users; the APC serves over 15,000 organizations and individuals in more than 90 countries, including:

Action Aid, ADIU, BASIC, CND, Central America Resources Network, Christic Institute, Climate Research Unit (Norwich), CRIES (Nicaragua), Dublin Portswatch, ECP, FoR, Findhorn, Finnish Peace Union, FoE, Global Challenges Network, Green Party (UK), Greenpeace, ITDG, Int'l Peace Bureau, IPPNW, Media Transcription Service, Nat'l Wildlife Fed., NATTA, Nat'l Peace Council, North Atlantic Network, NFIP support groups, Oxfam, Physicians for Social Responsibility, Quaker Peace & Service, Rainforest Info Ctr., SANE/Freeze, Sierra Club, Southscan, Survival Intl., Swedish Peace & Arbitration Soc., UNA, VERTIC, Vlaamse Vredesuniversiteit, War Resisters Int'l, WILPF, WISE, Worldwide Fund for Nature....

ukmail network & infocom interactive – services to be announced

The Davinson Group International
ukmail network
White Bridge House
Old Bath Road
CHARVIL
RG10 9QJ

Voice: +44 [0] 1734 344000 [office hours]
+44 [0] 1850 920041 [outside office hours]
Fax: +44 [0] 1734 320988
Data: +44 [0] 1734 340055 [v32bis]
Data: +44 [0] 1734 320055 [v32bis]

How to get up-to-date information

By Phone: 01734 344000 [office hours]
01850 920041 [outside office hours]

By FAX: 01734 320055
LOGIN using 'fax' and follow the instructions

By EMAIL: Send mail to info@ukmail.NET
with 'Subject: GENERAL' for a listing.

UUCP Software Server: Connect to 01734 320055, login using 'getuucp' follow the instructions to download UUCP software for your system.

PLEASE NOTE: infocom is NOT YET offering TCP/IP services, but will do so in the very near future. Points of Presence are planned for Belfast, Glasgow/Edinburgh, Leeds/Bradford, Liverpool/Manchester and London.

On-line – terminal based access

On-line Entertainment Ltd
  642a Lea Bridge Road
  London
  E10 6AP

Tel: 0181 558 6114
Fax: 0181 558 3914
Direct Dial number: 0181 539 6763 (8-N-1)
Internet: connect.on-line.co.uk (login: connect)
E-mail sysop@mail.on-line.co.uk

Information

On-line is a consumer leisure based service, offering Internet access (includes telnet, ftp and Usenet), and world-class multi-player entertainment. On-line can be accessed via Internet, Dialplus, Tymnet or by direct dial.

On-line offers the following multi-player games:

Air Warrior (by Kesmai): Multi-user flight simulator. Full, graphical flight simulator. Also runs on GEnie network.

MUD II (by Richard Bartle/MUSE): The latest version of the ORIGINAL multi-player fantasy adventure game.

FEDERATION II (Federation partnership): Adult space fantasy game. Buy a spaceship, explore the galaxy, or build your own planet! Fed also runs on GEnie.

LANDS OF THE CROWN: Multi-player fantasy role playing game.

INTERNECINE: Play-by-email game, set in a futuristic game show.

Pricing (including VAT)

On-line operates a flat rate of £2.00 per hour.

If you use Dialplus or Tymnet there is an addition network charge. Direct and Internet connections are free of charge.

PC User Group – terminal Internet access

PC User Group
E-mail: info@ibmpcug.co.uk
Voice: Alan, Jake on 0181 863 1191
CONNECT: 0181 863 6646 V.32bis, V.42bis (14,400 and below)

Information

The PC User Group has been offering Usenet News and Mail services since 1988 and provides services via a custom BBS interface and via UUCP for individual and site feeds. New users may register online and find out more about our services (including membership of the PC User Group) by logging in as 'register' at the nickname prompt (? for more help at the nickname prompt).

Pricing summary

All prices are in Pounds Sterling and exclude VAT.

Monthly (total cost per month):

	Members	Non-members
One-time joining fee	7.50 + VAT	10.00 + VAT
CONNECT (basic)	3.50 + VAT	5.00 + VAT
With external mail & IRC (admin charge)	5.25 + VAT	7.00 + VAT
With non-interactive FTP	6.50 + VAT	8.50 + VAT
With interactive FTP, and telnet	12.00 + VAT	14.00 + VAT

Monthly charges are billed in advance.
There are no volume charges relating to mail provided that your usage does not exceed 2.5 Mb per month.

Yearly (total annual cost in []):

	Members	Non-members
One-time joining fee	nil	10 + VAT
CONNECT (basic)	35 + VAT	50 + VAT
Options:		
External mail & IRC (admin. charge)	20 + VAT [55]	25 + VAT [75]
Non-interactive FTP	10 + VAT	15 + VAT

	Members	Non-members
(must have external email)	[65]	[90]
Interactive FTP,		
and telnet	65 + VAT	65 + VAT
(must have email	[130]	[155]
and non-interactive)		
UUCP connectivity	15 + VAT	20 + VAT
(in additional to any annual subscription)		

There are no volume charges relating to mail provided your usage does not exceed 2.5 Mb per month.

Access via non-London nodes

Access is available in the following areas: Cambridge (01223), Edinburgh (0131), Manchester (0161), Bristol (0117), Birmingham (0121).

Full details on registration. There is a communications surcharge for using these access points. Registration is only via the London direct dial node (0181 863 6646).

Other services

UUCP connections – sites: For larger users we also offer Site UUCP access at £250 for Mail and £400 for News and Mail (£225 and £350 for corporate members of the PC User Group). As a special offer to Site subscribers we are also offering one login account for interactive Internet access at an additional £100 per year. News only £200 per year. If you are interested in this service please mail us for an application form.

For Mail users we offer full MX record handling for mail sites and provide access to and from UK and overseas sites. The service also includes Application Relay to UK 'grey-book' JANET sites.

For News subscribers we offer a number of choices of feeds. Subscribers can choose the level of news they receive, allowing you to tailor your news requirements and so reducing your download time.

News-only subscriptions are available at £200 per year.

PC User Group – WinNET Mail and News – terminal Internet access

PC User Group

E-mail: help@win-uk.net
Voice: Alan, Jake on 0181 863 1191

WinNET Mail and News

WinNET Mail (TM) is a Windows 3.0/3.1 application for sending and receiving Electronic Mail and News articles with the worldwide Internet and Usenet networks using just your Windows system and a modem. The connection with the Internet and Usenet is provided through The PC User Group's computer system providing WinNET (UK) (SM) service.

The PC User Group has been offering Usenet News and Mail services since 1988 and provides services via a custom BBS interface and via UUCP for individual and site feeds.

Costs of using WinNET (UK) Mail

The WinNET (UK) Mail software is provided to you FREE of charge for the purpose of connecting with the WinNET (UK) system. The WinNET (UK) system is your connection with the Internet and Usenet networks and usage is billed to you on a connect-time basis (charges are plus VAT at the prevailing rate). The rate for online usage of the WinNET (UK) system is:

3.25 per hour (pounds sterling).

Subscribers can obtain a login account on our machine to use telnet, ftp, Gopher, IRC and other interactive Internet services at a monthly fee of £7.25 (with no time charges on this part of the account, except for telecom surcharges). Please mail help@win-uk.net for further details. To request an account mail info@win-uk.net.

Unlike many online services and bulletin boards, you are only connected to WinNET (UK) for just long enough to send or receive any pending email at speeds as fast as your modem will go. This results in connection times of typically 1 to just a few minutes. In our experience, customers average 1.25 hours of connect time per month or just £6.75 in charges (excluding online Internet services).

Non-London access nodes

Once a site is registered access is available via nodes in the following areas: Cambridge (01223), Edinburgh (0131), Manchester (0161), Bristol (0117), Birmingham (0121).

Full details on registration. There is a communications surcharge for using these access points. Registration is only via the London direct dial node (0181 863 6646).

Free Windows software

If you require a copy of the software, it is available for download from CONNECT 0181 863 6646, login as winnet (no password). Alternatively, if you already have an email address send a mail message to request@win-uk.net with the Subject: HELP for more information. You can use this method to request a copy of the software. WinNET software is also available via ftp from ftp.ibmpcug.co.uk /pub/WinNET/ and a number of other ftp sites around the world. The software is also available on disk; please call 0181 863 1191 or fax us on 0181 863 6095 and we will send you a copy.

WinNET (UK) Mail (TM)
Copyright 1992,1993 by Computer Witchcraft, Inc.
ALL RIGHTS RESERVED

PIPEX – full TCP/IP connections

PIPEX (Public IP Exchange Ltd.) –
part of Unipalm Group plc
216 Cambridge Science Park
Cambridge
CB4 4WA

Tel: +44 1223 250120
Fax: +44 1223 250121
Email: sales@pipex.net

Information

PIPEX offers commercial access to the Internet via a range of dial-up and leased-line services. These services are provided as a 'one-stop-shop' where equipment/telecom installation and rental costs are included within our charges.

PIPEX is directly connected to the USA, EBone (European Backbone), JIPS and SWIPnet networks. The network is designed to have no single point of failure and significant international bandwidth allows us to offer excellent performance and 99.5% network availability.

PIPEX is a member of the CIX (Commercial Internet Exchange) and EBone'94 and as such can route commercial traffic worldwide.

PIPEX does not restrict the type or volume of customer traffic in any way.

PIPEX has, mid-94Q2, nearly 200 leased-line customers in the UK and nearly 250 directly connected customers in all, representing 80% of the UK commercial leased-line market. PIPEX-style services are now available in France, Germany, Benelux, N. and S. Ireland, Hungary and Slovenia exclusively through our partners Oleane, MIS, INNet, Genesis, ODIN and Quantum, and a number of UK resellers (BBCNC, IBMPCUG, ExNet, CityScape, Almac, Microland, Direct Connection) also sell low-cost dial-up access across their PIPEX connections (details from sales@pipex.net).

Further information

Our FAQ (Frequently Asked Questions) is regularly updated and is available via anonymous ftp to ftp.pipex.net: /pub/FAQ or by emailing pipex-info-request@pipex.net, or via WWW server at: http://www.pipex.net

Tariff of services

Prices are in pounds sterling and exclude VAT.

Leased-line services

Service	Set-up	Annual	Bandwidth (kbps)	Equipment supplied
Worldwide +	1800	11500	64	Router
Worldwide + 128	3300	22000	128	Router
Worldwide + 256	3300	40000	256	Router
Worldwide	1000	9400	64	None
UK +	1800	9600	64	Router
UK	1000	7500	64	None
Local + (15–30km)	2800	8000	19.2	Router + Modem
Local (15–30km)	2500	7000	19.2	Modem
Local + (0–15km)	1800	6000	19.2	Router + Modem
Local (0–15km)	1500	5000	19.2	Modem
Worldwide + (0171 Area)	1800	10000	64	Router
Worldwide + 128 (0171)	3300	20000	128	Router
Worldwide + 256 (0171)	3300	35000	256	Router
Worldwide (0171 Area)	1000	8000	64	None
UK + (0171 Area)	1800	7100	64	Router
UK (0171 Area)	1000	6100	64	None
Local+ (0171 Area)	1800	5500	19.2	Router + Modem
Local (0171 Area)	1500	4500	19.2	None

PSTN dial-up services

Service	Set-up	Annual	Bandwidth (kbps)	Equipment supplied
Caller + Modem	1500	4000	19.2	Router +
Caller	250	2000	19.2	None
Solo	50	180	19.2	Software

X.25 dial-up services

Service	Set-up	Annual	Bandwidth (kbps)	Equipment supplied
X.25 Caller	250	2000	19.2	None
	500	5000	48/64	None
X.25 Caller +	1800	5200	19.2	Router

ISDN dial-up services

Service	Set-up	Annual	Bandwidth (kbps)	Equipment supplied
ISDN +	1800	6000	64	Router + Modem
ISDN	1000	4000	64	NB: For Sun equipment
ISDN Backup	1500	2500	64	Backup for 64K Leased services

Other services

Service	Set-up	Annual	Description
PAD/TELNET	–	1000	Protocol translation
WAN Management	1000	1000	Installation and remote management
RELAY	–	800	News feed, DNS, Store and forward
X.400 Conversion	–	1600	X.400 – SMTP/Greybook conversion

Notes

(1) All leased-line services include the installation and rental of the telecom circuit.

(2) All '+' services include the lease, installation and support of router and/or modem equipment.

(3) All services provide full TCP/IP access, that is, email, news, telnet, ftp.

(4) All services other than UK and UK + provide access to the worldwide Internet.

(5) The annual subscription is charged quarterly in advance. Prices are in pounds sterling and exclude VAT.

(6) Quotations for leased-line services at bandwidths 256K, and PIPEX VPNs (Virtual Private Networks) are available from sales@pipex.net.

PSILink – specialized terminal software required

PSILink
Performance Systems International, Inc.
Attn.: PSILink Information
P.O. Box 592
Herndon, VA 22070
(tel) +1.703.709.0300
(fax) +1.703.904.1207

PSILink – Personal Internet Access -
　　　Worldwide E-mail, Anonymous FTP, & USENET News

Introduction

Internet access is an important facet of all higher education institutions, and most corporations throughout the USA, North America, Western Europe and the Pacific Basin. It is also important for small organizations and individuals, yet both cost and usability have been barriers. The PSILink service is designed to remove these barriers for the indivdual.

PSI provides local dial-ups throughout North America, Europe and the Pacific Basin to provide PSILink service and provide access to the 25+ million people available through the Internet and electronic mail networks such as Compuserve, MCIMail, and so on. Over 300 cities are served.

The PSILink 'Lite' service today provides unlimited electronic messaging for a flat fee using our Class A dial-ups.

PSILink 'Basic', in addition to unlimited messaging, provides anonymous FTP access to thousands of archive sites as well as USENET News, the largest distributed bulletin board in the world. Both of these services allow the user offline composition and reading to decrease communications costs.

PSI provides the necessary software for MS-DOS based PCs to use this service at no additional cost – there are four platforms available:

PSILink for MDOS – Current version is 3.6
PSILink for the HP 95LX – Current version is 2.0
PSILink for the HP 100LX – Current version is 2.0
PSILink Electronic Mail for Windows – Version 1.1.9

PSILink service matrix

PSILink Platform	E-Mail	USENET ftp	1200– 2400bps	9600bps (V.32)	V.32bis	Wireless
DOS	*	*	*	*		*
HP 95LX	*		*			*
HP 100LX	*	*				*
Windows	*	*	*	*	*	F

* = Available today.
F = Available in the future.

Only PSI's software can access this service, but even the smallest PC with a Hayes compatible modem can use PSILink. This software is available via anonymous ftp or via the PSILink Bulletin Board System.

You may obtain PSILink software via the Internet anonymous file transfer protocol on ftp.psi.com in the 'psilink' directory as

psilink.zip   PSILink for DOS
psilinkw.zip   PSILink for Windows
psi95lx.zip   PSILink for the HP95LX
psi100lx.zip   PSILink for the HP100LX

Make sure you use binary transfer.

You may also obtain PSILink software via the PSILink Bulletin Board System. The telephone number to access the bulletin board from any standard communications software package – such as Kermit, ProComm or CrossTalk – is 703.904.4272. The login is 'psilink' and no password is necessary.

The software is also available on a 3.5" High Density (1.44 Mbyte) MSDOS floppy when you register for the service.

If you want to register for this service, send email to:

psilink-registration@psi.com

PostScript registration information will be automatically mailed to you; just fill it out and send it in by US Mail or fax.

If you can't print the PostScript documents, send complete contact information including postal address, name, and phone number to:

psilink-order@psi.com

You will receive materials via the US Postal system.

You can also call 1.800.fax.psi.1 in the USA for PSI's FAXBACK system to receive a marketing brochure and registration form. Call from any phone but have your fax number ready, as the system will require that.

Alternatively, you can call or write:

PSI, Inc.
Attn.: PSILink Information
P.O. Box 592
Herndon, VA 22070
+1.703.709.0300
(fax) +1.703.904.1207

PSILink Monthly Pricing (after the one-time $19 registration fee) is:

	@1200-2400baud	@9600baud (V.32)	@14400baud (V.32bis)
'Lite'	$9	$19	$29
'Basic'	$19	$29	$39

These flat fees apply to use of Class A dial-up cities which are available by sending email to:

classa-na-numbers@psi.com

The computer will automatically respond with the up-to-date list.

Class B North American dial-up cities have additional connection time costs – $6/hour prime time, $2.50/hour non-prime time. City lists are available by sending email to:

classb-na-numbers@psi.com

The computer will automatically respond with the up-to-date list.

Class B 'Rest of World' (from Paris to Tokyo, from Manila to Stockholm) are also available with a connection cost of $18/hour. City lists are available by sending email to:

classb-row-numbers@psi.com

The computer will automatically respond with the up-to-date list.

Basic Service provides 50 Mbytes of USENET per month, each additional Mbyte is an additional $1. It also includes 50 Mbytes of FTP per month, each additional Mbyte is an additional $1.

PSILink is billed on a monthly basis to your MasterCard, Visa or American Express credit card; no other payment plan is available.

Copyright 1991–1994 Performance Systems International Inc. All rights reserved.

Rev: 1/17/94

Sound & Vision BBS – terminal Internet access

Sound & Vision BBS +44 (0)1932 252323
6 lines, 24hrs, 300-14400 HST/V32b

Voice support on +44 (0)1932 253131
InterNet : Rob@sound.demon.co.uk
FidoNet : Sysop, 2:254/14

Information

Sound & Vision is a huge BBS with 6 lines and over 2000 members. A feed is set up for simple access to the non-interactive parts of the Internet, that is, Usenet and Internet Email. The cheapest way into this is £10/year, which will give you as much Internet Email and Usenet News as you can eat. There are currently over 350 newsgroups connected to S&V, and subscribers can request any others to be added to the BBS.

Services

- 6 Lines, 300–14400, 24-hrs
- 9 Gigabytes of software online including 12 CD-ROMs
- 110 Message echos in 5 Networks (Fido, SB, RANet, WAPOW, CDN)
- Full Usenet and Internet Email feeds
- Voice support on 01932 253131
- Internet/Usenet door allows:
  - Downloading of News/Mail in a ZIP
  - Uploading of reply News/Mail in a ZIP
  - Ability to Add/Remove/Request NewsGroups on the fly
- Mail/News is then read and replied to offline at your leisure, with Usenet-format software such as CPPnews

Costs (yearly)

> UKP/10.00+VAT for Internet/Usenet access + minimal BBS access
> UKP/17.50+VAT for Internet/Usenet access + 60 mins BBS access
> UKP/25.00+VAT for Internet/Usenet access + 120 mins BBS access
> UKP/50.00+VAT for Internet/Usenet access + unlimited BBS access

Specialix – terminal Internet access

> Specialix International
> 3, Wintersells Rd, Byfleet,
> Byfleet,
> Surrey,
> KT14 7LF
>
> Tel: 01932 354254
> Fax: 01932 352781
>
> Contact: Keith Oborn (keith@specialix.co.uk)

Specialix maintains a full Usenet news feed, sourced from PIPEX and one or more backups. As far as possible all known groups are carried. We will provide UUCP feeds of any subset of groups for a flat fee of £200.00 a year. Note, though, that a full feed is around 120 Mb per day, which is impractical over the available modems.

Currently we have Telebit Trailblazer (PEP) and USR Courier (HST, v.everything-except-fast) modems.

The annual fee is independent of volume. We are also quite happy to provide backup Ihave/Sendme links for free, as long as the 'normal' flow is small (<25K per day). If the flow on a backup feed increases significantly for more than a week we will charge the normal fee. We are also happy to set up nntp links where it seems mutually beneficial.

We don't currently provide mail feeds on a commercial basis, and as we are a private commercial site we have no public interactive services. We do keep copies of the releases of our current news software available to send to feed sites.

Spud's Xanadu – THE free news/mail provider for the UK – terminal access

> > SPUD'S XANADU > 01203 364436/362560 < Meeeeeooooww <

Information

Here is a brief description of Spud's Xanadu – the Sun network dedicated to the provision of a FREE mail and Usenet service for the UK. Login as 'new' at the prompt – there is an automatic server that will create your login shell.

Services

- Spuddy offers the only online full Usenet/mail service for free in the UK. A growing network, now consisting of five dedicated Sun Workstations, Spuddy represents a high-speed fast-expanding network. Why not give it a call ?!

- Over 2 gig of stuff to download or request by post. This includes a complete archive of GNU freeware, mirrored from prep.ai.mit.edu.

- Two 'MUD' games.

- FREE access to a full UNIX shell. The choices of shell are: sh, csh, bash, ksh, zsh, tcsh, rc, ssh and so on.

- If you don't like UNIX – you don't have to touch it! There is a menu system that allows user-friendly access to the world of usenet! Just request a 'menu' shell.

- Full access to Usenet news. This (obviously) includes posting.

- Your own mailbox for worldwide Internet/UUCP mail.

- No limit on downloading – no ratios or silly rules. You may request sources by post for free (providing you provide the media!).

- No restriction for time spent online.

- A friendly BBS.

Pricing

There is *no* restriction for time spent online, *no charges* for mail, news, disk usage or ANYTHING !!

Spuddy is a FREE news/mail service !!

Compiled ref: 94/6/9 inetuk.lng

Appendix 9

Email abbreviations

Abbrevations come and go (ACAG) so feel free to make up your own and inflict them upon the unknowing (ITUTU).

BCNU	Be Seein' You
BRB	Be right back
BTS	Better than s***
BTSOOM	Beats the s*** out of me
BTW	By the way
DYJHIW	Don't ya just hate it when…
FAQ	Frequently asked (or answered) question
FUBAR	Fouled Up Beyond All Recognition
FWIW	For what it's worth
FYI	For your information
GOMT	Gets on my t*ts
GR&D	Grinning running & ducking
IAE	In any event
IANAL	I Am Not A Lawyer
IMCO	In my considered opinion
IMHO	In my humble opinion
IMO	In my opinion
IOW	In other words
JASE	Just another system error
MUD	Multi user domain (or dungeon)
NFW	No f***ing way
NRN	No Reply Necessary
OTOH	On the other hand
PITA	Pain in the ass
ROFL	Rolling on floor laughing.
RSN	Real Soon Now [which may be a long time coming]
RTFM	Read the f***ing manual (or message)
SITD	Still in the dark
SNAFU	Situation Normal, All F***ed Up
SOL	S***! outta luck
TANSTAAFL	There ain't no such thing as a free lunch
TIA	Thanks In Advance (also AtDhVaAnNkCsE)

TIC	Tongue in cheek
TLA	Three letter acronym
TTFN	Ta-Ta For Now
WTF	What the f***
WRT	With Respect To
WYSIWYG	What You See is What You Get
YMMV	Your mileage may vary

Appendix 10

The Demon Internet Services – Meta-FAQ

Compiled by Michael Bernardi and reproduced here with kind permission

Author's note: This document is updated regularly and appears in the demon.answers newsgroup. It providers many valuable pointers to areas of interest on the 'Net, and I'm indebted to Michael Bernardi for permission to use it. Items marked 'last updates' were correct at print time, but will have changed by the publication date of this book. The document has been reformatted from the original to allow for typesetting, and 'Last Updated' fields removed. Readers are urged to download the latest copy of this document from any of the sources mentioned.

This is NOT a FAQ (Frequently Asked Questions – with Answers). It is a META-FAQ – that is, a place to point you to the FAQs and other information – and was created with help from other Demon users.

Introduction

This META-FAQ was started by Michael Bernardi <mike@childsoc. demon.co.uk> and originally posted to demon.ip.support on 14 Sep 1993; information from various other Demon users has also been incorporated. It was first archived on 28 Jan 1994 as version 1.6.

As from the beginning of Jan 94 it will be posted to demon.ip.support on a monthly basis, and possibly archived on ftp.demon.co.uk too. (If I remember). Comments on how it can be improved are encouraged. From the 20 Feb 94 version 1.7.2 it has been also posted weekly to demon.answers, and from 17 Jun 94 version 1.7.5 was made available as a WWW page from http://ftp.demon.co.uk/pub/doc/html/dis-meta.html.

It is for users of Demon Internet Services, particularly new users (or those changing computer and/or operating system).

It should point you to the place, on the Internet in general or ftp.demon.co.uk in particular, to find the information to solve your problems. It is in addition to the excellent Welcome.txt provided by Demon Internet. Welcome.txt explains how to use ftp to obtain files from the Internet, and so this is not repeated here. Please read Welcome.txt as it contains VERY useful pointers to using the Demon Service, including a brief overview of the directory structure of ftp.demon.co.uk, the demon hierarchy of Usenet news groups, and details on how to report problems. It also gives a brief precis of the various Internet tools available.

If you find this META-FAQ of use, an email message to this effect would be most encouraging :-)

Navigating the Internet

(a) Recently (in the past year) a number of interesting books on the Internet have been published. Many of these are listed in the 'Public Dialup Internet Access List' which is posted to the Usenet Newsgroups alt.internet. access.wanted, alt.bbs.lists, alt.online-service, and news.answers by kaminski@netcom.com (Peter Kaminski). Details of how/where to get such items is found below.

http://nearnet.gnn.com/GNN-ORA.html

For further details send an email to info@gnn.com.

(b) Also, certain RFC documents have been collected as FYI documents (For Your Information), which are less technical. These can be found in ftp.demon.co.uk:pub/doc/rfc.

The Internet Technology Handbook is a collection of the most pertinent RFCs, a table of contents for which can be found at ftp.nisc.sri.com:/netinfo/internet-technology-handbook-contents. There is a copy at ftp.demon.co.uk:pub/doc/general/netinfo.txt too.

The introduction includes:

RFC 1118	The Hitchhiker guide to the Internet
RFC 1175 FYI:3	A bibliography of internetworking information
RFC 1325 FYI:4	'new Internet user' Questions
RFC 1207 FYI:7	'experienced Internet user' Questions
RFC 1150 FYI:1	Introduction on FYI notes
RFC 1392 FYI:18	Internet User's Glossary
RFC 1087	Ethics and the Internet

NB: the FYI are sometimes updated (and thus get new RFC numbers) but their FYI numbers remain the same!

Other FYI documents of interest are:

RFC 1402 FYI:10   There's Gold in them thar Networks
RFC 1463 FYI:19   FYI on Introducing the Internet
RFC 1462 FYI:20   FYI on What is the Internet
RFC 1178 FYI:5   Choosing a Name for your Computer

The later the RFC number, the more recent the date of publication.

(c) Another useful source of information is the 'Internet Services Frequently Asked Questions & Answers (FAQ)' by savetz@rahul.net (Kevin Savetz). It is posted to the following Usenet newsgroups: alt. internet.services, alt. online-service, alt.answers, news.answers and is archived as internet-services/faq.

It gives details of what you can use to explore the 'Net, how to do so, and where to get the information from. (It too is supposed to be published as a book.) It gives detail on sending email to other systems. This info can also be found in rtfm.mit.edu:pub/usenet/news.answers/mail.

(d) Project Gutenberg contains several interesting works on the subject of beginners' guides to the Internet. There is a Project Gutenberg archive on ftp.cdrom.com (probably in /pub/gutenberg or /gutenberg). The following files are listed in the index:

Jul 1993 Email 101 by John Goodwin   [email025.xxx] 75C
Jan 1993 Surfing the Internet, Jean Armour Polly   [Surf10xx.xxx] 49C
Sep 1992 Hitchhiker's Guide to the Internet,
Ed Krol   [hhgi10xx.xxx] 39
Aug 1992 The Hackers' Dictionary of
Computer Jargon   [jargn10x.xxx] 38
Jun 1992 Zen & the Art of Internet,
Brendan P. Kehoe   [zen10xxx.xxx] 34
[Zen has NOT been withdrawn from circulation at the request of the author]
Mar 1994 Big Dummy's Guide To The Internet,
by EFF   [bigd22xx.xxx] 118C

Demon services

What do Demon deliver? See the file describing this as found in ftp.demon.co,uk:pub/doc/Services.Txt.

NB: The Demon Service consists SOLELY of an IP connection to the Internet, with email forwarding/routing, and access to a local/full Usenet News Server. ALL the software available (at ftp.demon.co.uk) for use with Demon Internet is USER supported.

Future plans for Demon Internet can be found in Press.txt.

A list of publicly available hosts/services available from Demon (for example, ftp.demon.co.uk, irc.demon.co.uk) with their Internet addresses can be found in Demon.txt (this also has the current list of available dial-in PoPs with their phone numbers).

Other information about Demon PoPs can be found in Pop.faq.

A list of all the NEWS groups that are fed by Demon can be found in ftp.demon.co.uk:pub/news/active.zip and an annotated list of NEWS groups can be found in the same directory as newsdesc.zip. This also includes information on mailing lists. Author/compiler: Christopher P Salter <chris@loncps.demon.co.uk>

Demon do NOT provide a CLARINET news Usenet feed. CLARINET WILL NOT GIVE DEMON INTERNET A BULK FEED. They tried to arrange this when they started up but Clarinet will not allow it. For further information contact info@clarinet.com, NOT Demon.

The problem is that Clarinet does user based accounting and Demon Internet does host based accounting. Unless and until one or the other changes its basis of accounting in order to accommodate the other then the only way to get a Clarinet feed is from Clarinet.

This is not Demon Internet Ltd policy, it is Clarinet Inc. policy. Arguing the toss with Demon Internet staff will change nothing. If you feel that arguing about it will change matters, argue with the people who have made this policy decision – that is, Clarinet.

Other Demon-provided documents also reside in this directory (including Welcome.txt, Modem.txt, Demon.txt, Services.txt, Press.txt, Problem.txt, Support.faq, Pop.Faq and Batchftp.txt). This file [dis-meta.faq] and other Demonite-supplied documentation can be found in ftp.demon. co.uk:pub/doc/general. The various Demon support documents are, also available for anonymous ftp from subdirectories in ftp.demon.co.uk:pub/doc/.

All the Demon authored _files_ in the pub/doc directory can be found in DISDOC.ZIP.

From Welcome.txt as of 9 May 1994: If you require more personal attention, please mail internet@demon.net or phone the support line. Details:

Monday–Friday (excluding Bank holidays) 9 a.m.–12:30 p.m. 2 p.m.– 9 p.m. 0181 343 3881 (Saturdays 10 a.m.–5 p.m.)

Emergencies Only at all other times 0181 343 3881 – this gets put through to a pager service. Please note that we cannot accept support queries by other methods (fax, posted mail and so on) If you want to contact us by email then please email internet@demon.net and use the problem template available from ftp.demon.co.uk:pub/doc/problem.txt or included in your installation.

NB: This is a precis of the FULL Demon phone switching arrangement. The FULL details can be found in Demon.txt.

Netiquette

This sort of material can be found (as FAQs) in the Usenet newsgroups news.newusers.questions, news.announce.newusers, news.answers and so on. It is worth joining these groups, at least for a short while when you start using

Usenet. There is now a demon.answers newsgroup where Demon-related FAQs will be regularly cross-posted (including this one).

TSFAQN41.ZIP 94 Jun 26 garbo.uwasa.fi:/pc/ts/tsfaqn41.zip

Questions from UseNet and Timo's answers including:

FAQFTP.TXT FAQs related to FTP, with answers.

FAQNEWS.TXT FAQs related to general Internet use, with answers.

FAQPROGS.TXT FAQs related to programs, with answers.

By ts@uwasa.fi (Timo Salmi)
How to get FAQs, and indeed why they matter:

- Wait for them to turn up in the newsgroup (usually once a month but sometimes more – especially if the group is going off topic!)

- ftp to rtfm.mit.edu (this archive is mirrored at src.doc.ic.ac.uk), cd /pub/usenet/xxxxx/ (where xxxxx is the newsgroup name) and get the FAQ. They are often there twice (under separate subdirectories) – and they usually have tricky names to spell! Try mget with a suitable wildcard!

- FAQs are important because, as the name implies, they answer questions that are regularly posted to a Usenet newsgroup. If you read the FAQ then (hopefully) you won't post the same question as everyone else for the 1000th time!

- Other useful introductory FAQs can be found using ftp (see below):

  ftp rtfm.mit.edu:pub/usenet/news.answers/news-newusers-intro
  ftp rtfm.mit.edu:pub/usenet/news.answers/active-newsgroups/part1
  ftp rtfm.mit.edu:pub/usenet/news.answers/active-newsgroups/part2

Software and help available

Connecting to the Internet using software found at ftp.demon.co.uk, with other useful pointers:

Subject	ftp.demon.co.uk dir	usenet news
General	pub	demon.ip.support
DIS PC/MSDOS	pub/ibmpc/DIS	demon.ip.support.pc*
Textwin	pub/ibmpc/textwin	demon.ip.support.pc*
View	pub/ibmpc/view	demon.ip.support.pc*
Cppnews	pub/ibmpc/cppnews	demon.ip.cppnews
Windows	pub/ibmpc/windows	demon.ip.support.pc*

Subject	ftp.demon.co.uk dir	usenet news
Winsock	pub/ibmpc/winsock	demon.ip.winsock
Windows NT	pub/nt	demon.ip.support.pc*
OS/2	pub/os2	demon.ip.support.pc*
Unix (general)	pub/unix	demon.ip.support.unix
Linux	pub/unix/linux	demon.ip.support.unix
386BSD	pub/unix/386BSD	demon.ip.support.unix
SCO	pub/SCO	demon.ip.support.unix
Sun	pub/sun	demon.ip.support.unix
Xenix	pub/xenix	demon.ip.support.unix
NeXT	pub/NeXT	demon.ip.support.unix ?
Macintosh	pub/mac	demon.ip.support.mac
Amiga	pub/amiga	demon.ip.support.amiga
Atari	pub/atari	demon.ip.support.atari
Archimedes	pub/archimedes	demon.ip.support.archimedes

Some of the software indicated above has had user guides on 'How to set-up and configure for various Operating Systems' written for them. Where known, a pointer to where these guides can be found is given below. A Demon Documentation Group (DDG) has recently been set up to attempt to document the tools, activities and cultural icons relating to the Internet as it appears to Demon users.

OS	ftp.demon.co.uk:pub/ directory/file	Author/Editor
General	doc/DISDOC.ZIP	Internet@demon.net
MSDOS	doc/ka9q/dispc.txt	Internet@demon.net
Winsock	ibmpc/winsock/DIS_docs/ws _bg_v5.txt	paul@paulwork.demon. co.uk
NeXT	NeXT/NeXT.Internet.rtfd. compressed	paul@seer.demon.co.uk
Mac	mac/help/*.*	?????
Linux	unix/linux/slack1.2.help.tar.gz	john@linux.demon.co.uk
OS/2	doc/os/OS2.txt	?????
Amiga	amiga/info/amiga-faq.txt	amiga-faq@blender. demon.co.uk

The following FAQs have been created by Demon users and are posted to the indicated usenet newsgroup demon.ip.* and they may be cross-posted to demon.answers as well. They can be found via ftp in ftp.demon. co.uk:pub/doc/general or in the appropriate application subdirectory within the pub/doc directory.

FAQ Name	demon.ip. * group	Frequency	Author/Editor
DIS-META.FAQ	support	Bi-Weekly	mike@childsoc.demon. co.uk
TUNING.FAQ	support.pc	Bi-Weekly	Tuning@locomotive.com
TOOTKA.TXT	support	?	Jim@gl-serv.demon.co.uk
HOTTOPIC.FAQ	support	Monthly	marcus@guitar.demon. co.uk

Important FTP sites and why!

The most important FTP site for Demon users is ftp.demon.co.uk. Information relating to the directory structure of this site can be found in ftp.demon.co.uk:pub/FTPVIEW.TXT.

See also the files in ftp.demon.co.uk:pub/doc/ftpsites. Many archive sites are mirrored at src.doc.ic.ac.uk, and as Demon has a direct line to this site it is worth looking here prior to searching across the Atlantic link (saving bandwidth). Also take a look at:

MODER37B.ZIP 94 May 21 garbo.uwasa.fi:pc/pd2/moder37b.zip A list of MS-DOS FTP sites and moderators, by ts@uwasa.fi (Timo Salmi) and rhys@fit.qut.edu.au (Rhys Weatherley)

FTP-LIST.ZIP 94 Jun 5 garbo.uwasa.fi:pc/doc-net/ftp-list.zipoakoakland. edu:SimTel/msdos/info/ftp-list.zip A list of FTP sites providing Anonymous FTP, including how to use ftp, by Perry.Rovers@kub.nl (Perry Rovers)

MIRRORS.INF 94 Jun 16 oak.oakland.edu:SimTel/msdos/filedocs/mirrors.inf List of FTP sites mirroring SimTel, Garbo and ULowell by w8sdz@ SimTel.Coast.NET (Keith Petersen)

NB: Most of the ftp servers are UNIX systems, which means that filenames are case sensitive. Other systems may or may not be. The recent release of a free FTP.NLM for Novell NetWare 3.1x means that more NetWare file servers are also appearing as ftp servers. Other systems such as VAX, OS/2 and even KA9Q can also be found.

UNIX boxes usually have a master listing of their contents called ls-lR (non-UNIX people would find this immediately intuitive :) and may look for files.txt or something like that).

Other useful information

Sending e-mail to services NOT directly connected to the Internet:

INTER-NETWORK MAIL GUIDE:

Further modifications and (C) 1994 by Scott Yanoff (yanoff@csd4.csd. uwm.edu) Inter-Network Mail Guide - Original Copyright (C) 1992 by John J. Chew

This guide is available via ftp: csd4.csd.uwm.edu

Also via WWW/Mosaic, URL is: http://alpha.acast.nova.edu/cgi-bin/inmgq.pl

Or by email request to the author Scott Yanoff.

Various Services available on the Internet via telnet, Gopher, Finger or mail:

SPECIAL INTERNET CONNECTIONS:
Compiled By: Scott Yanoff (yanoff@csd4.csd.uwm.edu). This list is available via ftp: ftp.csd.uwm.edu:pub/inet.services.txt.

HINTS FOR NEW AND LONG-TIME USERS:
Compiled By: Stan Brown (brown@ncoast.org). Available via email from the author, and via ftp from ftp.demon.co.uk:pub/doc/general/hints.new.

DARTMOUTH COLLEGE LIST OF MAILING LISTS:
This list gives details of many mailing lists being run. It is available via ftp: dartcms1.dartmouth.edu:siglists/Internet.Lists.
(This is a VAX, so this MUST be transferred in ASCII/TEXT mode. Binary gives garbage!) Also via email to list-serv@dartcms1.dartmouth.edu with a message of send listshrt package

The following needs checking:

E-ZINE-LIST Compiled By: John Labovitz (johnl@ora.com).
This list gives details of many electronic magazines being published. It is available by email from the author, and via WWW/Mosaic, URL is: http://www.ora.com:8080/johnl/e-zine-list

Other important stuff

File formats, and how to get stuff. For MS-DOS you absolutely need PKZIP/PKUNZIP 2.04g (old ZIPs won't do). Or the latest free Info-Zip version, which is available for some other machines including unix, from quest.jpl.nasa.gov:pub or preferred from ftp.uu.net:pub/archiving/zip as unzip51.tar.Z or unzip51.zip. Info-Zip unzip is supplied with the FULL Demon installation DOS package.

Collect stuff as you need it. For MS-DOS one would advise getting the SimTel directory file, as you can then scan through it (with just a text editor or from the same directory the SIMDIR reader) looking for the program and its directory OFFLINE. A slightly out-of-date version can be found mirrored in ftp.demon.co.uk:pub/simtel20/msdos/filedocs/simindex.zip.

Most MS-DOS material uses the FILENAME.ZIP format (see above), the filename.Z format is UNIX compress format, the filename.gz format is GNU zip format. Both can be extracted using GNU zip (source is available on multiple platforms), obtainable from oak.oakland.edu:pub/misc/unix, or from prep.ai.mit.edu:pub/gnu.

Some archiving methods are specific to a particular machine (eg Spark on the Archimedes), others are most common on a particular platform, but are also available for other systems (LHA is popular with Amiga users, and is also available for the PC/MS-DOS and Mac formats).

UUCODE is a method of transferring 8 bit data via a 7 bit path. Made up of UUENCODE and UUDECODE. Versions are available for most systems. Look under ftp.demon.co.uk:pub/ibmpc/uucode for MS-DOS version.

Further details on archive/file formats and so on, can be obtained by anonymous ftp from ux1.uiuc.edu:doc/pcnet/compression. An alternative can be found on SimTel mirrors via anonymous ftp oak.oakland. edu:SimTel/msdos/starter/00-files.doc.

Some archives support transfer of compressed archives, which are compressed on-the-fly. The Demon ftp.demon.co.uk has recently added this facility.

And finally...

Thanks to Richard Clayton richard@locomotive.com for encouragement, and suggestions. Also thanks to: John Washington <john@wash.demon.co.uk>, Paul Allen <pla@sktb.demon.co.uk>, Jim Webb <Jim@gl-serv.demon. co.uk>, Nikki Locke <nikki@trmphrst.demon.co.uk>, Neil Hoggarth <neil@ntl.com>, Robin Sermon <Rsermon@ashford.demon.co.uk>, Christopher Salter <Chris@loncps.demon.co.uk>, Paul Evans <paul@ paulwork.demon.co.uk>, Paul Lynch <paul@seer.demon.co.uk>, Anthony Naggs <amn@ubik.demon.co.uk>, Phil Hughes <phil@phcomp.demon. co.uk>, Giles Todd <giles@hel.demon.co.uk>, Neil Brewitt <neil@melkfri. demon.co.uk>, Fearghas McKay <fearghas@challis.demon.co.uk>, Richard Lamont <richard@stonix.demon.co.uk>, Stan Brown <brown@ncoast.org>, Keith Petersen <w8sdz@SimTel.Coast.NET> and Timo Salmi <ts@uwasa.fi>.

Copyright 1994 Michael Bernardi/The Children's Society. This file may be freely distributed provided that it remains unedited from its current form. Sections may be quoted for reference providing its source is given. The latest version is posted regularly to the newsgroup demon.ip.support and cross-posted weekly to demon.answers.

It can be obtained via ftp from:

ftp.demon.co.uk:pub/doc/general/dis-meta.faq

or via World Wide Web:

http://ftp.demon.co.uk/pub/doc/html/dis-meta.html

Michael Bernardi (mike@childsoc.demon.co.uk)
The Children's Society, Edward Rudolf House, Margery Street, London, WC1X 0JL, UK Voice: +44 171 837 4299 Charity Reg. No. 221124

Appendix 11a

Glossary of telecomms jargon

BABT British Approvals Board for Telecommunications. BABT Approval is provided by a number of independent testing labs to validate adherence of telecomms equipment to UK standards.

Baud rate After BAUDOT, who invented time division multiplexing in 1874. Baud rate is not applicable to contemporary modems equipped with data compression. Use BPS.

bis 'second working'. First revision of a CCITT recommendation.

BPS 'bits per second' – describes the throughput of modems. Divide bits per second by ten to come up with an estimate of the number of characters per second (CPS) transmitted.

CCITT 'Comité Consultatif International Téléphonique et Télégraphique'. International organization which ratifies recommendations for telecomms standards. Now the ITU.

DCE geek-speak for 'Data Communications Equipment'. It means 'modem'.

DTE geek-speak for 'Data Terminal Equipment'. It usually means 'computer'.

error correction used within modems (V42) to manage error-free comms.

handshake Inter-device system to prevent data loss due to data overflow. 'Soft' handshaking embeds GO/STOP codes into the data stream (XON/XOFF). 'Hard' handshaking raises and lowers voltages on the communications port. More properly called frame or over-run control.

Hayes compatible Denotes use of the Hayes 'AT' command set.

MNP Proprietary 'standard' for modem data compression/error correction. Early non-V42 bis modems use MNP 5 for both error correction and data compression, as does some communications software. Later modems offer MNP 10. V42/V42 bis is more common.

RS232 – Short for 'Electrical Industries of America Recommended Standard number 232'. Refers to the port through which a device communicates.

ter   'third working'. Second revision of an ITU recommendation.

TERBO   Non CCITT-ratified proprietary mode, despite the inference.

Transmission speed   the maximum rate at which data may be sent through the telephone system. Actual throughput is increased by use of data compression techniques.

Uses LAPM   'Link Access Procedure for Modems'. V42 also contains 'Alternative Protocol', which means that it's compatible with MNP classes 2 through 4.

V42   Error correction standard

V42 bis   Standard for error correction/data compression within modems. A modem equipped with V42 bis can multiply throughput by up to four times if the data is compressible.

Appendix 11b

Glossary of Internet terms

Distilled from RFC 1392, the 'Internet Glossary', and the 'Modem & Communications GuideBook'

acoustic coupler Means of connecting external devices to a telephone handset avoiding direct electrical connection; most commonly used for low-speed data terminals.

Acceptable Use Policy (AUP) Many transit networks have policies which restrict the use to which the network may be put. A well-known example is NSFNET's AUP which does not allow commercial use. Enforcement of AUPs varies with the network.

acknowledgment (ACK) A type of message sent to indicate that a block of data arrived at its destination without error. [Source: NNSC]

address There are three types of addresses in common use within the Internet. They are email address; IP, internet or Internet address; and hardware or MAC address. See also: email address, IP address, internet address, MAC address.

address mask A bit mask used to identify which bits in an IP address correspond to the network and subnet portions of the address. This mask is often referred to as the subnet mask because the network portion of the address can be determined by the encoding inherent in an IP address.

address resolution Conversion of an internet address into the corresponding physical address.

Address Resolution Protocol (ARP) Used to dynamically discover the low-level physical network hardware address that corresponds to the high-level IP address for a given host. ARP is limited to physical network systems that support broadcast packets that can be heard by all hosts on the network. It is defined in RFC 826.

administrative domain (AD) A collection of hosts and routers, and the interconnecting network(s), managed by a single administrative authority.

Advanced Research Projects Agency Network (ARPANET) – A pioneering longhaul network funded by ARPA (now DARPA). It served as the basis for early networking research, as well as a central backbone during the development of the Internet. The ARPANET consisted of individual packet switching computers interconnected by leased lines. [Source: FYI4]

anonymous FTP   Anonymous FTP allows a user to retrieve documents, files, programs, and other archived data from anywhere in the Internet without having to establish a user-id and password. By using the special user-id of 'anonymous' the network user will bypass local security checks and will have access to publicly accessible files on the remote system.

Archie   A system to automatically gather, index and serve information on the Internet. The initial implementation of Archie provided an indexed directory of filenames from all anonymous FTP archives on the Internet. Later versions provide other collections of information.

archive site   A machine that provides access to a collection of files across the Internet. An 'anonymous FTP archive site', for example, provides access to this material via the FTP protocol.

ASCII   American Standard Code for Information Interchange (ASCII). A standard character-to-number encoding widely used in the computer industry. ASCII is the standard used for sending non-binary messages over the Internet.

asynchronous   Occurring without central control or in an unpredictable time interval between successive elements; the typical mode of telegraphy, minicomputers and personal computers; requires transmission of start and stop bits to provide decoding synchronization at the receiver.

Asynchronous Transfer Mode (ATM)   A method for the dynamic allocation of bandwidth using a fixed-size packet (called a cell). ATM is also known as 'fast packet'.

BABT   British Approvals Board for Telecommunications. An independent body responsible for approval procedures for UK telecomms equipment. Only BABT-approved equipment may be connected to UK services, regardless of the supplier of these services.

backbone   The top level in a hierarchical network. Stub and transit networks which connect to the same backbone are guaranteed to be interconnected.

baud   A unit of signalling speed. The speed in baud is the number of discrete conditions or signal elements per second. If each signal event represents only one bit condition, then baud is the same as bits per second. Baud does not otherwise equal bits per second.

bis 'Second Working' or 'Second Implementation' as used in CCITT recommendations.

BinHex Program for the Macintosh computer which translates binary files into ASCII representations. Converted binary files can then be transferred as electronic mail. Used to get over the 7-bit limitations of the Internet.

Bitnet An academic computer network that provides interactive electronic mail and file transfer services, using a store-and-forward protocol, based on IBM Network Job Entry protocols. Bitnet-II encapsulates the Bitnet protocol within IP packets and depends on the Internet to route them.

bounce The return of a piece of mail because of an error in its delivery. [Source: ZEN]

bridge A device which forwards traffic between network segments based on datalink layer information. These segments would have a common network layer address.

bulletin board system (BBS) A computer, and associated software, which typically provides electronic messaging services, archives of files, and any other services or activities of interest to the bulletin board system's operator. Although BBSs have traditionally been the domain of hobbyists, an increasing number of BBSs are connected directly to the Internet, and many BBSs are currently operated by government, educational, and research institutions.

Campus Wide Information System (CWIS) A CWIS makes information and services publicly available on campus via kiosks, and makes interactive computing available via kiosks, interactive computing systems and campus networks. Services routinely include directory information, calendars, bulletin boards, databases.

CCITT Comité Consultatif International des Téléphones et Télégraphes, a major constituent of the International Telecommunications Union (ITU) that sets standards for the operation of telecommunications services across international boundaries. Many CCITT recommendations are adopted for use domestically. Now renamed to 'ITU'.

client A computer system or process that requests a service of another computer system or process. A workstation requesting the contents of a file from a file server is a client of the file server. [Source: NNSC]

client–server model A common way to describe the paradigm of many network protocols. Examples include the name-server/name-resolver relationship in DNS and the file-server/file-client relationship in NFS.

Comité Consultatif International de Télégraphique et Téléphonique (CCITT now ITU/T) – This organization is part of the United National International Telecommunications Union (ITU) and is responsible for making technical recommendations about telephone and data communications systems.

Computer Emergency Response Team (CERT)   The CERT was formed by DARPA in November 1988 in response to the needs exhibited during the Internet worm incident. The CERT charter is to work with the Internet community to facilitate its response to computer security events involving Internet hosts, to take proactive steps to raise the community's awareness of computer security issues, and to conduct research targeted at improving the security of existing systems.

cracker (USA)   A cracker is an individual who attempts to access computer systems without authorization. These individuals are often malicious, as opposed to 'hackers', and have many means at their disposal for breaking into a system.

CR (carriage return)   A control character causing the print or display position to move to the first position on the line, drawn from the typewriter and teleprinter function with similar action.

Cyberspace   A term coined by William Gibson in his fantasy novel *Neuromancer* to describe the 'world' of computers, and the society that gathers around them. [Source: ZEN]

cyclic redundancy check (CRC)   A number derived from a set of data that will be transmitted. By recalculating the CRC at the remote end and comparing it to the value originally transmitted, the receiving node can detect some types of transmission errors. [Source: MALAMUD]

data communications equipment (DCE)   Standards-body term for devices that perform signal conversion at the extremities of a data circuit. A data set (modem) or a CSU are common examples of a DCE. Compare to DTE.

data encryption key (DEK)   Used for the encryption of message text and for the computation of message integrity checks (signatures).

Data Encryption Standard (DES)   A popular, standard encryption scheme.

Defense Advanced Research Projects Agency (DARPA)   An agency of the US Department of Defense responsible for the development of new technology for use by the military. DARPA (formerly known as ARPA) was responsible for funding much of the development of the Internet we know today, including the Berkeley version of UNIX and TCP/IP. [Source: NNSC]

data terminal equipment   The standards-body term for a computer, user terminal, workstation or personal computer used for data communications; abbreviated DTE. Compare to DCE.

Defense Data Network (DDN)   A global communications network serving the US Department of Defense composed of MILNET, other portions of the Internet, and classified networks which are not part of the Internet. The DDN is used to connect military installations and is managed by the Defense Information Systems Agency.

Defense Data Network Network Information Center (DDN NIC) Often called 'The NIC', the DDN NIC's primary responsibility is the assignment of Internet network addresses and AutonomousSystem numbers, the administration of the root domain, and providing information and support services to the DDN. It is also a primary repository for RFCs.

Defense Information Systems Agency (DISA)   Formerly called the Defense Communications Agency (DCA), this is the government agency responsible for managing the DDN portion of the Internet, including the MILNET. Currently, DISA administers the DDN, and supports the user assistance services of the DDN NIC.

dial-up   A temporary, as opposed to dedicated, connection between machines established over a standard phone line.

digest   Instead of getting email messages from your listserv subscription one at a time as they are posted, the digest format gives you a compilation of the day's (week's, month's) messages. Some folk prefer this format since it helps to manage a large influx of mail and helps hold discussion on a certain topic together. Others prefer the more immediate and spontaneous 'heat' of receiving messages as they are posted. Note: not all listservs offer this distribution option.

domain   'Domain' is a heavily over-used term in the Internet. It can be used in the Administrative Domain context, or the Domain Name context.

Domain Name System (DNS)   The DNS is a general-purpose distributed, replicated, data query service. The principal use is the lookup of host IP addresses based on host names. The style of host names now used in the Internet is called 'domain name', because they are the style of names used to look up anything in the DNS. Some important domains are: .COM (commercial), .EDU (educational), .NET (network operations), .GOV (US government), and .MIL (US military). Most countries also have a domain. For example, .US (United States), .UK (United Kingdom), .AU (Australia). It is defined in STD 13, RFCs 1034 and 1035.

dweeb Slang (USA). Derogatory term for an unliked person, often young and unknowledgeable. Dweebs sometimes mature into nerds, and then into geeks.

E-journal (Electronic Journal)   Newsletters, zines, periodicals, scholarly journals same as the hard copy, except available over the net. You can access e-journals two ways: (1) a subscription will have the journal delivered to your e-mail box, or (2) you can look up the journal at its host site (via WAIS or Gopher) and if you want a copy you can have it delivered via FTP.

Ebone   A pan-European backbone service.

Electronic Frontier Foundation (EFF)   A foundation established to address social and legal issues arising from the impact on society of the increasingly pervasive use of computers as a means of communication and information distribution.

electronic mail (email)   A system whereby a computer user can exchange messages with other computer users (or groups of users) via a communications network. Electronic mail is one of the most popular uses of the Internet. [Source: NNSC]

email address   The domain-based or UUCP address that is used to send electronic mail to a specified destination.

emulate/emulation   Imitating a system or device such that a connected device accepts the same information, executes the same computer programs and achieves the same results as if the emulator were one of its own kind. Most often, emulation is a downward step in the capability of the device being used, as when a personal computer is used to emulate a mechanical teleprinter or a 'dumb' terminal on a computer network. While some degree of upward emulation is possible, it is less prevalent in the broad view of computer communications.

encryption   Encryption is the manipulation of a packet's data in order to prevent any but the intended recipient from reading that data. There are many types of data encryption, and they are the basis of network security.

Ethernet   A 10 Mb/s standard for LANs, initially developed by Xerox, and later refined by Digital, Intel and Xerox (DIX). All hosts are connected to a coaxial cable where they contend for network access using a Carrier Sense Multiple Access with Collision Detection (CSMA/CD) paradigm.

European Academic and Research Network (EARN)   A network connecting European academic and research institutions with electronic mail and file transfer services using the Bitnet protocol.

FARNET   A non-profit corporation, established in 1987, whose mission is to advance the use of computer networks to improve research and education.

FAQ   Frequently Asked Question. Either a frequently asked question, or a list of frequently asked questions and their answers. Many Usenet news groups, and some non-Usenet mailing lists, maintain FAQ lists (FAQS) so that participants won't spend lots of time answering the same set of questions.

Federal Information Exchange (FIX)   One of the connection points between the American governmental internets and the Internet. [Source: SURA]

file transfer   The copying of a file from one computer to another over a computer network.

File Transfer Protocol (FTP)   A protocol which allows a user on one host to access, and transfer files to and from, another host over a network. Also, FTP is usually the name of the program the user invokes to execute the protocol.

finger   A program that displays information about a particular user, or all users, logged on the local system or on a remote system. It typically shows full name, last login time, idle time, terminal line, and terminal location (where applicable). It may also display plan and project files left by the user.

flame   A strong opinion and/or criticism of something, usually as a frank inflammatory statement, in an electronic mail message. It is common to precede a flame with an indication of pending fire (that is, FLAME ON!). Flame Wars occur when people start flaming other people for flaming when they shouldn't have.

For Your Information (FYI)   A subseries of RFCs that are not technical standards or descriptions of protocols. FYIs convey general information about topics related to TCP/IP or the Internet.

flow control   In data communications, the use of buffering and other mechanisms that operate to avoid data loss in case the receiver cannot keep up with the transmitter. The ASCII control characters X-ON and X-OFF are frequently-used examples; they are returned in the reverse direction as an instruction for the sender to hold or restart held transmission.

freenet   Community-based bulletin board system with email, information services, interactive communications, and conferencing. Freenets are funded and operated by individuals and volunteers – in one sense, like public television. They are part of the National Public Telecomputing Network (NPTN), an organization based in Cleveland, Ohio, devoted to making computer telecommunication and networking services as freely available as public libraries. [Source: LAQUEY]

gateway   The term 'router' is now used in place of the original definition of 'gateway'. Currently, a gateway is a communications device/program which passes data between networks having similar functions but dissimilar implementations. This should not be confused with a protocol converter.

geek   Slang (USA). Derogatory term for computer user or enthusiast of some sort.

Gopher   A distributed information service that makes available hierarchical collections of information across the Internet. Gopher uses a simple protocol that allows a single Gopher client to access information from any accessible Gopher server, providing the user with a single 'Gopher space' of information. Public domain versions of the client and server are available.

hacker   A person who delights in having an intimate understanding of the internal workings of a system, computers and computer networks in particular. The term is often misused in a pejorative context, where 'cracker' would be the correct term. In the UK the terms Hacker and Cracker are used indiscriminately.

header   The portion of a packet, preceding the actual data, containing source and destination addresses, and error checking and other fields. A header is also the part of an electronic mail message that precedes the body of a message and contains, among other things, the message originator, date and time.

hierarchical routing   The complex problem of routing on large networks can be simplified by reducing the size of the networks. This is accomplished by breaking a network into a hierarchy of networks, where each level is responsible for its own routing. The Internet has, basically, three levels: the backbones, the mid-levels, and the stub networks. The backbones know how to route between the mid-levels, the mid-levels know how to route between the sites, and each site (being an autonomous system) knows how to route internally.

Integrated Services Digital Network (ISDN)   An emerging technology which is beginning to be offered by the telephone carriers of the world. ISDN combines voice and digital network services in a single medium, making it possible to offer customers digital data services as well as voice connections through a single 'wire'. The standards that define ISDN are specified by CCITT.

internet   While an internet is a network, the term 'internet' is usually used to refer to a collection of networks interconnected with routers.

Internet (note the capital 'I')   The Internet is the largest internet in the world. It is a three-level hierarchy composed of backbone networks (for example, NSFNET, MILNET), mid-level networks, and stub networks. The Internet is a multiprotocol internet.

internet address   An IP address that uniquely identifies a node on an internet. An Internet address (capital 'I'), uniquely identifies a node on the Internet.

Internet Assigned Numbers Authority (IANA)   The central registry for various Internet protocol parameters, such as port, protocol and enterprise numbers, and options, codes and types. The currently assigned values are listed in the 'Assigned Numbers' document [STD2]. To request a number assignment, contact the IANA at 'iana@isi.edu'.

Internet Protocol (IP)   The Internet Protocol, defined in STD 5, RFC 791, is the network layer for the TCP/IP Protocol Suite. It is a connectionless, best-effort packet switching protocol.

Internet Relay Chat (IRC)   A worldwide 'party line' protocol that allows one to converse with others in real time. IRC is structured as a network of servers, each of which accepts connections from client programs, one per user. [Source: HACKER]

International Telecommunications Union (ITU)   Anglicization of the proper French name of the Union Internationale des Télécommunications (UIT), resident in Geneva, Switzerland. ITU is the treaty-established world centre for agreements on telecommunications technical and operating standards and is a constituent body of the United Nations, engaging also in international development and education concerning telecommunications.

IP address   The 32-bit address defined by the Internet Protocol in STD 5, RFC 791. It is usually represented in dotted decimal notation.

KA9Q   A popular implementation of TCP/IP and associated protocols for amateur packet radio systems.

Kermit   A popular file transfer protocol developed by Columbia University. Because Kermit runs in most operating environments, it provides an easy method of file transfer. Kermit is NOT the same as FTP. [Source: MALAMUD]

listserv   An automated mailing list distribution system originally designed for the Bitnet/EARN network.

leased line   Any circuit or combination of circuits designated to be at the exclusive disposal of a given user. Synonym: Private line; Full Period Line; Dedicated Line, Tie Line (colloquial).

local loop   The local circuit connection between the end user and the user's nearest telephone exchange office; notorious for being the poorest, weakest link in data circuits.

mail gateway   A machine that connects two or more electronic mail systems (including dissimilar mail systems) and transfers messages between them. Sometimes the mapping and translation can be quite complex, and it generally requires a store-and-forward scheme whereby the message is received from one system completely before it is transmitted to the next system, after suitable translations.

mailing list   A list of email addresses, used by a mail exploder, to forward messages to groups of people. Generally, a mailing list is used to discuss a certain set of topics, and different mailing lists discuss different topics. A mailing list may be moderated. This means that messages sent to the list are actually sent to a moderator who determines whether or not to send the messages on to everyone else. Requests to subscribe to, or leave, a mailing list should ALWAYS be sent to the list's '-request' address (for example, ietf-request@cnri.reston.va.us for the IETF mailing list).

maximum transmission unit (MTU)   The largest frame length which may be sent on a physical medium.

moderator   A person, or small group of people, who manage moderated mailing lists and newsgroups. Moderators are responsible for determining which email submissions are passed on to the list.

modem   Modulator/demodulator. A piece of equipment that connects a computer to a data transmission line (typically a telephone line of some sort). Modems transfer data at speeds ranging from 300 bits per second (bps) to 19.2 Kbps. 28 Kbps modems will be here Real Soon Now (RSN).

Multipurpose Internet Mail Extensions (MIME)   An extension to Internet email which provides the ability to transfer non-textual data, such as graphics, audio and fax. It is defined in RFC 1341.

Multi-User Domain (MUD)   A game available on the Internet where multiple users can take part simultaneously.

Multi-User Dungeon (MUD) Adventure   Role playing games, or simulations played on the Internet. Devotees call them 'text-based virtual reality adventures'. The games can feature fantasy combat, booby traps and magic. Players interact in real time and can change the 'world' in the game as they play it. Most MUDs are based on the Telnet protocol. [Source: LAQUEY]

nerd   Slang (USA). See 'Dweeb'.

Netiquette A pun on 'etiquette' referring to proper behaviour on a network.

network   A computer network is a data communications system which interconnects computer systems at various different sites. A network may be composed of any combination of LANs, MANs or WANs.

network address   The network portion of an IP address. For a class A network, the network address is the first byte of the IP address. For a class B network, the network address is the first two bytes of the IP address. For a class C network, the network address is the first three bytes of the IP address. In each case, the remainder is the host address. In the Internet, assigned network addresses are globally unique.

Network File System (NFS)   A protocol developed by Sun Microsystems, and defined in RFC 1094, which allows a computer system to access files over a network as if they were on its local disks. This protocol has been incorporated in products by more than 200 companies, and is now a *de facto* Internet standard. [Source: NNSC]

Network News Transfer Protocol (NNTP)   A protocol, defined in RFC 977, for the distribution, inquiry, retrieval and posting of news articles.

Network Time Protocol (NTP)   A protocol that ensures accurate local timekeeping with reference to radio and atomic clocks located on the Internet. This protocol is capable of synchronizing distributed clocks within milliseconds over long time periods. It is defined in STD 12, RFC 1119.

Packet InterNet Groper (PING)   A program used to test reachability of destinations by sending them an ICMP echo request and waiting for a reply. The term is used as a verb: 'Ping host X to see if it is up!' [Source: RFC1208]

packet switching   The technique in which a stream of data is broken into standardized units called 'packets', each of which contains address, sequence, control, size and error checking information in addition to the user data. Specialized packet switches operate on this added information to move the packets to their destination in the proper sequence and again present them in a contiguous stream.

parity   A constant state of equality; one of the oldest and simplest methods of error checking data transmission. Characters are forced into parity (total number of marking bits odd or even as selected by choice) by adding a one or zero bit as appropriate when transmitted; parity is then checked as odd or even at the receiver.

parity bit   A check bit appended to an array of binary digits to make the sum of all the digits always odd or always even.

Point of Presence (PoP)   A site where there exists a collection of telecommunications equipment, usually digital leased lines and multi-protocol routers.

Point-to-Point Protocol (PPP)   The Point-to-Point Protocol, defined in RFC 1171, provides a method for transmitting packets over serial point-to-point links.

Post Office Protocol (POP)   A protocol designed to allow single-user hosts to read mail from a server. There are three versions: POP, POP2, and POP3. Later versions are NOT compatible with earlier versions.

postmaster   The person responsible for taking care of electronic mail problems, answering queries about users, and other related work at a site.

Privacy Enhanced Mail (PEM)   Internet email which provides confidentiality, authentication and message integrity using various encryption methods.

quad standard   Modem providing four CCITT modes, usually V21, V22/V22Bis, V23.

quin standard   Modem providing five CCITT modes, usually V21, V22/V22Bis, V23, V32.

RS-232   The most common technical specification for interconnection of DTEs to DCEs; extremely close equivalent to the suite of CCITT V.24/V.28 and ISO-2110.

remote login   Operating on a remote computer, using a protocol over a computer network, as though locally attached.

Request For Comments (RFC)   The document series, begun in 1969, which describes the Internet suite of protocols and related experiments. Not all (in fact very few) RFCs describe Internet standards, but all Internet standards are written up as RFCs. The RFC series of documents is unusual in that the proposed protocols are forwarded by the Internet research and development community, acting on their own behalf, as opposed to the formally reviewed and standardized protocols that are promoted by organizations such as CCITT and ANSI.

router   A device which forwards traffic between networks. The forwarding decision is based on network layer information and routing tables, often constructed by routing protocols.

Serial Line IP (SLIP) A protocol used to run IP over serial lines, such as telephone circuits or RS-232 cables, interconnecting two systems. SLIP is defined in RFC 1055.

server A provider of resources (for example, file servers and name servers).

SIG Special Interest Group. Called a forum on some systems, notably CompuServe.

signature The three or four line message at the bottom of a piece of email or a Usenet article which identifies the sender. Large signatures (over five lines) are generally frowned upon.

Simple Mail Transfer Protocol (SMTP) A protocol, defined in STD 10, RFC 821, used to transfer electronic mail between computers. It is a server-to-server protocol, so other protocols are used to access the messages.

Simple Network Management Protocol (SNMP) The Internet standard protocol, defined in STD 15, RFC 1157, developed to manage nodes on an IP network. It is currently possible to manage wiring hubs, toasters, jukeboxes, and so on.

TCP/IP Protocol Suite Transmission Control Protocol over Internet Protocol. This is a common shorthand which refers to the suite of transport and application protocols which runs over IP.

ter Means 'third working' or third implementation, as used in CCITT recommendations.

terminal (1) A point at which information can enter or leave a communications network; (2) Any device capable of sending or receiving information over a communications channel.

terminal equipment Devices, apparatus and their associated interfaces used to forward information to a local customer or distant terminal.

TTY (Teletype) (1) The registered trade name for teleprinters and data terminals of the Teletype Corporation; (2) Used generically in the telecommunications industry for teleprinters or data terminals that emulate teleprinter operations.

telnet Telnet is the Internet standard protocol for remote terminal connection service. It is defined in STD 8, RFC 854 and extended with options by many other RFCs.

terminal emulator A program that allows a computer to emulate a terminal. The workstation thus appears as a terminal to the remote host. [Source: MALAMUD]

Transmission Control Protocol (TCP)   An Internet Standard transport layer protocol defined in STD 7, RFC 793. It is connection-oriented and stream-oriented, as opposed to UDP.

Trojan Horse   A computer program which carries within itself a means to allow the creator of the program access to the system using it. See RFC 1135.

UNIX-to-UNIX CoPy (UUCP)   This was initially a program run under the UNIX operating system that allowed one UNIX system to send files to another UNIX system via dial-up phone lines. Today, the term is more commonly used to describe the large international network which uses the UUCP protocol to pass news and electronic mail.

UUEncode   Program for personal computers, which translates binary files into ASCII representations. Converted binary files can then be transferred as electronic mail. Used to get over the 7-bit limitations of the Internet. UUDecode is used to effect the reverse transformation.

URL   Uniform Resource Locator. Standard form of textual addressing used on the World Wide Web.

Usenet   A collection of thousands of topically named newsgroups, the computers which run the protocols, and the people who read and submit Usenet news. Not all Internet hosts subscribe to Usenet and not all Usenet hosts are on the Internet. See also: Network News Transfer Protocol, UNIX-to-UNIX CoPy. [Source: NWNET]

virus   A program that replicates itself on computer systems by incorporating itself into other programs which are shared among computer systems.

white pages   The Internet supports several databases that contain basic information about users, such as email addresses, telephone numbers and postal addresses. These databases can be searched to get information about particular individuals. Because they serve a function akin to the telephone book, these databases are often referred to as 'white pages'.

whois   An Internet program which allows users to query a database of people and other Internet entities, such as domains, networks and hosts, kept at the DDN NIC. The information for people shows a person's company name, address, phone number and email address. [Source: FYI4]

Wide Area Information Servers (WAIS)   A distributed information service which offers simple natural language input, indexed searching for fast retrieval, and a 'relevance feedback' mechanism which allows the results of initial searches to influence future searches. Public domain implementations are available.

World Wide Web (WWW or W3) A hypertext-based, distributed information system created by researchers at CERN in Switzerland. Users may create, edit or browse hypertext documents. The clients and servers are freely available.

worm A computer program that replicates itself and is self-propagating. Worms, as opposed to viruses, are meant to spawn in network environments. Network worms were first defined by Shoch and Hupp of Xerox in *ACM Communications* (March 1982). The Internet worm of November 1988 is perhaps the most famous; it successfully propagated itself on over 6000 systems across the Internet.

X.400 The CCITT and ISO standard for electronic mail. It is widely used in Europe and Canada.

X.500 The CCITT and ISO standard for electronic directory services.

Yellow Pages (YP) A service used by UNIX administrators to manage databases distributed across a network.

References

BIG-LAN 'BIG-LAN Frequently Asked Questions Memo', BIG-LAN DIGEST V4:I8, February 14, 1992.

COMER Comer D. (1991). *Internetworking with TCP/IP: Principles, Protocols and Architecture*. Englewood Cliffs, NJ: Prentice-Hall.

FYI4 Malkin G and Marine A. (1992). FYI on Questions and Answers: Answers to Commonly asked "New Internet User" Questions. FYI 4, RFC 1325, Xylogics, SRI, May 1992.

HACKER 'THIS IS THE JARGON FILE', Version 2.9.8, January 1992.

HPCC 'Grand Challenges 1993: High Performance Computing and Communications'. Committee on Physical, Mathematical and Engineering Sciences of the Federal Coordinating Council for Science, Engineering and Technology.

MALAMUD Malamud C. (1992). *Analyzing Sun Networks*. New York, NY: Van Nostrand Reinhold.

NNSC 'NNSC's Hypercard Tour of the Internet'.

LAQUEY LaQuey T. (with J. Ryer) (1992). *The Internet Companion: A Beginner's Guide to Global Networking*. Reading, MA: Addison-Wesley.

NWNET Kochmer J. and NorthWestNet (1992). *The Internet Passport: NorthWestNets Guide to Our World Online*. Bellevue, WA: NorthWestNet.

RFC1208 Jacobsen O. and Lynch D. (1991). *A Glossary of Networking Terms*. RFC 1208, Interop, Inc., March.

STD1 Postel J. (1992). *IAB Official Protocol Standards*. STD 1, RFC 1360, Internet Architecture Board, September.

STD2 Reynolds J. and Postel J. (1992). *Assigned Numbers*. STD 2, RFC 1340, USC/Information Sciences Institute, July.

TAN Tanenbaum A. (1989). *Computer Networks* 2nd edn. Englewood Cliffs, NJ: Prentice-Hall.

ZEN Kehoe B. (1992). Zen and the Art of the Internet.

Appendix 12

An epilogue for Internet users

Author's note: This is part of a Usenet message which appeared as we went to press. Change your passwords weekly, at least, and lock up your data....

Found in:

Newsgroups: comp.security.unix,comp.security.misc,alt.security
From: a2i support account <support@rahul.net>
Subject: intrusion at rahul.net and warning for affected sites
Sender: news@rahul.net (Usenet News)
Organization: a2i network
Date: Sat, 9 Jul 1994 03:51:07 GMT

AN INTRUSION AT RAHUL.NET AND A WARNING FOR POTENTIALLY AFFECTED SITES

On July 6 1994, at slightly after 2 am local time (PDT, 7 hours west of UTC), an intruder installed a TCP/IP-sniffing daemon on one of the machines at a2i communications (domain rahul.net). The sniffer was discovered and disabled on the evening of the same day, about 18 hours later. During this time, the daemon collected data including passwords.

Here is a summary of the intruder's tracks discovered in combination on the hosts bolero.rahul.net [192.160.13.1] and jive.rahul.net [192.160.13.2]. Both are SPARC machines running SunOS 4.1.3.

1. A number of setuid-root programs, which would instantly yield a root shell when executed. We found these with the command:

   find / -fstype nfs -prune -o -perm -04000 -print

2. Processes, one listening on UDP port 891, another listening on UDP port 937. We could detect this bound ports with the 'lsof' program.

3. A daemon that monitored the '/dev/nit' device, keeping the Ethernet interface le0 in promiscuous mode, and recorded the first few bytes of each telnet, ftp, and rlogin session, apparently to collect passwords. Output was collected in a log file. We could detect the promiscuous mode of le0 with the command '/usr/etc/ifconfig le0', which printed information similar to this:

le0: flags=163
<UP,BROADCAST,NOTRAILERS,RUNNING,PROMISC>
                        ^^^^^^^ note this

4. A daemon listening on TCP port 3011 which would accept a connection (no password needed) and immediately provide a root shell. The intruder could later connect to this port and use the root shell to collect the contents of the log file. We could detect these bound port with the 'lsof' program.

5. We were able to monitor the local network and observe incoming connections to port 3011 from the following hosts:

    joe.me.uiuc.edu   7:05 pm PDT July 6
    athena.brynmawr.edu   6:54 am PDT July 8

We believe that during the connection at 7:05 pm on July 6 from joe.me.uiuc.edu the intruder was able to collect the contents of the log file. The connection attempt at 6:54 am on July 8 was benign, because the intruder's processes were no longer active.

From the log file collected by the intruder's daemon, we have made a list of potentially affected hosts and it is given below. A numeric IP address indicates failure of the SunOS 4.1.3 gethostbyaddr routine to resolve the name – this usually means that either reverse resolution failed, or that reverse resolution yielded a name that could not be resolved back to the original IP address.

A quick script has been used to filter out from the log file entries for ftp sessions in which the target user was 'anonymous' or 'ftp', and entries for connections not involving any host external to our network. All other host names recorded by the sniffer are included in this list. Site administrators at all these hosts are advised to search their systems for possible intrusions. They should assume that if their users accessed a2i, or if any a2i user accessed their site, a password might have been logged. We are mailing a warning message to postmaster at each affected host. The message includes specific entries found for that host in the intruder's log.

A script was run to attempt to telnet to port 3011 on each host in the attached list, attempting to find out if a similar intrusion was in progress anywhere. No active port 3011 was reached on any of these hosts. There is, however, no guarantee that the intruder will always use port 3011.

All sites should look at their logs and search for connections to and from the domain rahul.net and/or from any host on the network 192.160.13.0, at any time before approximately 11:00 pm July 6. All clear-text passwords used in such sessions should be considered suspect.

For safety, it may be wise to assume that any password transmitted during the last 8 weeks has been compromised – since it cannot be guaranteed that previous undetected intrusions did not happen.

It is not yet clear by which mechanism the intruder gained access.

Appendix 13

Internet troubleshooting

If you've got this far without hesitation, repetition or deviation then you are doing well. The Internet, and the software and computer systems you need to master to become attached to it, are complicated beyond belief. A few punters are beginning to realize this now that some of the euphoria of UK computer journalists has worn off, and not a few letters are starting to appear in the computer press bemoaning the difficulty of hooking into the Global Garbage Dump. Even *Byte*, the once-respected American computer journal is hissing and spitting at the necessity of becoming a TCP/IP consultant before you can send your first email message. So for all those in trouble with the various bits and pieces of the Internet, this one is for you.

Troubleshooting Internet basics (Chapter 1)

The distinction between a 'full' Internet connection and a 'terminal' connection is being artfully blurred by not a few UK based purveyors of bulletin board systems. Full Internet services include those which need TCP based software to interact with them, whilst partial Internet services such as Internet-savvy electronic mail can be made to work in all sorts of devious ways without getting involved in TCP/IP. This may be a good thing, but don't get duped into believing that ASCII based terminal services offer 'full' Internet working.

The difference will become even more distinctive in 1995/96 when new ways of working with TCP/IP services over the Internet will appear. These will include video telephony, voice mail, digital voice and video bulletin boards (Usenet) and much more. To get the full benefit of these services you'll need a TCP/IP based account. Be wary of service providers who don't offer TCP/IP working but sell you offers of 'full' provision. If there's no TCP/IP on offer – then you'll be left behind on the digital dog-track, come the video revolution.

Access points

Service providers take time to react to influxes of new users. Generally they react either by adding more modems and phone numbers so remote users don't have to redial more than a couple of times to log in, or they react by ignoring pleas for more lines by frustrated users. Those who take the second approach will go broke in months. If you are signing up with an Internet provider look primarily for a local access point (PoP) near you. Then check how many lines it has. Check availability by dialling the number with an ordinary phone at peak time. This is normally 6:01 p.m. on any weekday. If you need to redial more than a couple of times to hear the modem, then you may be in for a frustrating time if you do sign up.

The most expensive type of dial-up account is one where all your calls are long distance, and where your service provider charges you by the minute for access time. (Internet browsing is time consuming.) The cheapest type is an account where there is a PoP on an exchange local to you, and you are not paying by the minute for access. If you do live in a remote area of the UK (like Sussex) then consider using Mercury 132 access if it's available to you. This costs around £10 a year, there's no tricky PIN to use, you simply add 132 in front of your normal dial string. Contrary to rumours by comms geeks Mercury 132 access does not degrade digital access by fast modems. Talk to Mercury on FreeCall Mercury for more details: 0500 500 196 for residential enquiries, 0500 700 102 for business enquiries.

Troubleshooting software (Chapter 2)

Getting hold of TCP/IP software is not easy at the moment. At the time of writing software for Windows is sparse. One Shareware route for Windows users is to use Trumpet Winsock, a Windows 'socket' for TCP/IP dial-up working, and then add utilities such as Netscape Mosaic for WWW browsing, and a mail program such as Eudora. Eudora only works with POP3 mail which isn't supported by some UK providers, for no good reason. DOS users are stuck with derivatives of KA9Q software (the call sign of the guy who wrote it), which works, but is clumsy when compared with commercial Windows products.

The best commercial product for PC Windows users is currently NetManage Chameleon 4.1, which works with both SMTP mail and POP3 mail; the best commercial software for Macs is VersaTerm Link. This works only with Internet providers who offer 'standard' SMTP send, POP3 receive accounts. These are standard in the USA, but not so in the UK – check with your provider before you buy.

Mac Shareware users can use Eudora for mail with a useful bolt-on called AddMail to make Eudora work with SMTP-only providers. TurboGopher, Anarchie, MacWeb and MacWAIS all do what they imply with great success, Mac PPP provides PPP dial-up. Mac users will also need the MacTCP control panel, free with this book and a Demon account, or included with System 7.5. (System 7.5 will not run on 68000 based Macs, although MacTCP will.) The ftp site at ftp.demon.co.uk provides all the Shareware software you need to get started, apart from the commercial versions.

Users of terminal accounts such as CIX and Delphi are stuck with whatever software is provided by the provider, or a third party, unless they want to type in clumsy commands at an ASCII terminal. CIX currently provide only Internet Mail and Usenet Support through their official Windows software (called Ameol); telnet, ftp and other Internet services are accessed by entering VT100 terminal mode. CIX themselves don't directly support the GUIs of Macs or Amigas, although some third party programs offer varying degrees of support.

CompuServe users can use CIM (pronounced with a soft 'c' as in Sim) for DOS, Mac and Windows platforms. This offers good mail handling, Usenet, and eventually, full TCP/IP access (mid 1995).

CityScape provide Windows software with Mail, Usenet and a WWW browser while the PC User group offer WinNet, an offline mailer and Usenet utility. Other providers seem to go down the cheap and cheerful route of providing basic email/Usenet utilities, and a Web browser. UK services will get a shock when Microsoft, IBM or BT launch cheap Internet access with fully figured software, sometime in 1995/96, although at the moment providers can get away with selling anything with an Internet label on it. Otherwise the UK software scene, (and support) is still parlous for users of anything other than DOS or Windows machines. Mac, Amiga, and Acorn computers don't exist for many service providers. At the moment Demon Internet provides the widest range of software and support for different computers, long may it stay that way, especially if they get their current odd position on POP3 mail provision sorted.

Troubleshooting TCP/IP technicalities (Chapter 3)

These don't seem to concern many recreational users of the Internet, once they've got over the learning curve of getting a dial-up workstation set-up – which is the main purpose of the Appendices in this book. TCP/IP hassles are of great concern to UK companies who want to use the Internet, or internal TCP/IP networking. The basic rule for corporates is not to employ cowboys to set up TCP/IP networks. The results can be catastrophically expensive to put right. In the UK corporates can either use software suppliers (often called consultants), Internet providers, Certified Novell Engineers (CNEs) with exposure to TCP/IP integration, or contract network engineers. In all cases business users will need a cohesive computer (mis)use policy (see Chapter 13) before they hook up their internal systems to the Internet. Before they even get that far, senior staff should be aware that any new internal TCP/IP installation should be Internet address aware, before they pay the invoice. Otherwise there will be a large expense for re-addressing workstations when the MD suddenly decides to put the internal TCP/IP net onto the Internet.

Internet providers are probably the best place to start for information and advice, and business users should be looking for turn-key installations, (supply, install, commission, handover) with penalty clauses for delays. Any decent installer will have third party liability cover, and will be able to provide you with a copy of this policy with his tender documents.

Troubleshooting email (Chapter 4)

Email is the largest Internet application, correspondingly it seems to cause the largest amount of trouble. The basic problems usually stem from setting up, after that users seem to have trouble in locating addresses of mail recipients. Setting up should be reasonably straightforward. You'll have a mail address, (as in *sue@s-sco.demon.co.uk*) which is the main address for mail in and mail out and often one or two other primary addresses for mail servers. A lot of set-up problems are caused by entering the wrong details for the server. Don't forget that you can use either the numerical address or the textual address for many providers, although programs such as Chameleon insist on numerical addresses. TCP/IP programs which accept text addresses often need a host table – a text file containing a look-up table of addresses. MacTCP works in this way and its host file (for Demon) looks like this:

```
s-sco.demon.co.uk A        158.152.24.10
gate.demon.co.uk.          IN 604800 A        158.152.1.65
ns.demon.co.uk.            CNAME
gate.demon.co.uk
demon.co.uk.               IN NS gate.demon.co.uk
```

Other mail complications are often caused by the way your supplier routes your mail. (See previous discussions about SMTP/POP3.) If you have only SMTP mail, as with Demon Internet, then your mail will be routed through a mail server (i.e. *post.demon.co.uk*). You'll need to have your mail application running *before* you kickstart your SLIP/PPP connection. This is so the remote mail server can search you out when your connection starts up, and send you what mail it holds. If you miss this and start your SMTP mail application late you'll miss your turn in the SMTP queue and have to wait a while to be recognized. SMTP users can send their mail at any time during the connection.

POP3 mail users can send their mail via SMTP at any time, and receive their mail any time. POP3 receives work by you logging into a POP3 server with a password. In my case I log into Demon's POP3 server (*pop3.demon.co.uk*) with my POP3 mail program, which I can do from any Internet connection in the world. I type in my name and password, and the mailer handshakes with the mail server and the mail arrives. POP3 is easy to use and ideal for anyone with say, access to an Internet terminal at college or work, and a dial-up computer at home. Hence its popularity in the USA.

When you are setting up your mail program remember that you'll need the address of the mail server you are using, your own mail address, and possibly a password for the remote mail server if you are using POP3. You'll also need to know exactly what your supplier is providing, be that SMTP or POP3 mail, or ideally a combination of both: SMTP receive/POP3 send – as seen from the server's end.

Mail addressing

Internet mail addressing is another bugbear. Briefly, if you want to find the address of your colleague in Australia the best way is to phone him and ask him to send you mail. There are a number of Internet mail address directories but they mainly cover US universities and colleges. Some address tracking systems store the address of everyone who has ever mailed a Usenet group, which will be of little use in tracking down anyone who hasn't.

The Finger command can be useful in tracking down users, but only if you can take a stab at a part of the address. If you thought that Sue-Sco worked at the Math department at Sussex University (she doesn't) you could try: *finger sue-sco@deptmath.sussex.ac.*

Most academic networks in the UK are hooked up to the Internet via the Joint Academic Network (JANET) or its successor Super-Janet. JANET addresses are now translated into Internet addresses and there's a list of JANET addresses for most UK educational bodies at ftp.demon.co.uk. Otherwise try Gophering for JANET – which may bring you an up to date list.

Whois is another way of tracking down users: try the command

finger -h whois.ripe.net schofield.

to find all the Schofields. Often *whois* doesn't work for a thousand reasons, and the advice to call or fax intended recipients of email for their address stands. Putting your email address on your letterheads and business cards is now accepted practice and needs to be encouraged.

Sending mail to other systems (such as CompuServe) can be daunting, but most Internet-savvy sites are adopting the Internet form of address. For those who don't go and get Scott Yanoff's list of mailing address conversions. There's a version of it on the disk enclosed with this book, as MAIL.TXT.

File fragmenting

Some email gateway systems break incoming files down into manageable chunks which causes problems for recipients who then have to fight with the prospect of using software utilities to join together the 32 files which make up the single spreadsheet binary which constituted the original. (Apple's Eworld is a typical culprit.) If this happens to you then all you can do is either ignore the messages and delete them, or try to use UUdecode (PC) or BinHex (Mac) to reconstitute the originals. You'll probably find that you'll also need a de-archiver such as LHA (PC/Mac/Amiga) Zip (PC/Mac) or Stuffit (Mac) to restore the file contiguity. The only sane recourse to this problem is to use a commercial MIME compliant email program to do the work for you, assuming that the program is available at both ends of the link. (MIME messages have the word MIME in the header.) Some programs such as VersaTerm Link (Mac) and Eudora use proprietary methods to overcome this problem. File fragmenting, especially on mailed binaries, and even more especially on encrypted mailed binaries complied by oddball methods, is quite common on the Internet. Businesses who need secure mailing of binaries should contact one of the commercial software companies in the UK such UniPalm or Ethix for a solution.

Other email problems include anonymous mail (ignore it), abusive mail, (send a copy to your Internet provider, and the *postmaster* at the site originating the message), and lost files – ask the originator to resend, rather than nagging your Internet provider.

Troubleshooting Usenet (Chapter 5)

Usenet has three main trouble-generating areas: the animosity of some Usenet moderators to newbies (new users), the availability of social trash of every description, and getting started with the software. The first two are covered in the news.answers group into which lists of Frequently Asked Questions (FAQs) are posted. The third is part of a commercial transaction between you and whoever provides your Internet connection, and the software to go with it.

You'll normally have to set your Usenet reader to point to a news server – there's one at news.demon.co.uk – to get your news. Then you have to join a news group – after you've downloaded a list of available groups. Most news software lets you type in the name of a group, rather than selecting it from a list of available groups, and there's a large list of newsgroups on the disk enclosed with this book. New users should watch out for Usenet software which tries to download a zillion new messages at startup. This takes forever.

(You can set the Demon DOS software to minimize its attraction for running up your phone bill. Before you connect for the first time select 'Configure News', 'Maintain Date you last got news'. Then press F4, F3, which sets the software to get only one day's news.)

Good Usenet Shareware in the UK is hard to find, most of the offerings limit the way you can reply or post messages, or forward them to other users. The two commercial offerings – Chameleon, and VersaTerm – offer off-line mail, again VersaTerm is by far the most flexible, if you have a Mac upon which to install it. Terminal account users often fare better – Usenet messages can be grabbed by most of the software for dial-up services such as CIX, CompuServe and Delphi.

Troubleshooting telnet (Chapter 6)

Many telnet problems are caused by means beyond the control of the Internet user. Remote sites disconnect themselves from the Internet at weekends or during local power surges, or when the operator takes the system down for repairs. Disconnects show up by your TCP/IP software not being able to find the address – you'll get messages saying site not found, or TCP/IP address unavailable, or such. Local errors are often caused by users operating the wrong kind of terminal emulator; one common example is using VT102 on an IBM 3270 equipped site. As with most other remote forms of access on the Internet, you, the punter, will generally have no idea what sort of computer you are remotely hooked in to, as everything from the humblest Mac Plus to a VAX can and does run UNIX and a set of TCP/IP utilities to make it talk over the 'Net.

In general many users get on fine with telnet, if only because they have learned the idiosyncrasies of their favourite sites. This also ties in with the willingness of users to equip themselves with decent TCP/IP-savvy terminal software such as Termite or Reflections (PC) or VersaTerm (Mac). Trying to hook yourself around the world on that old VT102 emulator provided by your Internet supplier can be frustrating. If you use telnet for anything other than recreation go buy a professional TCP/IP-savvy terminal emulator. It will save a lot of time and temper.

Command line prompts used on UNIX systems and telnet sites are equally confusing. Just about the only universal tip is to turn your disk capture on if you have it, and then type HELP, or /HELP at the prompt and refer to what you get. Some telnet sites need user IDs and passwords, and keeping a notebook and a pen by your computer is another obvious tip.

Troubleshooting Archie (Chapter 7)

Archie is such an antiquated method of trawling for files that it's a wonder it's still around. By and large problems are the same as for any other telnet based activity: lost sites, lost connections, and slow responses are the norm, especially when the Internet is busy.

In general try and brush up your Archie-by-email skills, especially if the information you want isn't urgent. Use Archie-by-mail to track down the sites which have the files you want – then add those sites straight into your ftp address list for later access. Archie-by-email is also often easier to handle than telnetting to an Archie site, as large messages and lists come into your mail system. You can then browse them at leisure. Running lengthy Archie searches over a phone connection is plain daft, especially when a Gopher search can often turn up the same information in half the time.

Troubleshooting FTP (Chapter 8)

FTP causes lots of headaches, partly because it's a highly popular Internet activity, and partly because it often uses UNIX based servers as a base. FTP also takes various forms. WWW browsers can covertly use FTP to send you files, as does Gopher.

Much confusion is caused by downloading binary files such as graphics and executable files as ASCII, and then wondering why the result doesn't work. Text files on UNIX servers are often labelled 'Index', HQX, 'Read.Me' or 'file.txt', almost anything else will be an ASCII file EXCEPT files with a suffix of **cpio**, **sea**, **lha**, **zip**, **x**, **tar**, **gif**, **pict**, **tiff**, **targa**, **jpeg**, **gz**, **gnu**, and **zoo**. All of these are binary files and need to be downloaded (FTPd) by issuing a **binary** or **image** command first. Often there's a help file called **read.me** at the root level which explains how the site organizes and archives its files, and this file should be your first grab from an unfamiliar site.

Other FTP nightmares include using UNIX directory commands to navigate up and down directories, and having to remember that UNIX filenames can be long, and are case sensitive. Some of the most difficult sites to work are those where the site manager or operator provides files such as **'Really-Long_fileName_no&&42_.HQX'**. You will have to type all of this in accurately to get the file, unless you're blessed with a decent GUI based FTP program, where you simply point at the file and double-click, to receive it.

FTP also suffers from the curse of the Internet – 30 million other users. If you're trying to FTP a file from a US or other long distance site at peak times you'll wonder why you ever bought a fast modem. In general you can preserve most of your phone bill and your sanity by keeping your FTP sessions to mornings in the UK, when 20 million Americans are still abed.

Remember also that you can multitask FTP and other Internet sessions on Windows, UNIX, Mac and Amiga computers. On a slow download go and get your mail, or join IRC for a fight, or send a message to the Author. TCP/IP will manage all the sessions without you losing any data. It's also possible to pick up your TCP/IP sessions if your modem drops the phone lines although this depends to a large extent on your software. On Macs you can reconnect to sessions – as long as the sessions don't time out internally or Mac TCP bombs out.

Troubleshooting Gopher (Chapter 9)

Gopher gives so little trouble that it's hardly worth mentioning here. You can streamline Gopher sessions by building a set of bookmarks (see your software documentation) and by using Veronica searches to a European university site such as Pisa or Cologne where you'll stand a better chance of getting a connection. Remember that Gopher multitasks, and the solution for a slow response is to go and open another session. Graphical Gophers are the most fun, and many can be fine tuned to interact with other applications. Download a GIF graphic file, and up pops your GIF viewer software, for instance. Gopher can be fun, but it can also be expensive as it encourages online browsing. Watch those phone bills.

Troubleshooting the World Wide Web (Chapter 10)

There are two sides to the World Wide Web. The client software, which lives on your computer, is one source of tribulations, the server software, comprising Web 'pages', is another. Web client software still isn't very good, despite a few years of development. It still attempts to download large graphics files over slow modems on a whim, and as yet there's little in the way of file compression to help data on its way. By the end of 1995 we'll see some rather flashier Web software which will handle video clips such as digital video mail, but at the moment you'll spend a lot of time watching your Web software run up your phone bill. Tips are to use the address book or bookmark facility to file your Universal Resource Locators. (URLs) and to leave the Display Graphics option turned off. Look also for software from EiNet, such as MacWeb and WinWeb. These programs offer a Web search facility which lets you type in a name and search, either GopherSpace, WAIS, or the WWW, for a name. Type in Telegraph, for instance, and the software will find the UK Daily Telegraph site, and take you straight there. WinWeb is currently under development – but the MacWeb version is a winner.

For those developing Web pages – watch out for Web Hypertext Mark-up Language options in forthcoming software. Microsoft and WordPerfect are currently preparing offerings to allow the easy construction of Web pages.

Troubleshooting your abilities

The first edition of this book brought me about 500 emails in three months. All but one of them proclaimed that the writer had been able to use *The UK Internet Book* to get connected to the Internet via a variety of services. The one grumble was from a user unable to make sense of help-line services from a provider despite '20 phone calls'. While most of these readers were presumably computer-literate quite a few weren't and admitted that there was still a need for the Internet-in-a-box concept, where you plug in and go. Some of the UK providers are offering rapid set-up systems, but the majority still expect you to get involved with the intricacies of TCP/IP. If this worries you then remember that there's a lot of help out there in the virtual community, and if you do need help (and – catch 22 – you have access to email) you can always mail me. Pleas for technical help are forwarded directly to the information providers concerned, who generally reply very quickly.

My only concern is that not one female appears to have mailed me. Perhaps they are all busy writing communications handbooks.

Index

For your records

This is a **summary** of the special offers that are available to you through the revised edition of *The UK Internet Book*. Please note that you **must complete the original tear-out cards** in order to receive your special offer from each of the companies listed.

Demon voucher offer

Do you want to explore the Internet?

For a limited time only, Demon Internet Ltd offers you the opportunity to connect to the Internet for up to **ONE MONTH FREE** with no cost.

Take the chance while you have it,

**THIS OFFER IS ONLY VALID UP TO AND INCLUDING
31st DECEMBER 1995.**

Macintosh Users:
MacTCP will be provided by Demon free of charge for the duration of this offer when taking a Demon Internet Account.

(See Reverse side for details)

Please Read Carefully

In order to get connected to the Internet for **ONE MONTH FREE, starting on the first day of any calendar month,** fill out this order card indicating how you would like to pay for continued Demon Internet Service. If you decide to stay connected to the Internet after your month's free access you will be charged a joining fee (see details of charges below). If you decide NOT to remain connected to the Internet, you **MUST** inform Demon Internet Ltd, **in writing**, before the end of the month. This will prevent you from being charged the joining fee. Please note that without receipt of either a cheque or credit card information you will NOT be connected for this trial offer.

Charges if you stay connected:

By credit card (Mastercard, VISA...)   £12.50 + VAT joining fee, plus £10 + VAT monthly charge

By cheque (cheques should be postdated, for the first day of a calendar month and **MUST** be submitted with this offer)
   £155.68 (includes 12 months' connection, £12.50 joining fee and VAT)

If you have submitted a cheque and you decide not to continue your Demon account it will be returned to you if you have included an SAE otherwise it will be destroyed. VAT receipts can only be issued for people paying annually.

Your Name (Full name please).. Company Name (if applicable)..

Address:...

.... Business Tel No:...................................... Home Tel No:....................................

Credit Card No:.. Expiry Date...................... Monthly or Annual account?...........
(if paying by Mastercard or Visa).

Credit Card address:(if different from above) ....

Machine name 1st choice _____ .demon.co.uk 4 to 8 characters

Machine name 2nd choice _____ .demon.co.uk 4 to 8 characters

I am a Macintosh user but don't have MacTCP. Please send me my **free** copy of MacTCP.   Please Tick Box ☐

Signed .... Date...

Please complete this original voucher only (photocopies are not acceptable) and post to
Demon Internet Ltd, Gateway House, 322 Regents Park Road, Finchley, London N3 2QQ.
Cheques should be made payable to Demon Internet Ltd.   Tel 0181-371 1234.   Please dial carefully.

Terms of special voucher offer

(The "small print")

Demon Internet Ltd offer a trial connection to the Internet making use of our full services and support lines for up to one calendar month via a Standard Dial Up account.

We work in calendar months so to make the best use of this offer, you should apply at the start of the month. By accepting this offer you are subscribing to the service on an on-going basis until you cancel. Cancellation should be made to us in writing and if you cancel during the first month you will have paid nothing. If you carry on, as we hope you will, you will then pay the joining fee and start paying the monthly fee which is due in advance of using the service.

Joining fee £12.50 plus VAT   Monthly fee £10.00 plus VAT

There are no usage or online time charges. When joining you must send payment details in the form of one of the following:

1) Credit Card details (Visa or Mastercard)

2) Post-dated cheque for £132.50 + VAT = £155.68 for the 1st of the following calendar month

3) 12 post-dated cheques. The first is for £12.50 + £10.00 + VAT and is to be made for the 1st of the following month. The 11 others should be for £10.00 + VAT = £11.75 and dated the 1st of each of the subsequent months.

In any event you will not be paying for the first month.

We regret that no other forms of payment are acceptable. Accounts are deemed to be annual but you may pay monthly as described above. We do not issue VAT receipts for monthly accounts and businesses are therefore advised to join annually.

We regret that we cannot accept vouchers that do not enclose payment and these may be returned or destroyed.

Ethix voucher offer

Ethix Distribution Ltd are pleased to offer:

1 copy of

Net*Manage* Internet Chameleon

at a special price of £99 *plus VAT, shipping*

Normally £139 *plus VAT, shipping*

Internet Chameleon includes:

- WebSurfer, Archie, Gopher, Email, NewsReader, FTP client & server, Telnet and more!
- Windows user interface
- 5 minute installation
- Easy dial-up; supports SLIP, CSLIP, PPP and ISDN
- 256+ colour support

This offer is valid until 31st December 1995.

Internet Chameleon Order Form:

Please send me a copy of the Internet Chameleon!

Quantity	Product	Price
1	Internet Chameleon	£99 special price plus VAT
	VAT	£17.32
	Shipping	£8.00
Total		**£124.32**

Credit Card Information:

☐ VISA ☐ Access/Master Card

Card Number .... Expires ....

Full Name on Card (Please Print) ....

Please Ship to:

Name: ....

Address: ....

....

Postcode: .... Telephone Number ....

All orders and enquiries to be sent to:

Ethix Distribution Ltd, Ethix House, Meadow Court, South Normanton, Derbyshire DE55 2BN

Tel: +44 (0)1773 863666   Fax: +44 (0)1773 863919   E-mail: sales@calibra.demon.co.uk

Pace voucher offer

25% OFF

Pace Micro Communications are the UK's leading supplier of personal modems offering a range of products to suit a wide range of needs.

The **MICROLIN 34 fx** is the latest addition to this award winning series, and with full 28,800bps connection it's blisteringly quick. On top of that it has a full send and receive fax facility, and is portable enough to travel with you when you need.

For further information and to order your discounted MICROLIN, call Probrand Limited, a Pace authorised reseller on **0800 262629**

MICROLIN 34

pocket modems

This offer is valid until 31st December 1995.

PACE

The **Personal Connectivity** Company

ORDER FORM

NAME *(AND COMPANY NAME IF APPLICABLE)*

ADDRESS

POST CODE   TEL NO:

PLEASE SUPPLY _____ MICROLIN 34fx(s) AT £ _____:_____ (RRP EACH)

LESS 25% PACE DISCOUNT £   :

DELIVERY £   :

VAT £   :

SIGNED _____

TOTAL £   :

TO OBTAIN THIS SPECIAL DISCOUNT PRICE YOU MUST PRESENT THIS CARD *(PHOTOCOPIES ARE NOT ACCEPTABLE)* TO:

PROBRAND LIMITED,
49 CAMDEN STREET
BIRMINGHAM, B1 3BP
TEL: 0800 262629
FAX: 021 626 0268

E & O E

PACE

The **Personal Connectivity** Company